THE ECONOMICS OF CHILD LABOUR

The Economics of
Child Labour

Alessandro Cigno and Furio C. Rosati

OXFORD
UNIVERSITY PRESS

331.31
C57e

OXFORD
UNIVERSITY PRESS

Great Clarendon Street, Oxford OX2 6DP

Oxford University Press is a department of the University of Oxford.
It furthers the University's objective of excellence in research, scholarship,
and education by publishing worldwide in

Oxford New York

Auckland Cape Town Dar es Salaam Hong Kong Karachi
Kuala Lumpur Madrid Melbourne Mexico City Nairobi
New Delhi Shanghai Taipei Toronto

With offices in

Argentina Austria Brazil Chile Czech Republic France Greece
Guatemala Hungary Italy Japan Poland Portugal Singapore
South Korea Switzerland Thailand Turkey Ukraine Vietnam

Oxford is a registered trade mark of Oxford University Press
in the UK and in certain other countries

Published in the United States
by Oxford University Press Inc., New York

British Library Cataloguing in Publication Data
Data available

Library of Congress Cataloging in Publication Data
Data available

Typeset by Newgen Imaging Systems (P) Ltd., Chennai, India
Printed in Great Britain
on acid-free paper by
Biddles Ltd., King's Lynn, Norfolk

ISBN 0-19-926445-7   978-0-19-926445-2

1 3 5 7 9 10 8 6 4 2

To Enrico, Nicola,
Paola and Tommaso,
who do not know child labour

Contents

Acknowledgements

The book was written while Furio Rosati was director of the joint UNICEF-ILO-World Bank Understanding Children's Work project <http://www.ucw-project.org>, and uses some of the research carried out and published by it. However, the book is not a publication of UCW, and the views expressed in it should not be attributed to the project, or to any of the participating agencies. We thank Partha Deb, Lorenzo Guarcello, Scott Lyon, Fabrizia Mealli, Owen O'Donnell, Roland Straub, and Eddy van Doorslaer for allowing us to draw on joint empirical work. Thanks are due also to Kaushik Basu, Jean Fares, Frank Hagemann, Robert Holzmann, Frans Roselaers, and Zafiris Tzannatos for valuable comments. Chapter drafts served as teaching material for courses at the universities of Florence and Tor Vergata. Student reaction helped us to improve the presentation.

List of Figures

List of Tables

xii

List of Tables

Introduction

Children throughout the world are engaged in a great number of activities classifiable as work. These range from fairly harmless, even laudable, activities like helping out in the home, to physically dangerous and morally objectionable ones like soldiering and prostitution. In the middle, we have the bulk of what is generally called 'economic activity'. According to currently available ILO estimates (see Table 0.1), throughout the world, 211 million children between the ages of 5 and 14 were 'economically active' in the year 2000. That is a very large proportion, 18 per cent, of the age group. The participation rate is even higher, 23 per cent, if we include youngsters up to the age of 17.

Most of the economically active children are in developing countries, where the participation rate of the 5–14 age group ranges between 15 and 29 per cent (see Table 0.2). The great majority of these children work on the family farm, or otherwise helping parents in their daily businesses. Only a small minority, less than 4 per cent of all working children, are estimated to be engaged in what international conventions call 'unconditional worst' forms of child labour (Table 0.3). But the absolute number, 8.4 million, is stunning. Should we be concerned only about these worst cases?

Child abuse certainly needs to be extirpated, but there are arguments for being concerned also about child labour in general. Child labour at a very young age, especially for long hours or in poor conditions, interferes with education and is likely to harm health. On the other hand, formal education is not the only means of accumulating human capital. Most forms of child labour have learning-by-doing elements. Furthermore, child labour generates current income. If a family is credit rationed, child labour thus serves to relax the liquidity constraint on current consumption. If a family cannot buy insurance,

Table 0.1. *Global estimates of economically active children aged 5–17 in 2000*

Age Group	Total Population (000s)	Number at work (000s)	Work ratio (%)
5–9	600,200	73,100	12.2
10–14	599,200	137,700	23.0
5–14	1,199,400	210,800	17.6
15–17	332,100	140,900	42.4
Total	1,531,100	351,700	23.0

Source: ILO (2002).

Table 0.2. *Regional estimates of economically active children aged 5–14 in 2000*

Region	Number of children (millions)	Work ratio (%)
Developed economies	2.5	2
Transition economies	2.4	4
Asia and the Pacific	127.3	19
Latin America and Caribbean	17.4	16
Sub-Saharan Africa	48.0	29
Middle East and North Africa	13.4	15
Total	211	18

Source: ILO (2002).

Table 0.3. *Estimated number of children in unconditional worst forms of child labour*

Unconditional worst form of child labour	Global estimate (000s)
Trafficked children	1,200
Children in forced and bonded labour	5,700
Children in armed conflict	300
Children in prostitution and pornography	1,800
Children in illicit activities	600
Total	8,400[a]

[a] The total excludes the category of trafficked children because of the risk of double counting.

Source: ILO (2002).

child labour serves also as a buffer against severely adverse events. There are thus trade-offs. To the extent that current consumption has a positive effect on future health (hence, on the child's future earning capacity), the trade-off between present and future consumption may be lower than one might think. In certain circumstances, it might conceivably be negative. In other words, there may be circumstances in which a child and his family are better off working than not working.

This raises two questions. Should child labour be abolished or curtailed, and if so how? International conventions[1] define child labour that should be eliminated not in terms of content of the activities carried out by the child, but in terms of the consequences that such activities have on education, health, and more generally on the welfare of the child. Fig. 0.1 illustrates the basic

---

[1] The international conventions most relevant for child labour are: the UN Convention on the Rights of the Child (CRC), the ILO Convention 138 (minimum age) and the ILO convention 182 (worst forms of child labour).

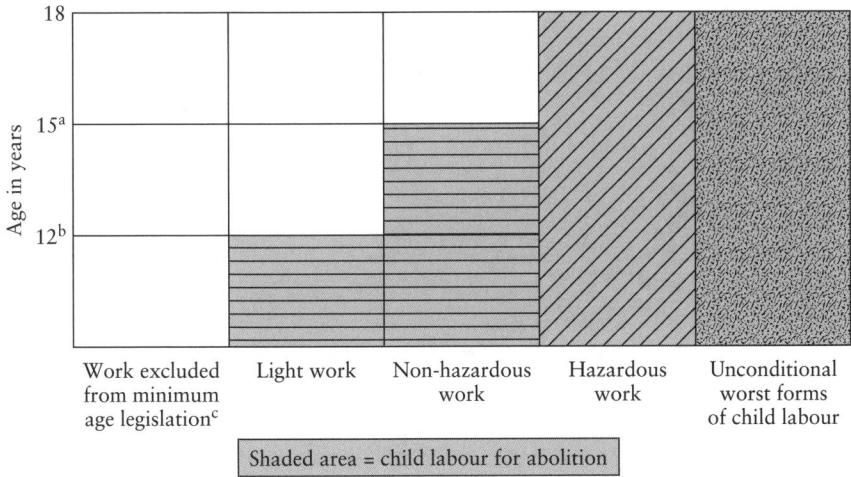

Figure 0.1. *Basic distinctions in ILO child labour standards*

Note: The size of the areas in the above figure does not represent quantitative proportions.

[a] The minimum age for admission to employment or work is determined by national legislation and can be set at 14, 15, or 16 years.

[b] The minimum age at which light work is permissible can be set at 12 or 13 years.

[c] For example, household chores, work in family undertakings, and work undertaken as part of education.

Source: Global Report under the follow-up to the ILO declaration on Fundamental Principles and Rights at Work, ILO, Geneva, 2002.

distinctions embodied in ILO Conventions Nos. 138 and 182.[2] It shows that it is the interaction between the type of work and the age of the child that defines the boundaries of child labour due for abolition. While setting objectives, these conventions offer no precise indication of how these objectives can actually be achieved.

What has economics got to say on the matter? The individual optimization assumption underlying most economic reasoning implies that one does (on average) what is best for oneself. Public intervention is thus justified only if it can be shown that it helps remedy a coordination failure, or on equity grounds. That is true also in relation to child labour (Grootaert and Kanbur, 1995). Since child labour prevails in less developed countries, there is no shortage of coordination failures (as evidenced by widespread market imperfections) and lack of social justice. But there is an additional argument. Young children are not free agents. Their parents decide for them, and not necessarily in their best interest.

There is no short answer as to how to go about reducing child labour either. It is widely believed that child labour is caused by poverty. Some economists thus maintain that income redistribution, from rich to poor countries and from

[2] See ILO Global Report 2002, fig. 2 and paragraph 25.

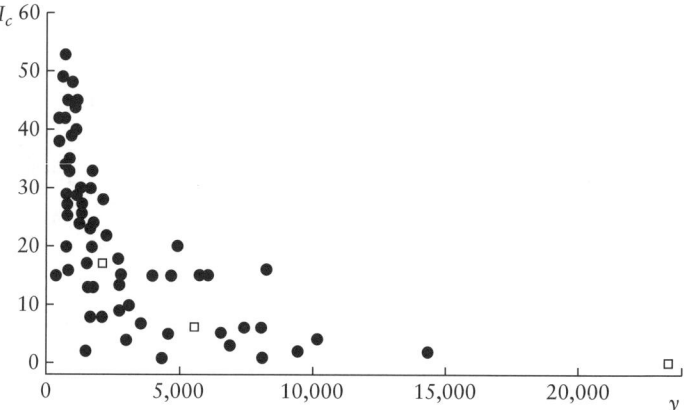

Figure 0.2. *Cross-country correlation between child labour and per capita income*
Source: Strulik (2004).

rich to poor households, would do the job. Others (fewer and fewer) still believe that growth in itself will take care of poverty, hence of child labour. The scatter diagram in Fig. 0.2 associates a measure of child labour (the participation rate of children aged 10–14) with per capita income in the year 2002 across sixty-nine countries. The dots represent countries, the squares are averages of low-, middle-, and high-income countries. It is clear that income and child labour are negatively correlated, but the correlation is not strong. Countries with similar per capita income can have very different levels of child labour, especially at low levels of income, and even relatively prosperous countries present a high incidence of child labour. The same will be shown to be true at the household level.

More to the point, income and child labour are co-determined. The fact that they are observed to move in opposite directions is thus no guarantee that income redistribution or income growth would be accompanied by a reduction in child labour. What is true rather is that child labour, especially in its more unsavoury forms, is part and parcel of the general problem of economic underdevelopment. Does that mean that child labour will only disappear when the general underdevelopment problem is solved? The present book argues that patient policy intervention on a number of fronts, guided by a good understanding of the theory and supported by sound empirical evidence, can substantially reduce child labour ahead of other features of underdevelopment.

In most of the book, child labour is modelled from the supply side. We use theory to predict, and data to measure, household responses to a given environment. There are three justifications for this research strategy. The first is that most of our micro-data come from household surveys. The second is that closing the model by the introduction of an aggregate demand for child labour would not advance our knowledge very much. For it to be really worthwhile, a market equilibrium analysis would have to take into account the specific technology of the industries that employ child labour. Were we to follow that approach, the book would break down into a series of sectoral studies (peasant farming in the Indian subcontinent, carpet making in the middle East, cocoa plantations in Latin America, etc.). The third justification is that, in an increasingly globalized economy, it is not too far fetched to assume that the local demand for child labour is virtually horizontal. In other words, that the relevant wage rates (of child labour, uneducated adult labour, and educated adult labour) are internationally determined.

The first three chapters develop a fairly comprehensive theory of child labour and closely related variables such as education, fertility, and infant mortality. They deal also with the effects of credit, insurance, and different forms of government intervention. The approach is essentially positive, but produces the elements for a normative judgement. Chapter 4, concerned with the effects of trade, reviews some recent theory, and brings some cross-country evidence. The last five chapters are country studies, aimed at illustrating and testing different aspects of the theory in different cultural and geographical contexts. They look, in particular, for the effects (on fertility, child labour, school attendance, nutritional status, etc.) of a range of policies ranging from the very specific, like building schools or providing running water, to the very general, like reducing risk or improving access to credit. These empirical chapters use the latest developments in microeconometric methodology for identifying causal relationships, and evaluating the effects of public intervention. A sketch of the methodology is given in the General Appendix at the end of the book.

1

Prolegomena

The present chapter sets the scene by presenting three contributions, one specifically concerned with child labour, the other two dealing primarily with the allocation of household resources between parents and children. The first contribution is due to Kaushik Basu,[1] the second to Gary S. Becker and Richard Barro,[2] the third to the present authors.[3] Basu's analysis of child labour has the merit of presenting what is a very complex problem in a relatively simple and compact way. It is thus a good point of entry into the subject. Its limitation lies in the highly restrictive assumptions on which it is based. The Becker–Barro approach has had an enormous influence on the way economists and policy makers think of child-related issues. Its attraction, but also its limitation, is that it reduces family decision making to a single optimization by a single decision maker. A host of other authors have attempted to remedy that by modelling the allocation of household resources as a game between husband and wife. That, however, is a game that only adults can play. While fruitful in many other respects, that approach is thus unsuited to deal with intergenerational interactions. Our own contribution to the field is based on the idea that it may be in each generation's own interest to abide by a set of minimal rules (a 'family constitution'), and optimize subject to those rules. Subsequent chapters will use these contributions as a basis on which to build a fairly comprehensive theory of child labour.

1.1 A MODEL OF THE MARKET FOR ADULT-EQUIVALENT LABOUR

Basu focuses on the interaction between adult and child labour markets in a closed economy. There are N_h identical households and N_f identical firms. Each household consists of one adult worker and n children. Each person is endowed with one unit of time. Adults throw their time endowment inelastically onto the labour market, $L_a^S = 1$. The amount of labour supplied by a child may be equal to or less than the endowment, $0 \leq L_c^S \leq 1$. The amount consumed by an

---

[1] The original exposition is in Basu and Van (1998). See also Basu (1999).

[2] The original exposition is in Becker (1960). See also Becker and Barro (1988).

[3] The original exposition is in Cigno (1993). The extensions are in Rosati (1996), Cigno and Rosati (2000), and Cigno (2005, 2006).

adult is represented by a. The amount consumed by a child is a given fraction, $0 < \beta < 1$, of the amount consumed by the adult family member. The total consumption of a household with n children is thus $(1 + \beta n)a$. The household budget constraint is given by

$$(1 + \beta n)a = w_a + nL_c^S w_c, \tag{1}$$

where w_a is the adult wage rate, and w_c the child wage rate.

Decisions regarding consumption and child labour are taken by the adult family member. Her preferences are summarized in the following *axioms*. Let a_s denote the subsistence level of adult consumption (the subsistence level of child consumption is βa_s). For any $a \geq 0$ and $\delta > 0$, the adult prefers

(i) the plan $(L_c^S, a + \delta)$ to the plan (L_c^S, a),
(ii$a$) the plan $(1, a + \delta)$ to the plan $(0, a)$ if $a < a_s$,
(ii$b$) the plan $(0, a)$ to the plan $(1, a + \delta)$ if $a \geq a_s$.

Axiom (ii) delimits the feasible set (the set of consumption and labour plans that allow the family to survive). Axiom (i) provides a partial ordering of feasible plans. Plans with the same amount of child labour are ranked according to the amount of consumption (the higher the consumption, the higher the ranking). Plans with different amounts of child labour are not comparable. Therefore, we cannot draw indifference curves in the $(1 - L_c^S, a)$ plane, and there is no utility function.[4]

Suppose that n is given. If the adult wage rate is sufficient to provide the whole family with at least the subsistence level of consumption, the household does not supply child labour,

$$L_c^S = 0 \quad \text{if } w_a \geq (1 + \beta n)a_s.$$

Otherwise, the household supplies n units of child labour,

$$L_c^S = 1 \quad \text{if } w_a < (1 + \beta n)a_s.$$

The output produced by a firm is $f\left(L_a^D + \gamma L_c^D\right)$, where $f(.)$ is the production function, assumed concave. L_a^D and L_c^D are, respectively, the amount of adult labour and the amount of child labour employed by the firm. The parameter $0 < \gamma < 1$ is the marginal rate of technical substitution of child for adult labour. Assuming this to be constant, the two types of labour are perfect substitutes in production.

If $w_a < w_c/\gamma$, firms employ only adult labour. Therefore, the ith firm sets $L_c^i = 0$, and chooses L_a^i to satisfy

$$f'\left(L_a^D\right) = w_a.$$

---

[4] That would be true, notice, even if the feasible plans were ranked first according to the amount of child labour (less child labour, higher ranking), and second according to the amount of consumption. That would in fact give us a *lexicographic* preference ordering.

By contrast, if $w_a > w_c/\gamma$, the ith firm sets $L_a^i = 0$, and chooses L_c^i to satisfy

$$f'\left(\gamma L_c^D\right) = w_c.$$

If $w_a = w_c/\gamma$, the ith firm is indifferent between hiring one adult, or $(1/\gamma)$ children. It will then hire

$$L^D \equiv L_a^D + \gamma L_c^D$$

adult-equivalent workers to satisfy

$$f'(L^D) = w_a.$$

In equilibrium, (w_a, w_c) is such that the market demand for adult labour is equal to the aggregate supply,

$$L_a^D N_f = N_h,$$

and the market demand for child labour is equal to the aggregate supply,

$$L_c^D N_f = n L_c^S N_h.$$

Since the two types of labour are perfectly substitutable, we may safely assume that

$$w_c = \gamma w_a.$$

The possible equilibria are illustrated in Fig. 1.1.

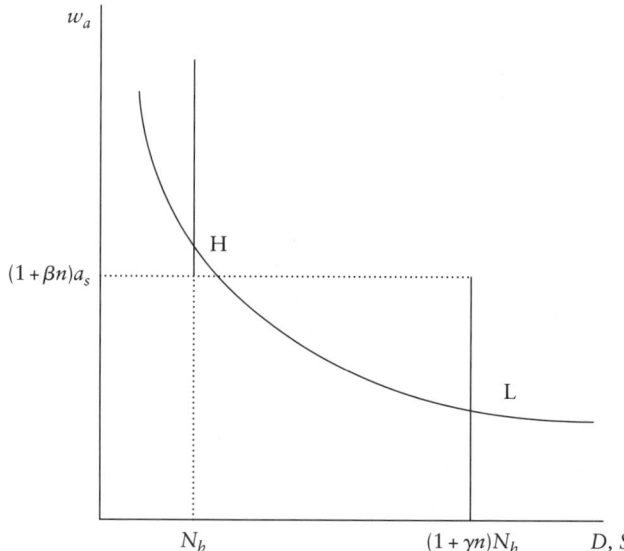

Figure 1.1. *The market for adult-equivalent labour*

The downward-sloping curve tracing the marginal productivity of adult-equivalent workers is the graph of the market demand for adult-equivalent labour. The market supply of adult-equivalent labour consists of two vertical segments. For w_a greater than or equal to subsistence, the supply is equal to the number of adult workers, N_h. For w smaller than subsistence, the supply is equal to the amount of adult-equivalent labour, $(1 + \gamma n)N_h$, provided by N_h adults and nN_h children working full time. As the aggregate supply is 'backward bending', there may be up to two equilibria.

One of the possible equilibria looks like point **H**. There, the adult wage rate is above the subsistence minimum, and only adults work. Household consumption is equal to w^L. The other possible equilibrium looks like point **L**, where the adult wage rate is below the subsistence level, and children are made to work. Household consumption is equal to $(1 + \gamma n)w^L$. Depending on demand elasticity, consumption could be higher at point **H**, where fewer people work for a higher wage, or at point **L**, where more people work for a lower wage. If the demand curve is sufficiently high, only an equilibrium such as **H** is possible. By contrast, if the demand is sufficiently low, the only possible equilibrium will look like **L**.

Is one equilibrium preferable to the other? Employers clearly prefer **L**, where profits are high, to **H**, where profits are low. By contrast, workers prefer **H** to **L**, because no amount of extra consumption can compensate for even a small amount of child labour. Therefore, the two equilibria are not Pareto-comparable. A value judgement is required to say that one is better.

Let us now suppose that adults can choose how many children to have. Fig. 1.2 illustrates the possible equilibria under the simplifying assumption that there are only two possible fertility levels, n^L and n^H, with $n^L < n^H$. The labour market supply curves are now two, each consisting of two vertical segments. If the fertility level is n^L, the labour supply consists of N^H adult workers for $w_a \geq (1 + \beta n^L)a_s$, of $(1 + \gamma n^L)N_h$ adult-equivalent workers for $w_a < (1 + \beta n^L)a_s$. If the fertility level is n^H, the labour supply consists of N^H adult workers for $w_a \geq (1 + \beta n^H)a_s$, of $(1 + \gamma n^L)N_h$ adult-equivalent workers for $w_a < (1 + \beta n^H)a_s$. The first segment of the high-fertility labour supply thus overlaps with the first segment of the low-fertility labour supply, but not completely, because the subsistence level of the adult wage rate is obviously higher if there are more children to support.

Given two possible fertility levels, there are up to three possible equilibria. One looks like point **HL**, where only adults work, and the adult wage rate is higher than the subsistence level. Here, fertility choice does not affect the wage rate, because children do not work, but it does affect adult and child consumption. Since the latter is obviously higher if fertility is lower, adults will then choose n^L. Adult consumption is

$$a^{HL} = \frac{w^{HL}}{1 + \beta n^L}. \tag{2}$$

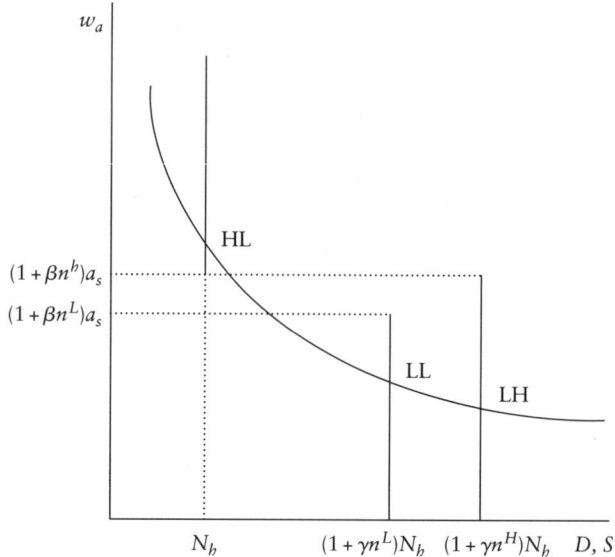

Figure 1.2. *The market for adult-equivalent labour with two fertility levels*

The second possible equilibrium is at a point like **LL**, where the adult wage rate is lower than subsistence. Parents still choose to have are n^L children, as at **HL**, but they now send them to work. Adult consumption is

$$a^{LL} = \frac{(1+\gamma n^L)w^{LL}}{1+\beta n^L}. \tag{3}$$

The third possible equilibrium looks like **LH**. As the adult wage rate is even lower than at **LL**, children will again work. The difference is that parents now choose to have more children. Adult consumption is

$$a^{LH} = \frac{(1+\gamma n^H)w^{LH}}{1+\beta n^H}. \tag{4}$$

Again, we cannot say at which of these equilibria adult consumption is higher. That depends on demand elasticity, and on the value of γ. Notice that, if a^{HL} is lower than either a^{LL} or a^{LH}, this does not disqualify **HL** from being an equilibrium. Since the wage rate w^{HL} is large enough to provide subsistence for one adult and n^L children, adults will in fact have that number of children, and keep them at home. By contrast, if it turns out that a^{LH} is higher than a^{LL}, then **LL** is not an equilibrium. Since the wage rate is w^{LL}, not large enough to keep an adult and n^L children above subsistence, parents will in fact have n^H children.[5]

If the demand curve is sufficiently high, the only possible equilibrium will look like **HL**. By contrast, such an equilibrium will not be possible if the demand curve is sufficiently low. A sufficiently flat (elastic) demand curve could leave either **LL** or **LH** as the only possible equilibrium. If more than one equilibrium exists, there is again the question of their possible ranking. Again, the alternatives are not Pareto-rankable.[6] Again, a value judgement is required to say that one is preferable to another.

Suppose that such a value judgement has been made, and that child labour is deemed to be socially undesirable. Basu and Van maintain that a ban on child labour would be self-enforcing, in the sense that it would not be in anyone's interest to try to circumvent it. Once the adult wage rate is higher than subsistence, they argue, parents have in fact no interest in sending their children to work. The problem with this argument is that it may take some time before the desired equilibrium gets established.

Suppose that the economy is originally in equilibrium at point **LH**. The government forbids child labour. The only legitimate equilibrium is then **HL**. Let the demand for labour be such, that

$$(1 + \beta n^L)a_s \leq w^{HL} < (1 + \beta n^H)a_s \tag{5}$$

as in Fig. 1.2. Since there are n^H children in each household, the adult wage is not sufficient to keep children and parents alive. Adults have then no choice but to accept employment for their children at a wage rate lower than γw^{HL}. Indeed, they have no choice but accept employment for themselves at a wage rate lower than w^{HL} (no firm will be willing to pay w^{HL} for an adult, when it can hire a child for less than γw^{HL}). Therefore, **HL** cannot be reached before the present children have become adults. Until that time comes, the ban will have to be enforced by coercive means. If the alternative to child employment is starvation for the whole family, however, public authorities will be inclined to close their eyes to child labour. As this will give households the wrong signal, parents will then continue to have n^H children, and the situation will tend to perpetuate itself (until and unless some external factor shifts the demand for labour upwards enough to rule out any equilibrium involving child labour).

The problem disappears if it so happens that, in the equilibrium without child labour, the adult wage rate is sufficient to support the existing number of children. It promptly reappears, however, if we drop the assumption that adult and

[5] The argument does not work the other way round. Suppose that a^{LL} is higher than a^{LH}. If the wage rate is w^{LH}, the best adults can do is have n^H children, because the lower fertility level would give them less than a^{LH}. Therefore, **LH** is an equilibrium even if it gives every household member less consumption than **LL**.

[6] Employers prefer **LH** to **LL**, and **LL** to **HL**. Workers prefer **HL** to **LL**, and **LL** to **LH**, if a^{LL} is higher than a^{LH}; **HL** to **LH**, and **LH** to **LL**, otherwise.

child workers are perfect substitutes in production. Then, firms cannot replace child with adult workers without changing the technique of production. As the necessary investments take time, firms will then want to continue employing children for a while, and this will again send the wrong signal to the households. Of course, the adjustment problem is much greater in the real world, where there are different types of firm producing the same product, many different products, and many different types of household.

Basu's approach leads to the conclusion that there may be a multiplicity of equilibria, some of which are inefficient. The a dynamic equivalent of this argument is developed by Dessy (2000), who uses a dynamic general equilibrium model to show the possible existence of a 'poverty trap' characterized by child labour and low wage rates, and of a take-off point beyond which per capita income grows and child labour eventually disappears. The author uses this result to suggest that legislation prohibiting child labour would become self-enforcing once the virtuous equilibrium without child labour became established. The growth context underscores the point we made in connection with the Basu model, that it may take a very long time before this equilibrium is established.

Using a richer dynamic general equilibrium model, Strulik (2003, 2004) also shows the possibility of two long-run equilibrium paths, one characterized by high child mortality, high fertility, high child labour, low educational investment, and low per capita income growth, the other with the opposite characteristics. The two equilibria are connected by an adjustment path interpretable as a 'demographic transition'. This dynamic literature is reminiscent of an older one, based on the simple neoclassical growth model, which also explained underdevelopment with the possible existence of a low-income trap, and came to the simplistic policy conclusion that development could be kick-started by injecting enough capital into the economy.

1.2 A MODEL OF FERTILITY AND INTERGENERATIONAL TRANSFERS

In its stark simplicity, the Basu model has the merit of highlighting the complex set of interactions that lies behind the child labour issue. In particular, it throws light on the connection between fertility and child labour. It leaves one wondering, however, about the extent to which the results can be generalized. We have just seen that a small change in the technological postulates (dropping the seemingly harmless assumption that a child does a given fraction of the work done by an adult) throws doubt on one of the model's more optimistic implications. The same applies, with greater force, to the representation of parental preferences.

Basu's assumption that parents are willing to let their children work only if the alternative is starvation reflects the widely held belief that child labour is the consequence of extreme poverty, but contrasts with the evidence that child labour persists at levels of household income well in excess of subsistence. Be that as it may, the assumed attitude of parents towards children is somewhat schizophrenic. On the one hand, parents appear to be willing to pay any price other than death by starvation to avoid their children working. On the other, if circumstances are such that children have to work in order to survive, parents do not limit themselves to making their children work the minimum required to reach subsistence, but send them to work full time! Parents thus seem to be saying to themselves, 'I wish my children did not have to work. Given that they do, however, I may as well get all I can out of them.'

A further contradiction comes to the surface when we look at fertility behaviour. Adults are supposed to have perfect control over fertility, and not to derive utility from children *per se*. If it is true that keeping children from working is highest in people's minds, why is it that people have children when the circumstances are such that they will have to work? Ignorance is not the explanation. Given a choice between having few or many children, parents do in fact choose to have many, if that gives everyone a higher consumption.[7]

There is then the question of what it is that children do when they do not work. If they do nothing, it is an open question whether a little work is worse than an empty stomach. If the alternative to work is school, the rationale for not letting a child work is that it reduces the child's future earning capacity. In that case, however, one should look for the best mix of education and present consumption, not only because future consumption substitutes for present consumption at a diminishing rate, but also because future earning capacity does not depend just on education. It may depend also on muscle power, and is in any case conditional on health status. Since both muscle power and health status are positively affected by nutrition at the early stages of life, there is then a clear trade-off between education and present consumption.

A way of synthesizing these contrasting effects of parental decisions on a child's well-being is to define $U^*(\Omega)$ as the maximized value of a child's lifetime utility, where Ω includes the endowments with which this person entered adult life, as well as his consumption before becoming an adult, and $U^*(\Omega)$ is a concave indirect utility function. The elements of Ω may be anything from money and capital goods to human capital, and even health status. If we assume that parents have their children's well-being at heart, we can make U^* an argument in the utility function of the person's parents. That is indeed the route followed by Gary Becker and associates, and by many others after them.[8] The model that follows captures the essence of that approach.

The simplest assumption we can make is that Ω is above-subsistence expenditure incurred by the parents on each of their children's behalf, and that the utility

---

[7] Similarly, if circumstances are such that children do not need to work in order to survive, people have few children, because that will allow everyone in the family to consume more.

[8] See Barro (1974), Becker (1960, 1981), Becker and Barro (1988), Becker and Tomes (1976).

of an adult (or couple) is given by

$$U = u(a) + \beta U^*(\Omega)n, \quad 0 < \beta \leq 1, \tag{6}$$

where $u(.)$ is a concave function, representing the non-altruistic component of parental utility, and β is a measure of parental altruism. We are thus retaining the assumptions of parental benevolence and perfect fertility control made in the last section, but we are now allowing for some degree of substitutability between a child's well-being, U^*, number of children, n, and parental consumption, a. We further assume that parents can procure up to a maximum of n^m births by incurring a fixed cost p for each birth. The positive constant p is defined to include all the unavoidable expenses and opportunity costs associated with the birth of a child, including the child's subsistence consumption.

Parents choose (a, n, Ω) to maximize (6), subject to the budget constraint

$$a + (p + \Omega)n = w_a, \tag{7}$$

where w_a is again parental income, and to the physiological constraint

$$0 \leq n \leq n^m. \tag{8}$$

If (8) is binding, the number of children is either zero or n^m. If it is zero, Ω is obviously zero too. In view of the budget constraint, a is then set equal to w_a. If the number of children is n^m, parents allocate their budget between their own and their children's consumption so as to equate their marginal utilities,

$$u'(a) = \beta U^{*\prime}(\Omega). \tag{9}$$

If (8) is not binding, (9) must still hold, but it must then also be true that the opportunity cost of an extra child is equal to the benefit,

$$(p + \Omega)u'(a) = \beta U^*(\Omega). \tag{10}$$

In view of (9), (10) now implies that parents allocate resources so as to equate the marginal and the average return to money spent on children,

$$U^{*\prime}(\Omega) = \frac{U^*(\Omega)}{p + \Omega}. \tag{11}$$

Since (11) fixes Ω, a and n are now determined by (9) and (7).

The implications are best understood if one looks at the effects of a reduction in w_a. If fertility is held at zero, a will obviously fall. If fertility is held at n^m, both a and Ω will fall (these are pure income effects). If neither of the constraints in (8) is binding, Ω will stay put, because it must still satisfy (11). In view of (9), a will remain the same too. In view of (7), parents will then have fewer children. In contrast with the predictions of the model considered in the last section, parents thus respond to a reduction in the adult wage rate by having less children, not more as in the model of the last section. They will reduce transfers to children (the equivalent of sending them to work) only if n is pressing against the physiological ceiling, and continues to do so despite the reduction in w_a.

Another and less obvious implication of the Becker approach is that fertility may be too high for the children's good. In other words, descending altruism does not necessarily imply that parents act in their children's best interest. To see that, it is convenient to re-cast the analysis in a two-date framework. At date 1, parents are adults, earn w_1, and can have children. At date 2, the children have become adults, earn w_2, and can in turn have children. Their parents have meanwhile become old, and can no longer earn.

Let us then reinterpret a as a vector,

$$a = (a_1, a_2),$$

where a_i is parental consumption at date i ($i = 1, 2$). Let us similarly interpret Ω as a vector,

$$\Omega = (c, y),$$

where c stands for a child's date-1 consumption, and y for the child's date-2 income. The latter is given by

$$y = w_2 + m,$$

where m stands for parental transfers.

Parental consumption at date 1 is given by

$$a_1 = w_1 - (p + c)n - s, \tag{12}$$

where s denotes saving. At date 2, it is determined by

$$a_2 = sr - mn, \tag{13}$$

where r is the interest factor.

Parents now choose (c, m, n, s) to maximize

$$U = u(w_1 - (p + c)n - s, sr - mn) + \beta n U^*(c, w_2 + m), \quad 0 < \beta \le 1, \tag{14}$$

subject to (8), and to two further constraints. The first of these restrictions,

$$mn \ge 0, \tag{15}$$

says that parents cannot make negative transfers to their adult children. This follows from the assumption implicit in (14) that parents do not receive gifts from their children, and from the legal principle that a child is not obliged to accept a negative bequest.[9] The other restriction,

$$s \ge -b, \tag{16}$$

says that parents cannot borrow more than some non-negative amount b.

---

[9] There are exceptions, for example the Terai region of Nepal.

Assume that (8) is not binding. If (15)–(16) is not binding either, the parental plan satisfies

$$\frac{U_c^*(c,m)}{U_m^*(c,m)} = r = \frac{u_1(a_1,a_2)}{u_2(a_1,a_2)} \tag{17}$$

and

$$\frac{\beta U^*}{u_1(a_1,a_2)} = p + c + \frac{m}{r}. \tag{18}$$

Condition (18) tells us that parents go on having children until the marginal benefit (the income equivalent of the altruistic pleasure they get from an extra child) equals the marginal cost. Condition (17) says that parents equate both their own marginal rate of substitution of future for present consumption, and their children's marginal rate of substitution of future income for present consumption, to the interest factor. The allocation of consumption is thus a Pareto optimum conditional on the number of children chosen by the parents.

If either (15) or (16) is binding, however, (17) does not hold, and the allocation of consumption is consequently not a Pareto optimum.[10] Baland and Robinson (2002) further argue that the number of children will be inefficiently high, in the sense that the utility of the parents *and* the average utility of the children would be higher if fewer children were born. The argument may be put as follows.

If the non-negative transfers constraint is binding, the second equation in (17) will still hold, but the first one will be replaced by

$$\frac{U_c^*(c,m)}{U_m^*(c,m)} = \frac{u_1(a_1,a_2)}{u_2(a_1,a_2) - \lambda}, \tag{19}$$

where λ is the Lagrange-multiplier of (15). As λ is positive, children value their current consumption, at the margin, more than their parent values hers. There is thus scope for mutually beneficial trade between parents and children. But there will be no trade, because young children have no current income, and cannot credibly commit to make payments out of future earnings. The point can be illustrated with the help of Fig. 1.3. The horizontal axis measures a child's consumption at date 1. The vertical axis measures a child's income at date 2. The convex-to-the-origin curves are the contours of $U^*(\Omega)$. If (15) were not binding, the parent would maximize her utility by procuring n^A births, and allocating the resources under her control in such a way that each of her children consumes c^A now, and enjoys income y^A in the future. Suppose, however, that

---

[10] The possibility that (15) might be binding is recognized in Becker and Murphy (1988), where it is pointed out that 'operative bequests' are necessary for an efficient allocation of consumption.

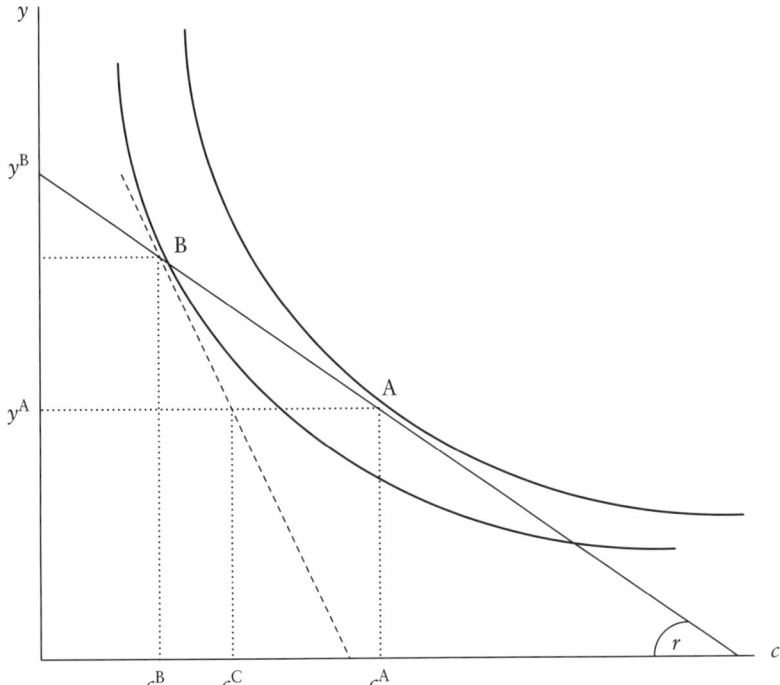

Figure 1.3. *The altruistic model with non-negative transfers and credit-rationing constraints*

any value of y lower than y^B implies a negative m (recall that y includes the child's own earnings). As (15) is binding, the parent will then maximize her utility by procuring a larger number of births, say n^B, and giving each child (c^B, y^B). In Gary Becker's language, the parent has substituted of 'quantity' for 'quality' of children. Clearly, a child is better-off consuming (n^B, c^B, y^B) will give the parents, and each of the children, lower utility than (n^A, c^A, y^A).

Let us now imagine that children are born sequentially, and that n^A of them are already born. Each of these children would clearly be willing to trade $(y^B - y^A)$ units of future income for $(c^A - c^B)$ units of current consumption. If they could credibly commit to make the future payment, the parent would accept the trade, because that would allow her to implement her preferred plan (n^A, c^A, y^A). As there is no way of holding a young child to her word, however, the parents can do no better than have another $(n^B - n^A)$ children, and deploy the resources under their control so that each of their children consumes c^B now, and has income y^B next period. The fertility level n^B is inefficient in the sense that the parents, and each of the children already born, would be better off if no more children were born.

218

If the borrowing constraint (16) is binding, the parental plan satisfies:

$$\frac{U_c^*(c,m)}{U_m^*(c,m)} = +\frac{\mu}{u_2(a_1,a_2)} = \frac{u_1(a_1,a_2)}{u_2(a_1,a_2)}, \tag{20}$$

where μ is the Lagrange-multiplier of (16), instead of (17). Parents and children then have the same marginal rate of substitution, but the allocation is still inefficient because their common marginal valuation of current consumption is higher than the interest factor. The problem, in this case, is not that insufficient commitment prevents a mutually beneficial trade between parents and children, but rather that neither party can borrow as much as they would like. The issue can again be illustrated with the help of Fig. 1.3. If credit were not rationed, parents would choose the plan (n^A, c^A, y^A). But, suppose that a child's current consumption cannot rise above c^B without violating (16). Parents then maximize their utility by choosing (n^B, c^B, y^B) as in the previous case. Fertility is inefficiently high.

The approach outlined in this section offers an alternative argument for regarding child labour as possibly a symptom of economic malfunctioning. The argument, here, is not that there may be a multiplicity of Pareto-rankable market equilibria as in Basu, Dessy, and Strulik, but rather that certain types of trade are not feasible.

1.3 FAMILY CONSTITUTIONS

In the models examined in the last two sections, decisions are taken by just one person, or by a couple acting as if they were one person. There is thus no coordination problem. Models of this kind, in particular those inspired by the work of Gary Becker, are referred to as the *unitary* model. A coordination problem arises, however, if there is more than one effective decision maker. The so-called *collective* model of Pierre-Andre Chiappori *assumes* that the domestic allocation of resources, and the distribution of the benefits, are Pareto-optimal. Such an outcome is consistent with a number of different decision mechanisms, among them the Nash-bargaining process that makes the final distribution of benefits dependent on the outside options available to the players.

The collective model is appropriate for portraying the behaviour of adults who can credibly threaten to break the family sodality if they do not get at least as much as they would under an alternative arrangement. In developed countries, this model is widely used to estimate the unobservable distribution of consumption between marriage partners from data regarding an observed partner-specific variable such as individual labour supply. It is less useful in a developing country context, where the marriage relationship is typically subject to more constraints than just the law of the country. The model is in any case inappropriate for explaining the allocation of goods between parents on the one hand, and young children who cannot credibly threaten to break the sodality on the other. In any case, it cannot be used to explain fertility behaviour in an altruistic context, because children are then a kind of local public good. An alternative approach, more appropriate to a developing country context, is that of Neher (1971).

Elaborating on an idea of Leibenstein (1957), that the demand for children may be derived from the demand for old-age support (the so-called 'pension motive'), Philip Neher imagines a situation where property rights are vested in families, not individuals, and family income is distributed according to a '*share alike ethic* whereby all members of the family have equal claim to the product whether they work or not'. Instead of assuming an efficient outcome like Chiappori, Neher thus assumes the rules of the game. But these rules are clearly not conducive to an efficient outcome, because they leave scope for free riding. Indeed, they result in excess fertility, and under-accumulation of assets. The model has some descriptive validity for those parts of the developing world where the rules assumed by Neher are reported to be prevalent, but does not explain why these rules were adopted and persist despite being inefficient. In this chapter, we shall look in some detail at a model of the family where the rules are endogenously determined.

A useful way of characterizing an organization is to describe its fundamental rules, its *constitution*. Economic theory tells us that it may be in everyone's interest to agree first on a constitution, allowing agents to safely renounce the dominant strategy in a prisoner's dilemma type of situation, and then optimize individually subject to the constitution (Buchanan 1987). Although originally conceived with reference to city or nation states, the constitution concept can be applied also to smaller groupings, such as clubs, professional associations, or, indeed, families. Cigno (1993) puts forward the idea of a 'family constitution', and establishes conditions under which this is self-enforcing in the sense that it is in the best interest of every family member to obey it, and to have it obeyed. Cigno (2005, 2006) identifies circumstances in which a constitution is self-enforcing also in the stronger sense that, once established, it will never be amended.

Let the life-cycle consist of three periods, labelled $i = 0, 1, 2$. A person is said to be young in period 0, adult in period 1, old in period 2. Adults are able to produce income, and to reproduce. The young and the old can do neither. We retain the assumption that parents can have as many children as they like, subject to (8), by bearing a fixed cost p for each birth. Let c_i denote a person's consumption, and c_i^s the subsistence level of consumption, in period i. Assuming that people derive utility only from their own lifetime consumption, a person's lifetime utility is given by

$$U = u_0(c_0) + u_1(c_1) + u_2(c_2), \tag{21}$$

where $u_i(.)$ is a concave function, with $u_i'(c_i^s) = \infty$.

At any given date, a family consists of individuals at three different points of the life-cycle. That is important, because it provides an opportunity for mutually beneficial deals. Differences of sex and other personal characteristics also provide scope for cooperation, but we assume them away to concentrate on intergenerational relations. A family constitution is defined as a set of (unwritten, typically unspoken) rules prescribing that each present adult must pay

(i) at least $z \geq c_0^s$ to each of her children, if she has any, and
(ii) $x \geq c_2^s/n^{-1}$ to her parent, where n^{-1} is the number of children the parent had, conditionally on the parent having complied with the constitution.

The condition attached to (ii) makes it in every adult's interest to punish transgressors. In general, x and z will be contingent on n^{-1}, r and w. Here, however, we assume for simplicity that r and w, hence n^{-1}, are certain (we shall look at the effects of uncertainty in a moment) and constant over time. Therefore, z and x will be constant too. How will an adult respond to such a constitution?

1.3.1 *Family constitutions as Nash equilibria*

If an adult does not have access to asset and credit markets, she can survive into old age only if her grown-up children will support her. She has then no option but to comply with the constitution. As she is not an altruist, she will not give her children and parent more than the minimum required. She will thus give x to her parent, z to each of her children, and choose the number of children n that maximizes her own utility over what is left of her life,

$$u_1(w - x - zn) + u_2(xn),$$

subject to (8).

This adult will choose either the value of n that equates her marginal rate of substitution of adult for old-age consumption to the marginal return on money spent for children,

$$\frac{u_1'(w - x - (p + z)n)}{u_2'(xn)} = \frac{x}{p + z}, \tag{22}$$

or, if that violates the second constraint in (8), its highest possible value n^m. The first constraint in (8) will never be binding, because the agent needs children to survive in old age.

The constitution is feasible if it satisfies (8) and

$$c_1^s + x + n(z, x, w)(p + z) \leq w. \tag{23}$$

If it is feasible, it is also self-enforcing in the limited sense that the best individual response to every other family member complying with the constitution is to do the same. The allocation of resources that results from everybody complying with the constitution is thus a Nash equilibrium. Since complying implies threatening one's own parent with punishment if she does not also comply, and given that the threat is credible because carrying it out is in the complier's own interest,[11] the equilibrium is sub-game perfect.

The story becomes more complicated if the adult has access to asset and credit markets, because she can then provide for her own old age by buying assets, or lending money. She then has a choice of two strategies: *comply* with the constitution, or *go it alone* in the market. Can a feasible constitution (z, x) be self-enforcing in these circumstances? Before we go into that, we need to make a preliminary consideration, and then write down the pay-off functions associated with the two strategies.

Since children have a cost (at least p) but yield no benefits unless the family constitution is complied with, go-it-aloners have no children. By contrast, compliers have children, for otherwise they would not get any benefit from paying x to their parents. For reasons that will become clear in a moment, compliers have no interest in saving (buying assets), and are not allowed to borrow from the market more than a certain quota (normalized to zero).

The pay-off to going it alone is

$$v(r, w) = \max_s u_1(w - s) + u_2(rs),\tag{24}$$

where s is the amount of assets ('savings') accumulated in period 1, and $r - 1$ the return on these assets. For any given (r, w), the choice of s satisfies

$$\frac{u_1'(w - s)}{u_2'(rs)} = r.\tag{25}$$

The effects of changes in r or w on the pay-off of this strategy are

$$v_w = u_1'(w - s), \qquad v_r = su_2'(rs).\tag{26}$$

The pay-off to complying, provided that the agent's children also comply, is

$$v^*(w, x, z) = \max_n u_1(w - x - (p + z)n) + u_2(xn).\tag{27}$$

For any given (x, w, z), the choice of n satisfies (22).

The effects of changes in x, w, or z on the pay-off of this strategy are

$$v_x^* = -u_1'(w - x - (p + z)n) + nu_2'(xn),\tag{28}$$

$$v_w^* = u_1'(w - x - (p + z)n),\tag{29}$$

$$v_z^* = -nu_1'(w - x - (p + z)n).\tag{30}$$

The necessary and sufficient condition for a feasible constitution to bring about a sub-game perfect Nash equilibrium is

$$v^*(w, x, z) \geq v(r, w).\tag{31}$$

---

[11] In equilibrium, the threat is never carried out because everybody complies.

This is automatically satisfied if adults do not have access to asset and credit markets, as in the case examined earlier, because the right-hand side of (31) is then identically zero. If adults do have access to asset and credit markets, however, (31) can be true only if the marginal return to money spent on children is strictly higher than the return to buying conventional assets from (or lending to) the market,

$$\frac{x}{p+z} > r. \tag{32}$$

Since a complier must pay a fixed amount x to her parent, *irrespective of how many children she has*, there is in fact no way that she could recover the fixed cost of complying if (32) were not true. Given (32), a complier will not save.[12]

While making it disadvantageous for compliers to lend to the market, (32) makes it advantageous for them to borrow from the market in order to finance additional births. But there are limits to this arbitrage operation. First, fertility cannot increase without bound because it will eventually hit its physiological ceiling, n^m. Second, there is no legal mechanism through which entitlements arising from an informal family arrangement can be transferred to another person. Since an entitlement that cannot be legally transferred from one person to another cannot be used as collateral to obtain credit from the market, we assume that compliers cannot borrow from the market at all. Nothing of substance changes if we allow them to borrow up to some positive amount smaller than $(p+z)n$.

Figure 1.4 illustrates the properties of the set of constitutions that can be supported by a sub-game perfect Nash equilibrium. This set is bounded to the right by the curve through point (z^*, x^*). All the points on this curve satisfy (31) as an equation; those to the left of it satisfy (31) as an inequality. Let us see why this boundary line has the shape shown. Since young children have no income, and cannot consequently make transfers to their parents, z cannot be negative. It can be zero, however, because agents are past childhood, and have already received z from their own parents. They would thus be happy to subscribe to a constitution that did not oblige them to *make* transfers to children (in addition to paying p) in the current period. On the other hand, agents would not countenance a constitution that did not entitle them to *receive* transfers from their children in the next period. Therefore, all points of the set satisfy $z \geq 0$, and $x > 0$.

The slope of the boundary is

$$\frac{dz}{dx} = \frac{(p+z)n - x}{nx}. \tag{33}$$

---

[12] Strictly speaking, that is true only if the physiological ceiling on fertility is not binding. Were it binding, the agent could not procure as many children (acquire as many entitlements to future transfers) as she would like, and would then find it optimal to top up her stock of domestic credits with market assets. As this complicates the analysis without bringing any additional insight, we assume that the chosen n is never greater than n^m.

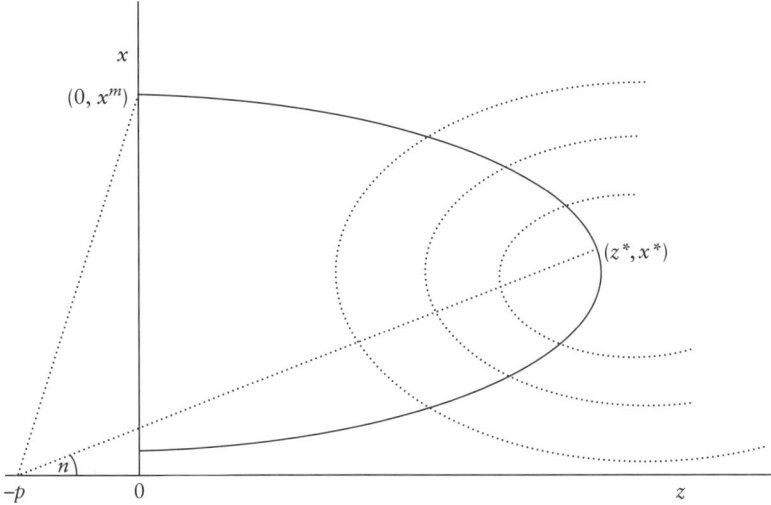

Figure 1.4. *The Nash frontier and the self-enforcing family constitution*

Since

$$\frac{d^2 z}{d(x)^2} = -\frac{p+z}{(x)^2} \tag{34}$$

is negative, z is maximized at the point, shown in Fig. 1.4 as (z^*, x^*), where

$$\frac{x}{p+z} = n. \tag{35}$$

As v_r is positive in view of (26), a rise in r will shift the boundary inwards. Intuitively, that is because the lowest marginal rate of return to money spent on children that makes complying with the constitution at least as attractive as going it alone in the market increases with the market rate of interest. By contrast, a rise in w shifts the boundary outwards. In view of (26) and (29) v_w and v_w^* are in fact positive. In view of (32), however, the rate of return to children is higher than the rate of return to capital. As a consequence, compliers consume less than go-it-aloners in the current period, and the marginal utility of current income is thus higher for the former than for the latter. Therefore, v_w^* is higher than v_w. While an exogenous rise in the interest rate would make the set of sustainable constitutions smaller, an exogenous rise in the wage rate would thus make it larger. For w/r sufficiently low, the set may be empty.

Let us now consider the effects of an actuarially fair pension scheme, that exacts a contribution T from each adult, and pays a pension Tr to each old person.[13] The pay-off to going it alone is now

$$v(r, w, T) = \max_{s} u_1(w - s - T) + u_2((s + T)r). \qquad (36)$$

The pay-off to complying is

$$v^*(w, x, z, T) = \max_{n} u_1(w - x - (p + z)n - T) + u_2(xn + Tr). \qquad (37)$$

The introduction or expansion of the scheme has no effect on the pay-off to going it alone, because

$$v_T = -u_1'(w - s - T) + r u_2'((s + T)r) \qquad (38)$$

is zero in view of (25).[14] By contrast, its effect on the pay-off to complying,

$$v_T^* = -u_1'(w - x - (p + z)n - T) + r u_2'(xn + Tr), \qquad (39)$$

is negative in view of (22) and (32). The policy thus shifts the boundary of sub-game perfect Nash equilibria inwards. Intuitively, that is because the policy hurts only compliers, who are obliged to participate in a scheme that offers a lower marginal return than the family one.

It is thus clear that an increase in either the market rate of interest, or in public pension coverage, would lower the proportion of adults who find it advantageous to comply, and raise the proportion of adults who find it advantageous to go it alone. Since go-it-aloners have no children, an increase either in the market rate of interest, or in public pension coverage, would reduce aggregate fertility. Since pensions satisfy at least part of the demand for old-age consumption, an increase in pension coverage would reduce aggregate fertility not only by reducing the number of compliers, but also by reducing the fertility of those that are left.

1.3.2 *Renegotiation-proof family constitutions*

Given that an infinite number of (x, z) pairs may satisfy (31), and that an infinite number of constitutions might thus be sustained by a sub-game perfect Nash equilibrium, which will prevail? Cigno (2005, 2006) offers a criterion akin to the renegotiation-proofness concept developed by Bernheim and Ray (1989), and Maskin and Farrell (1989).

At any date, the adult members of a family are at liberty to propose a new constitution. Will future adults take any notice? Not if (i) the old constitution satisfies (31), and (ii) there is no other constitution satisfying (31) that makes generations $t, t + 1, t + 2, \ldots$ better-off. In other words, a constitution

---

[13] In the absence of uncertainty, one should say simply 'fair'. As the expression is standard, however, and the results carry over to an uncertainty context, however, we continue to say 'actuarially fair'.

[14] Assuming either that T is no greater than the optimal s, or that the agent is free to borrow. If neither of these assumptions is true, T has a negative effect on the pay-off to going it alone.

is renegotiation-proof if, in addition to being a sub-game perfect Nash equilibrium, it is not Pareto-dominated by any other constitution which is itself a sub-game perfect Nash equilibrium. If the existing constitution is undominated, the only way a person can offer her children a better deal, and not lose in the bargain, is in fact to pay her parent *less* than the existing constitution requires, in other words to default on the existing constitution. But that would make her liable to punishment at the hands of her own children. The latter would in fact be better-off upholding the existing constitution, which entitles them to pay nothing to their parent, than acquiescing to the proposed new one. Once established, a constitution satisfying the double requirement of being a sub-game perfect Nash equilibrium, and undominated by any other constitution itself a sub-game perfect Nash equilibrium, is thus unamendable.

At any given date, the adults of the day are only interested in adult and old-age consumption, but their children are interested also in youthful consumption. A family constitution is then renegotiation-proof if it maximizes,

$$U(x, z, w) = u_0(z) + u_1(w - x - (p + z)n) + u_2(xn), \qquad (40)$$

subject to (31).

If the constraint is not binding, the renegotiation-proof constitution satisfies

$$\frac{u_0'(z)}{u_1'(w - x - (p + z)n)} = n = \frac{u_1'(w - x - (p + z)n)}{u_2'(xn)}. \qquad (41)$$

and (35). It thus equates the marginal rate of substitution of youthful for adult consumption to that of adult for old-age consumption. In this case, the point representing the renegotiation-proof constitution could be located anywhere below the Nash frontier.

If (31) is binding, a renegotiation-proof constitution satisfies

$$\frac{u_0'(z)}{u_1'(w - x - (p + z)n)} = (1 + \lambda)n, \qquad (42)$$

$$\frac{u_1'(w - x - (p + z)n)}{u_2'(xn)} = n \qquad (43)$$

and (35), where λ is now used to denote the Lagrange-multiplier of (31). The marginal rate of substitution of youthful for adult consumption is then higher than that of adult for old-age consumption. In this case, the renegotiation-proof constitution is represented by a point on the Nash frontier. Since the only point of the frontier satisfying (35) is (x^*, z^*), the renegotiation-proof constitution is the one that maximizes transfers to the young.

In Fig. 1.4, the broken curves, with slope $(u_0' - u_1'n)/(-u_1' + u_2'n)$, are the contours of $U(., ., w)$. The picture is drawn under the assumption that U happens to reach a maximum just inside the Nash frontier, close to (z^*, x^*).

Since the Nash frontier shifts inwards as the interest rate rises relative to the wage rate, the probability of such a solution increases with r/w. Notice that $(0, x^m)$, the constitution favoured by the family founder, could never be renegotiation-proof.

Since the return on children is greater than the return on capital in view of (32), the allocation brought about by a renegotiation-proof constitution is not a Pareto optimum conditional on the number of children. Furthermore, if (31) is binding, and a child consequently values current consumption more than the parent, the number of children is inefficiently high in the Baland–Robinson sense. In conclusion, a family constitution makes up to some extent for the unavailability of legally enforceable contracts between adults and young children (see the discussion at the end of section 1.2), but it is only an imperfect substitute because it must distort marginal incentives in order to be self-enforcing. We shall look at the child labour implications in the next chapter.

1.3.3   *Altruism, uncertainty, and personal services*

Before concluding the exposition of the family constitution model, it will be useful to look at a number of extensions of the basic framework that make the whole approach more realistic,[15] without fundamentally altering its conclusions. An obvious one is to allow for altruistic feelings among members of the same family. Suppose, as in the Becker-style model examined in the last section, that parents derive utility from their children's well-being, but not the other way round (*descending altruism*). Unless we assume that parents are always generous and rich enough not to want transfers from their adult children, this does not eliminate the need for a family constitution. The only difference this form of altruism makes is then that not only compliers, but also go-it-aloners, may have children. Since go-it-aloners get only direct utility from children, however, while compliers get also indirect utility (*via transfers*), the latter will still have more children than the former as in the basic model.

Let us then consider the possibility that children, too, love their parents (*bilateral altruism*). The most optimistic assumption one can make in this respect is that all members of the same dynasty unanimously maximize the same dynastic utility function, subject to the same dynastic budget constraint. Then, clearly, there is no coordination problem. There are many decision makers, but they all want the same thing. A less optimistic assumption is that the utility functions of different generations are *symmetrical*, rather identical. Let the

---

[15] A test based on Italian data could not reject the hypothesis that the behaviour of a statistically relevant proportion of the adult population is governed by a family constitution; see Cigno et al. (2004).

utility functions of parents and children be, respectively,

$$U^p = u_1\left(c_1^p\right) + u_2\left(c_2^p\right) + \gamma n U^c, \quad 0 < \gamma \le 1. \tag{44}$$

and

$$U^c = u_0\left(c_0^c\right) + u_1\left(c_1^c\right) + u_2\left(c_2^c\right) + \frac{\gamma}{n}U^p, \quad 0 < \gamma \le 1, \tag{45}$$

where c_i^j is the amount consumed by family member $j = c, p$ in period $i = 0, 1, 2$ of her life.

Suppose that, at any given date, the family includes only one adult with an exogenously given number of children, n. Suppose that there will be no grandchildren, so the story ends with the children's generation. The parent would then like to maximize (44) subject to the budget constraint,

$$c_1^p + \left(p + c_0^c\right)n + \frac{c_2^p + c_1^c n}{r} + \frac{c_2^c n}{r^2} \le w^a + \frac{w^c n}{r}. \tag{46}$$

Each of her children would like to maximize (45) subject to the same budget constraint. If $\gamma = 1$, we are back to the unanimity case. Parent and children want the same thing. If $\gamma < 1$, however, there is a conflict of interest. Stark (1993) suggests that the intergenerational allocation will be the solution to a non-cooperative game between the parent and the child, and finds that this is generally inefficient. That need not be the case if the child generation can in turn have children. If that is the case, however, a self-enforcing family constitution may again exist.

Another obvious extension is to drop the assumption that the future is known with certainty. Suppose that, for reasons beyond their control (low ability, ill health, premature death), today's young might not be in position, tomorrow, to pay their parents a fixed amount x. Rosati (1996) examines the case, particularly relevant in a developing country context, where a child's survival into adulthood is uncertain. If the constitution does not allow for all possible contingencies—for example, if it relies on some simple rule of the kind that a child is excused from supporting her parent if her own income falls below a certain level—it may then be worthwhile for a risk-averse complier to do some precautionary saving, in addition to having children. Provided that risks are not positively correlated, that remains true even if the return on capital is uncertain too. There could thus be some saving even if all agents are the same, and they all comply. That eliminates an unrealistic feature of the basic constitution story.

Another unrealistic assumption of the basic model is that market goods are the only source of utility. To remedy that, Cigno and Rosati (2000) allow for the possibility that the market does not provide perfect substitutes for the personal services of the agent's own parent or children, and reword the constitution to the effect that each adult is now required to give her elderly parent a combination of money and personal services yielding the same utility as x, and each young child a combination of money and personal services yielding the same utility as z. By permitting agents to substitute time for money, this reduces both the fixed cost of complying, and the marginal cost of children. Since the money equivalent of the utility that an old person derives from services without a perfect market substitutes can be very high, it thus makes it much more likely that a self-enforcing family constitution will exist. The argument acquires special significance in a development context, where an elderly person might need the assistance of adult children for security purposes, and in order to physically gain access to consumption and medical care.

2

Child Labour, Education, and Saving

In this and the next chapter, we capitalize on the insights gained from the previous one to construct a comprehensive theory of household behaviour with the focus on child labour. To do that seriously, one has to take account of the sequential nature of domestic decisions, and of the fact that parents do not perfectly control the number of children of an age to work. Failing to account for that misses out crucial aspects of the child labour problem. The simplest decision sequence includes three steps, or decision stages (see Fig. 2.1). At stage 0, would-be parents choose the level of birth control. This conditions the probability that a child is born. Stage 1 comes if and when a child is actually born. At that point, parents decide how much food, attention, and medical care to give each child. That will in turn condition the child's probability of surviving to the next stage. Stage 2 occurs if and when a child reaches school age. At that stage, parents decide whether to send their children to school or work, and how much food, education, and medical care each child should get. Since premature mortality is heavily concentrated in the early years, we shall assume that, if a child survives to school age, he will live to be an adult. Stage-2 decisions determine the stock of human capital and other assets with which the child will enter adult life. Beyond that, decisions will be taken by the children themselves. The decision problem is solved by backward induction.

Our representation of parental preferences is analogous to that adopted in the Becker-style model of section 1.2. Parental utility is determined *ex post* by

$$U = \sum_i u_i(a_i) + \beta U^*(c_2, y)n, \quad 0 < \beta \leq 1, \tag{1}$$

where a_i denotes parental consumption at stage i $(i = 0, 1, 2, 3)$, c_2 is a child's stage-2 consumption (including medical care, as well as food and clothing, but excluding education), y a child's stage-3 income, and n the number of children who live to be adults. The functions $u_i(.)$ are taken to be increasing and concave, with $u_i(a_s) = 0$ and $u_i'(a_s) = \infty$, where a_s is again the subsistence level of adult consumption. The function $U^*(.)$ is similarly assumed to be increasing and concave, with $U^*(c_s, .) \equiv U^*(., a_s) \equiv 0$ and $U_{c_2}^*(c_s, .) \equiv U_y^*(., a_s) \equiv \infty$, where c_s is the subsistence level of school-age consumption.

The first right-hand-side term of (1) is again to be interpreted as the self-regarding component of parental utility. The second right-hand-side term is the altruistic component, proportional to the children's maximized utility, U^*.

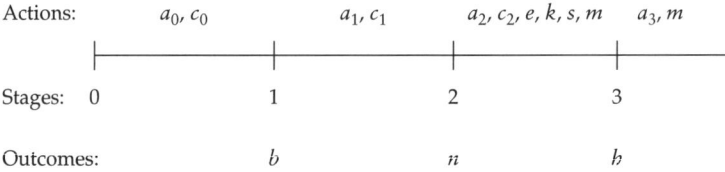

Figure 2.1. *Decision stages*

Notes:
a_i = parental consumption at state $i(i = 0, 1, 2, 3)$
c_0 = level of birth control
c_j = child's consumption at state $j(j = 1, 2, 3)$
e = time that a school-age child spends studying
k = inputs (other than own time) used for a child's education
s = parental saving per child
m = net transfers to each grown-up child
b = number of births
n = number of school-age children
h = human capital of each grown-up child

By interpreting n as the number of children who reach adulthood, we are in effect saying that children who die prematurely are not a source of utility. The restrictions on the form of $u_i(.)$ and $U^*(.)$ imply that selfish considerations have more weight if parental consumption is low at any point of the life-cycle, and become paramount as parental consumption approaches subsistence. By contrast, altruistic considerations will tend to prevail if parental consumption is consistently high. In the present chapter, we place ourselves at stage 2 of the decision process.

2.1 HUMAN CAPITAL

The stock of human capital, h, with which a person enters adult life is partly innate, and partly the result of education. We thus write

$$h = h_0 + g(e, k), \tag{2}$$

where h_0 is a positive constant representing natural talent, e the amount of time that this person spent in education (including not only school attendance, but also individual study outside school hours), and k is other educational inputs (books, tuition, writing material, etc.). Assuming that both e and k are essential to the educational process, and that the production of human capital is characterized by constant returns to scale, we take the production function $g(.)$ to be linear-homogeneous, with $g(0, k) \equiv g(e, 0) \equiv 0$.

Let w_c be the opportunity cost of a child's time (the child wage rate, or the marginal product of this child's labour if higher than the market wage), and p_k the price of other educational inputs. Normalizing a child's time endowment to unity, we may write the full cost of providing a future adult with h units of human capital as

$$Q(h, w_c, p_k) \equiv \min_{e,k}(ew_c + kp_k) \quad \text{s.t. } h_0 + g(e, k) \geq h, 0 \leq e \leq 1. \quad (3)$$

The function $Q(., ., .)$ is defined for

$$h \geq h_0. \quad (4)$$

Like all cost functions, it is increasing in output, and increasing and concave in input prices.

By the constant-returns-to-scale assumption, each unit of h is produced with the same cost-minimizing combination of e and k up to the point where the child's time is fully occupied attending school and doing homework. From that point onwards, any increase in the production of human capital will require an increase in the quantity of other factors used in conjunction with the fixed amount of time. That is illustrated in Fig. 2.2, where the convex-to-the-origin curves are isoquants, and the vertical line through points E and F represents the constraint that the time spent in education cannot exceed the endowment. For any given (w_c, p_k), the production of human capital will expand along a given isocline (in the figure, the one through point F) to the point where the child's time is fully used for educational purposes ($e = 1$). From that point onwards, h can be increased at a rising marginal cost by moving to a steeper isocline (in the figure, to the one through point E).

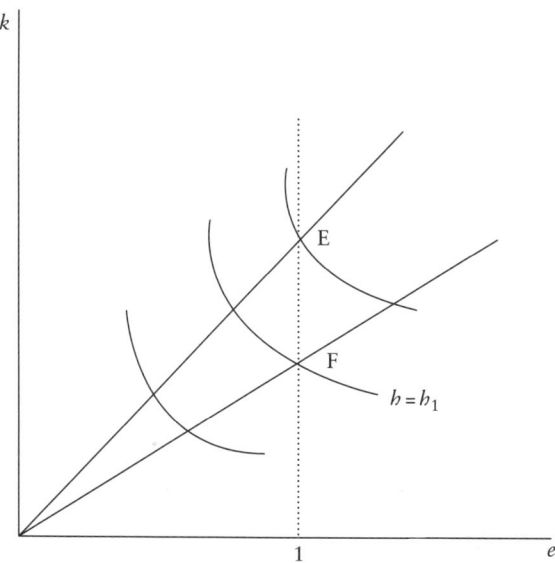

Figure 2.2. *Production of human capital*

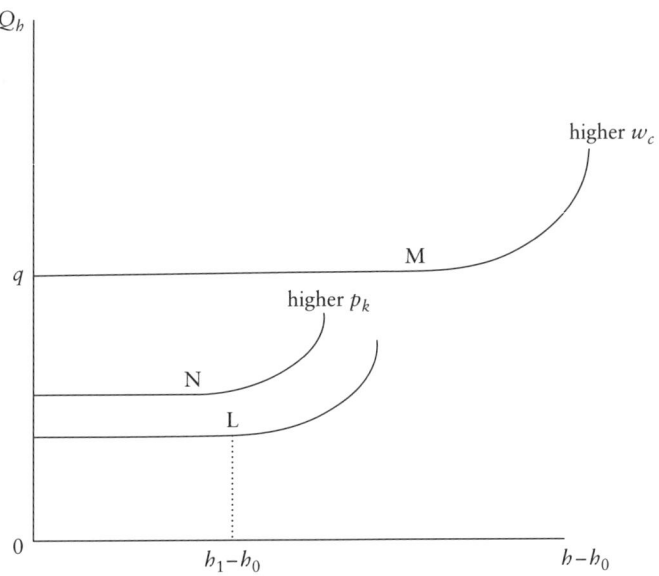

Figure 2.3. *The marginal cost of human capital*

Let h_1 denote the level where the child's time becomes fully employed in education (given w_c and p_k). Between h_0 and h_1, the marginal cost of human capital is then a constant determined by input prices,

$$Q_h(h, w_c, p_k) \equiv q(w_c, p_k) \quad \text{for } h_0 \leq h \leq h_1. \tag{5}$$

At higher levels, the marginal cost of human capital is increasing in h.

Fig. 2.3 shows the behaviour of the marginal cost of human capital for a given (w_c, p_k). Point L is where the child's time becomes fully employed in education. The kinked line through point L may be interpreted as the domestic supply of human capital. Had we assumed decreasing returns to scale, the supply curve would have been convex over its entire domain, but there would still have been a discontinuity at point L. Therefore, the assumption that human capital production is characterized by constant returns to scale does not affect the substance of the argument.

If w_c rises, the horizontal segment of the supply curve shifts upwards. The point where the child starts to study full time moves to the right, because the parents economize the child's time. The new supply curve then looks like the kinked line through **M**. Alternatively, suppose that p_k rises. The horizontal segment of the supply curve will again shift upwards, but the point where the child starts to study full time will now move to the left, because parents economize educational inputs. The new supply curve will then look like the kinked line through **N**.

2.2 PARENTAL DECISIONS

At stage 2, (a_0, a_1, c_1) is a bygone, and n is given. The income that a child will enjoy at stage 3 is assumed to be

$$y = h\omega + m, \tag{6}$$

where m is again the amount of net transfers that the future adult will receive from his parents, h the amount of human capital with which the child will enter adult life, and ω the return to this asset. In contrast with the model of paragraph 1.2, the child's future earning capacity is thus taken to vary with education.[1] The items of expenditure included in c_1 and c_2 are defined to include food and medical care, but not education (that enters into the determination of h).

We assume that a self-enforcing family constitution (see section 1.3) pre-scribing adults to give at least z to each of their young children, and at least x to their elderly parents, is in place. Adults thus give their parents exactly x. Being altruistic towards their children, however, they *may* give each of their young children more than z at stage 2,

$$c_2 + Q(h, w_c, p_k) \geq z. \tag{7}$$

For the same reason, at stage 3, they *may* give back to their adult children some of the x they are entitled to receive from each of them, or even give them more than x. If the latter, m will be positive. If the former, m will be negative. In contrast with the model of section 1.2, parents can thus make negative net transfers to their children, but *gross* transfers must still be non-negative for the reasons already discussed. Hence,

$$x + m \geq 0. \tag{8}$$

Parental old age consumption is determined by

$$a_3 = sr - mn, \tag{9}$$

where s is the amount saved by parents at stage 2, and r is the interest factor. The 'constitutional' model examined in Chapter 1 predicts that, in the absence of uncertainty, compliers will not save because the marginal return on children is higher than the return on conventional assets. This is not true here, however, because the number of children who survived until stage 2 is given. At earlier

---

[1] In general, y could be a function of c_1 and c_2, as well as h, because pre-school and school-age consumption may affect the child's future health status, hence his future ability to produce income. Indeed, the child's future ability to produce income may depend also (positively if there is learning by doing, negatively if work is bad for the child's health) on the amount of labour supplied while of school age. For simplicity, however, we assume at this stage that c_1 and c_2 affect U^* only directly, not through y, and that child labour affects U^* only indirectly, through the budget constraint. The hypothesis that a child's health is adversely affected by his labour supply is considered and tested in Chapter 7.

stages, parents may well have chosen the level of birth control, and then the level of pre-school expenditure per child born, that maximized expected parental lifetime utility. The realization of n, however, may be 'too high' or 'too low'. If it is too high, parents may want to borrow money or sell assets. If it is too low, they may want to lend money or buy assets.

Let w_c denote the child wage rate (or the marginal product of a child's labour in the family business if higher). Define W_2 as the sum of parental earnings and assets (inclusive of bequests received), *net* of the amount x due to the grandparents under the family constitution, and of any other fixed charges such as rents or taxes. The stage-2 budget constraint is then

$$a_2 + [c_2 + Q(h, w_c, p_k)]n + s = W_2 + w_c n. \qquad (10)$$

The left-hand side of this equation represents the full cost of a family with n school-age children. The right-hand side is the household's full disposable income (i.e. the household's income if assets are disposed of, and all family members, including children, work full time).

Additionally, asset and credit market imperfections may impose upper and lower bounds on the choice of s,

$$s_0 \leq s \leq s_1, \qquad (11)$$

where s_0 is a non-positive, and s_1 a non-negative number. In the presence of adverse selection, the lower bound may reflect lack of assets to sell or offer as collateral (Stiglitz and Weiss 1981, Hoff and Lyon 1995). The upper bound, unusual in a developed economy, may well arise in a developing country context, where some individuals do not have access to financial markets, and there may also be a shortage of assets, particularly land, worth buying (Biswanger et al. 1995).

Given n, parents choose (a_2, c_2, h, m, s) to maximize

$$U_2 = u_2(a_2) + u_3(sr - mn) + \beta U^*(c_2, h\omega + m)n, \quad 0 < \beta \leq 1, \qquad (12)$$

subject to (4),(7)–(11) and

$$a_2 \geq a_s, \; a_3 \geq a_s, \; c_2 \geq c_s, \; y - x \geq a_s. \qquad (13)$$

Since ω is not yet known, (12) implies that parents are subjectively certain about the future value of this parameter. If parents had probabilistic expectations, they would maximize the expected value of (12). As the concavity of $U^*(.)$ would then imply aversion to risk, and realistically assuming that parents cannot insure against the risk of a low ω for the usual moral hazard problem, parental decisions would then be affected by the degree of risk aversion. If risk aversion is decreasing in full income, poor parents will then invest in their children's education less than rich parents. This carries the implication that labour market policies aimed at reducing the riskiness of private educational investment would induce poor parents to invest more in their children's education. We shall come back to this point in Chapter 8.

2.2.1 *Saving or dissaving*

Suppose that (7)–(8) and (11)–(13) are not binding. The solution then satisfies

$$\frac{u_2'(a_2)}{u_3'((sr-m)n)} = r = \frac{U_{c_2}^*(c_2, h\omega + m)}{U_y^*(c_2, h\omega + m)} \tag{14}$$

and

$$\text{either } \frac{\omega}{Q_h} = r, \text{ or } h = h_0. \tag{15}$$

The first set of conditions tells us that parents equate their own and their children's marginal rate of substitution of current for future consumption to the interest factor. The second says that, if parents invest in their children's human capital at all, they do so to the point where the marginal return to education, ω/Q', is equal to the interest factor, r. Notice that (14)–(15) are also the conditions for a Pareto-optimal allocation of resources between parents and children.

Figs 2.4 to 2.7 illustrate the properties of the solution under four possible configurations of parameters. In all these pictures, the amount currently consumed by each child, c_2, is measured on the horizontal axis. The vertical axis measures the child's adult earnings, $h\omega$, and adult income, y. If y is higher than

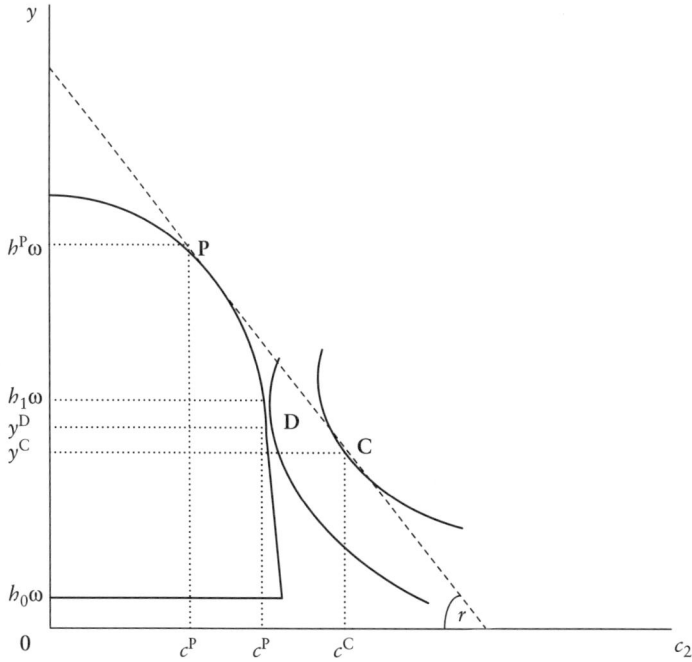

Figure 2.4. *Low interest rate, parents dissave*

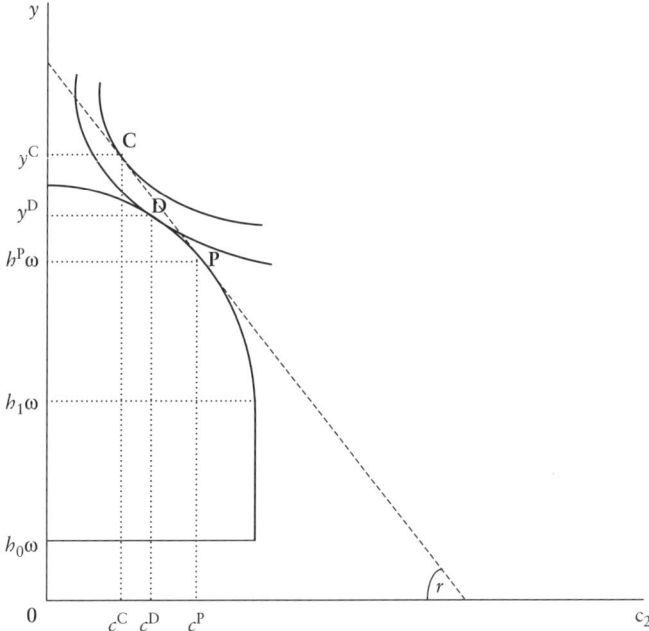

Figure 2.5. *Low interest rate, parents save*

$h\omega$, this implies that the net transfer from the child's parents, m, is positive. If y is lower than $h\omega$, it means that m is negative.

The kinked curve through point **P** is the domestic production frontier. The slope of this curve is the marginal return to education, ω/Q_h, equal to ω/q up to h_1, lower than ω/q above it. The straight line with slope r represents the intertemporal budget constraint of parents who are free to save or dissave. This line has only point **P** in common with the domestic production frontier. The ordinate of that point, h^P, is the future human capital of a child whose parents are free to save or dissave. The convex-to-the-origin curves are the children's indifference curves. If parents are free to save or dissave, the solution is at point **C** of the intertemporal budget line, where the children's marginal rate of substitution of current for future consumption, U_c^*/U_y^*, is equal to r.

Suppose that the interest rate is relatively low, in the specific sense that the interest factor is larger than the marginal return to education up the point where the child starts to study full time,[2]

$$r < \frac{\omega}{q}. \tag{16}$$

[2] Recall that the marginal cost of h, hence the marginal return to education, is assumed constant up to that point. As already noted, this is a harmless simplification. Even if the marginal cost increased throughout, there would still be a discontinuity at h_1.

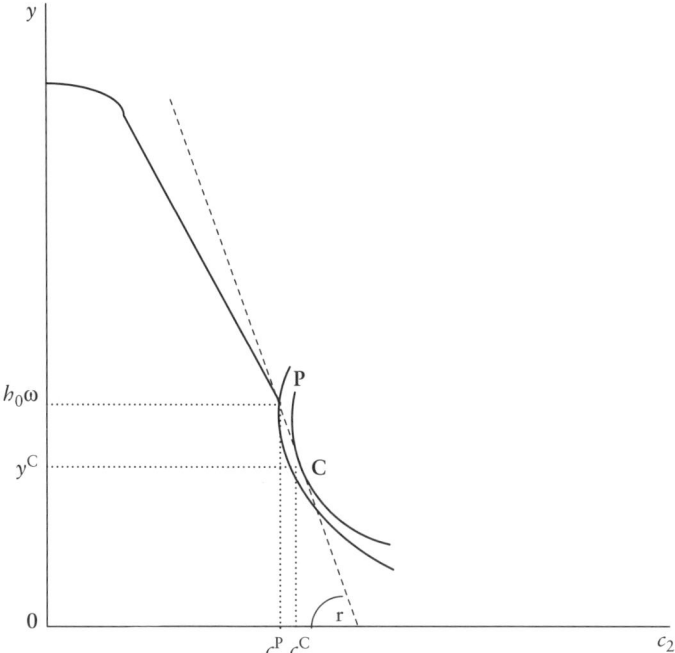

Figure 2.6. *High interest rate, parents dissave*

In this situation, parents invest in their children's education to the point where the marginal return to education is equal to its opportunity cost. Since parents wish to increase their children's human capital, (4) is clearly not binding. Given that all points below **P** have slope greater than r, the ordinate of this point, h^P, is higher than h_1. Therefore, children study full time.

In Fig. 2.4, preferences and endowments are such that **C** lies south-east of **P**. As $h^P \omega$ is then higher than the ordinate of point **C**, y^C, this tells us that parents are planning to recover part of the cost of their children's education by making negative net transfers (bequeathing each child less than x). The abscissa of point **P**, c^P, is to be interpreted as the amount of current consumption that the child would get if the parents were *not* borrowing money, or selling assets, to pay for h^P. Since the abscissa of point **C**, c^C, is higher than c^P, however, parents are doing precisely that.

In Fig. 2.5, by contrast, **C** lies above **P**. Since y^C is now larger than $h^P \omega$, this means that, in addition to giving their children an education, parents plan to make them also a positive net transfer (bequeath each child more than x). The abscissa of point **P**, c^P, is then to be interpreted as the amount of current consumption that a child would get if the parents were not lending money, or buying assets. Since c^C is lower than c^P, the parents are doing that on top of

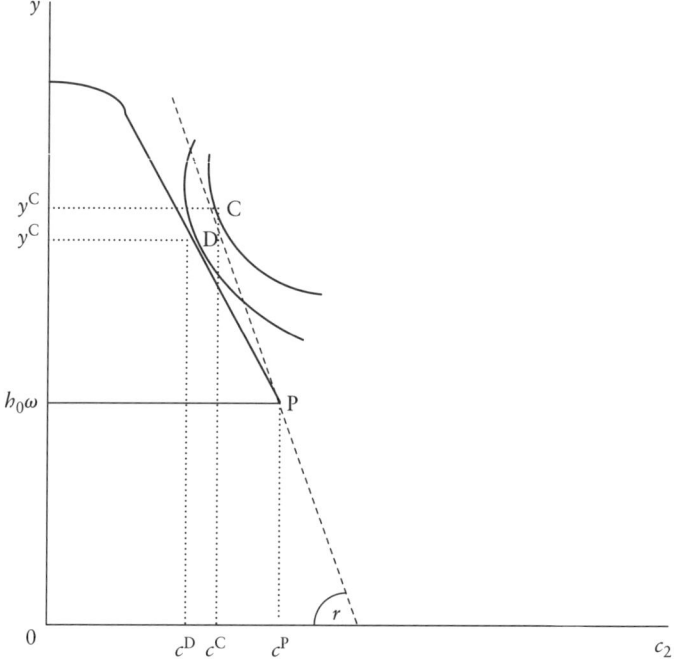

Figure 2.7. *High interest rate, parents save*

investing in their children's human capital. The configuration of preferences and endowments that could give rise to a situation like that portrayed in Fig. 2.5 could differ from that portrayed in Fig. 2.4 in a number of respects, among them that the parents are richer or more generous (have either W_2 or β) in the the former than in the latter.

Alternatively, suppose that the interest rate is relatively high, in the sense that

$$r > \frac{\omega}{q}. \tag{17}$$

Parents would now sell off their children's natural talent if only they could. Therefore, (4) is always binding, and the ordinate of point **P** is always equal to $h_0\omega$. If parents give their children anything, it is money or other conventional assets, but never education. School-age children now work full time.

In Fig. 2.6, point **C** lies south-east of point **P**. When they grow up, children will thus find themselves without an education. Since y^C is lower than $h_0\omega$, they will also get a negative m. Parents are thus doing the next best thing to selling off their children's natural talent; they are borrowing against it. In Fig. 2.7, by contrast, **C** lies north-west of **P**. Therefore, parents are still keeping their children ignorant. Since y^C is higher than $h_0\omega$, and c^C lower than c^P, they are however saving with a view to making positive net transfers when their children grow up. Children will thus enter adult life ignorant but rich. The difference between Fig. 2.7 and Fig. 2.6 can again be explained in terms of parental wealth or generosity, but another plausible explanation in that the marginal return to education is lower in the latter than in the former.

2.2.2 *No saving or dissaving*

In reality, it may be difficult to borrow against one's own future earnings, because financial institutions are generally reluctant to lend without adequate security. Since human capital cannot be mortgaged like a building or a piece of land, a person without conventional assets will thus find it difficult to get credit for educational purposes. If the person who would like to borrow is a parent, and the one who would get the education is a child, there is also an insufficient commitment problem. Parents may in fact be confident that they would be able to pay back the loan out of the transfers they will be entitled to receive from their own grown-up children under the terms of the family constitution. But an entitlement arising from an informal intra-family arrangement cannot be legally transferred to a third party, and cannot thus be used as collateral.

In developing countries, these problems are aggravated by the high incidence of parents without conventional assets, by the insufficient development of the financial sector, and by the government's inability to act as insurer of last resort. In these countries, parents may also find it difficult to accumulate assets. Access to an ordinary bank may in fact be restricted by ignorance, or travel costs. Access to real asset markets—particularly to the market for land, if landlords are reluctant to surrender the power and status that land confers—may be restricted too. Let us then look at what happens if (11) is binding. To avoid carrying an extra constant around, we shall simply assume that s is effectively constrained (either from above, or from below) to be zero.

Continuing to assume that neither the family constitution nor the subsistence constraints (13) are binding, parents now choose (a_2, c_2, h, m) to satisfy the budget constraint (10),

$$\frac{u_2'(a_2)}{u_3'(-mn)} = \frac{U_{c_2}^*(c_2, h\omega + m)}{U_y^*(c_2, h\omega + m)} \tag{18}$$

and

$$\text{either } \frac{U_{c_2}^*(c_2, h\omega + m)}{U_y^*(c_2, h\omega + m)} = \frac{\omega}{Q_h}, \text{ or } h = h_0. \tag{19}$$

Condition (18) tells us that the marginal rates of substitution of parents and children are still equalized. Since parents are excluded from the asset and credit markets, however, there is nothing to ensure that the two marginal rates of substitution will be equated to the interest factor. The solution in not a Pareto optimum. It is, nonetheless, a constrained Pareto optimum (i.e. given that certain markets are not available). Condition (19) says that, if parents invest in their children's human capital at all, they do so to the point where the marginal return to education equals the children's marginal rate of substitution of present consumption for future income. Let us now go back to Figs 2.4–2.7, to see what this implies for child labour and education. Since parents can neither save nor dissave, the solution is now a point on the domestic frontier, denoted by **D**.

In Fig. 2.4, the parameter configuration is such that (4) is not binding. In other words, circumstances are such that parents do not wish they could sell off their children's natural talent. Their children's marginal rate of substitution is then equated to the marginal return to education. In the figure, **D** lies north-west of **C**. This means that parents are giving their children too little current consumption, and too much future income. Since the ordinate of point **D**, y^D, is not only lower than $h^P\omega$, but also lower than $h_1\omega$, children work and study at the same time. This is the case, remember, where the efficient solution, **C**, has children studying full time. It thus follows that child labour is inefficiently high. But that is not the only possibility. If y^D were higher than $h_1\omega$, children would study full time even though their parents are not allowed to dissave. If that were the case, educational investment would still be inefficiently low, but only in the sense that there is too little educational expenditure. In general, therefore, we can only say that permitting parents to borrow money, or giving them assets to sell, would increase educational investment, but would not necessarily reduce child labour.

In Fig. 2.5, (4) is still not binding, but point **D** lies south-east of **C**. Parents are now giving their children too much current consumption, and too little future income. Since **D** must necessarily lie above **P**, parents are letting their children study full time, but are spending too much on their children's education. In this case, educational expenditure is inefficiently high. While, in Fig. 2.4, the source of inefficiency was that parents could not dissave enough to finance the efficient amount of human capital investment, the problem in Fig. 2.5 is rather that lack of conventional investment opportunities induces parents to overinvest in their children's human capital. Permitting parents to lend money, or buy assets, in such circumstances would reduce educational investment, and have no effect on child labour.

In Fig. 2.6, the parameter configuration is such that parents do wish they could sell off their children's natural talent. As (4) is now binding. the solution is at point **P**. In this case, parents give their children too little current con-sumption, and too much future income. Allowing parents to dissave in such circumstances would remove the inefficiency, but would have no effect on either child labour or education. In Fig. 2.7, by contrast, the solution is represented by point **D**. Since this point lies south-west of the efficient allocation, **C**, current consumption is again too low, but the reason is not that parents cannot dissave (they would save if they could). It is rather that, as they cannot lend money, or buy conventional assets, parents overinvest in their children's education. In this case, child labour is inefficiently low, and educational expenditure inefficiently high. Allowing parents to save would remove the inefficiency, but would also raise child labour.

Lack of access to credit and asset markets may thus result in an inefficiently high supply of child labour by certain families. This result was first established in Baland and Robinson (2000). Using a richer model, however, we have shown that asset and credit market imperfection may also result in an inefficiently low supply of child labour, or excessive educational expenditure, by other families. The latter is unlikely to concern the very poor, but it may occur in families only just comfortably off.[3] In any case, it is a misallocation of resources, and thus an obstacle to development. These conclusions, and those of the next subsection, rest on the assumption that child labour affects utility only through consumption. If there are other effects, and they are adverse, the probability that child labour may be inefficient is obviously higher. Bommier and Dubois (2005) show that, if child labour yields direct disutility, an equilibrium with child labour may be inefficient even if parents are altruistic, transfers are not at a corner, and there are no market imperfections. The same is obviously true if child labour has an adverse effect on health.

2.2.3 *Binding family rules*

Let us now see what happens if the family constitution imposes effective constraints on parental choice, still assuming that the subsistence constraints are not binding. Let preferences and endowment be such that parents would like to spend less than z for each school-age child. As (7) is then binding, the allocation satisfies (19) and

$$\frac{U_{c_2}^*(c_2, h\omega + m)}{U_y^*(c_2, h\omega + m)} = \frac{u_2'(a_2) - \lambda}{u_3'(sr - mn)}, \tag{20}$$

where λ is the Lagrange-multiplier of (7). The marginal rate of substitution of present for future consumption is thus lower for the children than for the parents. If parents have access to asset and credit markets, they will equate their own marginal rate of substitution to the interest factor, otherwise they will not. But the allocation will be inefficient in either case, because the two marginal rates of substitution are not equalized. Both parties would be better off if parents could reduce the amount spent for each child at stage 2, and increase the net amount transferred to each child at stage 3, until the two marginal rates of substitution became the same. That will not happen, however, because the family constitution allows adults to punish elderly parents who spend less than z for each school-age child.

Alternatively, suppose that, at stage 3, parents would like to receive more than x from each of their grown-up children. As (8) is then binding, m is no

---

[3] A recent *New York Times* article documents the outburst of household spending for private education in India (Waldman 2003).

longer a choice variable $(m = -x)$. In this case, the allocation satisfies (19) and

$$\frac{U^*_{c_2}(c_2, h\omega - x)}{U^*_y(c_2, h\omega - x)} = \frac{u'_2(a_2)}{u'_3(xn) + \mu}, \tag{21}$$

where μ is the Lagrange-multiplier of (8). In this case too, the marginal rate of substitution of present for future consumption of the children is thus lower than that of the parents. If parents have access to asset and credit markets, they again equate their own marginal rate of substitution to the interest factor, otherwise they do not. In either case, the allocation is again inefficient. Parents and children would be better off if the latter could credibly commit to give the former more than x at the next stage. For the reasons discussed in section 1.2, that will not happen.

Figs 2.4 to 2.7 can again be used to illustrate the solution. In the first two figures, where parents invest in their children's education, the solution is represented by point **D**. In the other two, where human capital is at a corner, the solution is represented by point **P**. Point **C** is now irrelevant because, even if parents have access to credit and asset markets, the children's consumption is in any case distorted by constitutional requirements. As we already knew from section 1.3, family constitutions may thus be a source of inefficiency. In the absence of a family constitution, however, the elderly would get no support from their grown-up children, and poor adults would spend very little on their young children.

2.3 THE EFFECTS OF ACCESS COSTS

The model we have developed so far does not allow for the possibility that children do nothing. As we shall see in later chapters, however, household surveys report a large proportion of school-age children, as much as a quarter, who neither work, nor attend school. That is puzzling in areas where a large number of families live close to the subsistence line. Comparing surveys relating to different countries, we also find that combining work with study is common in some places, for example in Latin America, but uncommon in others, for example in rural India. The theory predicts that children will not work and study at the same time if (i) their parents are free to save or dissave, and (ii) the non-negative-bequest constraint is not binding. Were it true that the places where combining work with study is unusual are also the places where (i) and (ii) are more likely to be satisfied, that would be consistent with the theory. But we have no reason to believe that. Scarcity of part-time work opportunities could be another explanation. Since most children work either for their parents or in unregulated labour markets, however, that is not a very plausible hypothesis.

Both phenomena, widespread idleness and low incidence of part-time work, can be explained with the presence of fixed costs of access to either school or work. In the present context, fixed means that the cost must necessarily be incurred if a child is to carry out a certain activity, but does not vary with the number of hours allocated to the activity. Such costs may include travel to school or the place of employment, and living expenses away from home. In the case of education, they may further include school fees, expenditure for basic educational material, and possibly also for clothing (in some surveys, children give lack of decent clothing as a reason for not attending school). The fixed costs of getting a job may include search costs, or paying off a labour 'recruiter'.

Let t_w denote the fixed cost of access to work, and t_s the fixed cost of access to education. Disregarding the possibility of saving and dissaving in order to focus on the effects of these entry barriers, we write the budget constraint as

$$a_2 + \gamma n = W_2, \qquad (22)$$

where γ represents the net cost of a child. Since the time not spent studying $(1 - e)$ may now be used either to work, or to do nothing,

$$\gamma \equiv \begin{cases} c_2 & \text{if } h = h_0, w_c < t_w \\ c_2 + t_w - w_c & \text{if } h = h_0, w_c \geq t_w \\ c_2 + t_s + Q(h, w_c, p_k) & \text{if } h \geq h_1 \\ c_2 + t_w + t_s + Q(h, w_c, p_k) - w_c & \text{if } h_0 < h < h_1 \end{cases}.$$

Fig. 2.8 illustrates the case where children will either work full time, or study full time. The broken line through points **F** and **G** is the domestic production frontier. The convex-to-the-origin curve through **E** and **G**. is an indifference curve. There are two solutions, one represented by point **E**, where children study full time and consume

$$c^E \equiv \frac{W_2 - a_2}{n} + w_c - t_w,$$

the other represented by point **G**, where children study full time and consume

$$c^G \equiv \frac{W_2 - a_2}{n} + w_c - t_s - Q(h, w_c, p_k).$$

If the indifference curves were steeper than the one assumed here, the only possible solution would be at **G**. If the indifference curves were flatter, it would be a point on the domestic frontier, north-west of **G**, where children consume less than c^G. In any case, children would not combine work with study.

Fig. 2.9 illustrates the case where work is effectively precluded by high access costs. The domestic production frontier looks like the concave-to-the-origin curve through points **F** and **G**. There are again two possible solutions. One is at point **E**, where children do nothing and consume

$$c^E \equiv \frac{W_2 - a_2}{n}.$$

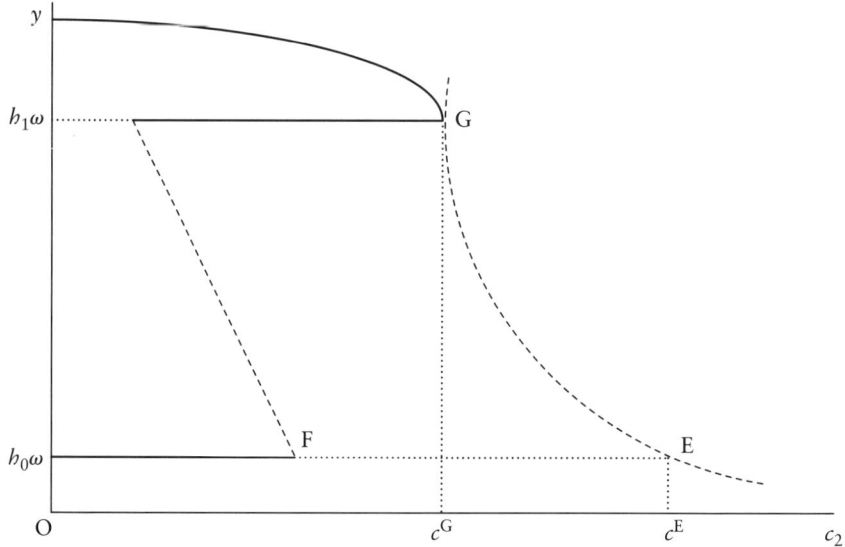

Figure 2.8. *Children work full time, or study full time*

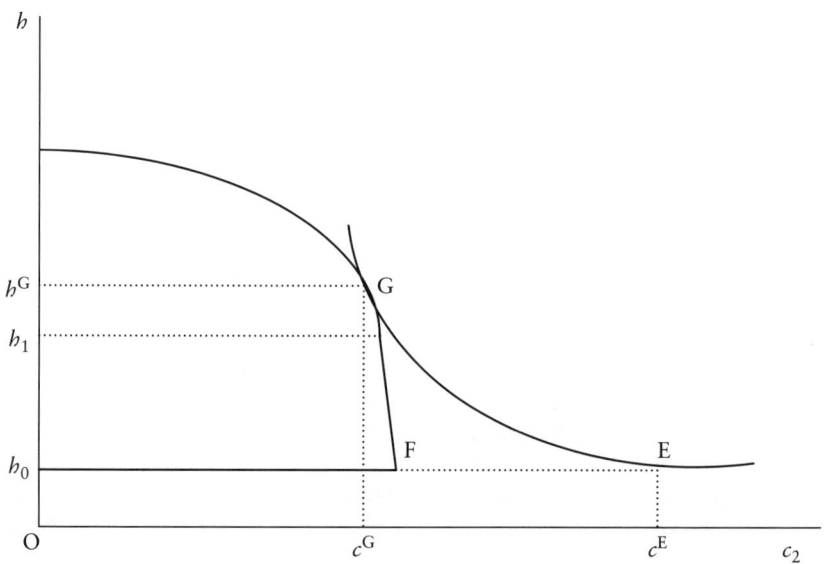

Figure 2.9. *Children study full time, or do nothing*

The other is at point **G**, where they study full time and consume

$$c^G \equiv \frac{W_2 - a_2}{n} + w_c - t_s - Q(h, w_c, p_k).$$

If the indifference curves were steeper, the only solution would be at **E**. If they were flatter, the only solution would be a point on the frontier north-west of **G**. Whatever their preferences, children will either spend a substantial amount of time studying (not necessarily full time as assumed in the figure), or do nothing.

Both the low incidence of children working and studying at the same time, and the high number of children reportedly doing nothing, may thus be explained with the existence of fixed costs of access to education or work. The probability that children combine work with study increases, and the probability that they do nothing decreases, as $W_2 + nw_c$ increases. The lower full household income, the higher is in fact the incidence of the fixed access costs.

2.4   THE EFFECTS OF EXTREME POVERTY

Extreme poverty cannot be defined with reference to a single family characteristic such as full income. We characterize it as a configuration of initial assets, interest and wage rates, marginal return to education, and number and preferences of children, such that parental choice is effectively constrained by one or more of the subsistence constraints in (13).

Figs 2.4 to 2.7 were drawn under the assumption that a_2 and a_3 are at their utility-maximizing levels. To represent the consequences of extreme poverty in the (c_2, y) plane, we now imagine that the figures are drawn holding a_2 and a_3 at their subsistence levels, $a_2 = a_3 = a_s$. We then consider the point, call it **S**, with coordinates (c_s, a_s). The position of this point determines whether a feasible solution exists, and which of the subsistence constraints is binding. If parents are free to save or dissave, a feasible solution exists if and only if **S** lies on, or inside, the intertemporal budget line. Otherwise, it will exist if and only if **S** lies on, or inside, the domestic production frontier. If a feasible solution exists, extreme poverty may still prevent an efficient allocation of resources. If it does not exist, the family cannot survive under the assumptions made so far.

Let us consider the situation portrayed in Fig. 2.4. The efficient solution is represented by point **C**, where parents dissave to pay for their children's education, and children study full time. Suppose that parents are able to borrow, or have assets to sell. If **S** is located inside the intertemporal budget line, south-east of **C**, plan **C** is not feasible. The solution will be a point on the intertemporal budget line, where children work more than would be efficient. Alternatively, suppose that parents can neither borrow, nor sell assets. If **S** lies inside the domestic production frontier, south-east of **D**, the plan represented by this point is not feasible. Children will then work even more than at **D**. It is thus clear that extreme poverty is another source of inefficiency, in addition to those already considered.

In the case illustrated, a lump-sum income subsidy would have a strong negative effect on the incidence of child labour in households close to subsistence, a weaker one in other strata of society. This carries the important policy implication that a government primarily concerned with child labour should give priority to bringing families out of extreme poverty, rather than try to reduce some overall measure of income inequality. Using data from Vietnam, Edmonds (2005) finds by non-parametric methods that improvements in household income status (proxied by per capita expenditure) explain 80 per cent of the decline in child labour observed between 1993 and 1997 in households that moved out of poverty over that period. The effect on non-poor households is much weaker. This is consistent with the proposition that extreme poverty is a cause of child labour. But the finding could also reflect the fact that household income must reach a certain level in order to get over the fixed cost of access to education. Beyond that level, the fixed cost becomes irrelevant, and the effect of a further income increase is much weaker.

What happens if the family is so abjectly poor that a feasible solution does not exist? Slavery, 'tied' labour, or 'bonded' labour may then be the only means of survival. The difference between the first and the other two forms of labour is the same that there is between outright sale and a long lease. We talk of tied labour if a person is committed to work for a certain employer over a very long period of time in exchange for a stream of predetermined wage payments. On the face of it, a tied labour arrangement does not look any different from an ordinary long-term employment contract. But modern labour legislation makes a long-term employment contract binding only on the employer. In developed countries, the worker can thus walk out of it at any time with little or no penalty. In developing countries, by contrast, lack or imperfect enforcement of modern legislation may effectively tie a worker down to a lifelong work commitment.

We talk of bonded labour if the worker gets a lump-sum payment at front. Consider a family living close to subsistence at the best of times. Suppose that a catastrophic event (crop failure, serious illness, or the birth of too many children) brings it below the subsistence threshold. Assume that the family cannot afford to buy insurance, or insurance is not available, and that the government will not step in to compensate them for the consequences of a catastrophic event. If they cannot get credit any other way,[4] parents may have no option but to deliver themselves, or some of their children, into bondage in order to repay the loan.

There was a time, not very distant from ours, when such arrangements were legal. A young London-trained barrister, the future Mahatma Gandhi, made his first appearance on the international political scene campaigning for the

---

[4] Certain institutions do make small unsecured loans to particular categories of persons with a reputation for credit worthiness. In Pakistan, for example, the Grameen Bank makes small loans to women. But that is typically a drop in the ocean compared with the total demand for unsecured credit.

rights of bonded labourers in South Africa. Nowadays, bonded labour is mostly illegal, but debt bondage is still an important phenomenon. The UN Working Group on Contemporary Forms of Slavery puts the number of persons in debt bondage around the world at about 20 million (United Nations Organization 1998). The incidence is particularly high in areas like the Terai region of Nepal, where debts can be inherited (a case where the non-negative-bequests constraint does not apply).

Genicot (2002) argues that the possibility of delivering oneself or one's children into bonded labour makes it *less* likely that assetless households will get credit from legitimate lenders. If a borrower defaults on his repayments to a bank, he will in fact be denied credit by that and every other bank the next time round. If bonded labour were effectively outlawed, potential borrowers would then know that the penalty for defaulting is death by starvation when bad luck strikes again. If bonded labour is only nominally outlawed, however, it is possible for a defaulter to survive. The existence of this safety net makes the borrower's commitment to pay back a debt a little less credible, and consequently restricts the range of loan applications that financial institutions will be willing to accept. This argument is indeed right, but there is no guarantee that the range of acceptable loan applications will ever be wide enough to include families on the verge of starvation. Effectively outlawing bonded labour would thus condemn the extremely poor to death.

Given the focus of the present book, we shall concentrate on tied or bonded *child* labour. An example of the former are young country girls delivered into residential domestic service a long way from home by parents who, in many cases, will show up only to collect the wage. The Moroccan *petites bonnes* have recently attracted the attention of the international agencies, but similar cases abound in parts of Latin America, and were common in southern Europe not so very long ago. Examples of the latter are the boys delivered to unscrupulous farmers or quarry owners, and the girls delivered to brothel keepers, all over the developing world, in exchange for a lump sum. Where the bonded person is a child it seems pedantic to make a distinction between bondage and slavery. Bales (1999) calls them simply the new slaves.

In the Introduction, we reported statistics on 'unconditional worst' forms of child labour. Many of these cases are associated with tied or bonded labour arrangements. The worst ones are likely to be associated with the latter, because the at-front payment removes the necessity of any further contact between parents and children.[5] In what follows, we shall thus concentrate on bonded child labour. Since children are more docile than adults, and easier to restrain by force if need be, we shall assume (though it is not universally true) that only children are acceptable as bonds. Even though it is unfortunately not always true, we shall also suppose that parents resort to bonding their children only

---

[5] In the limiting case, that of children sold to be killed, and have their organs explanted, there is no 'labour'.

if the family cannot survive by any other means.[6] This brings us into an area where it is difficult to make Paretian statements.

Suppose that full household income is not enough to keep the parents and all existing children alive. In such circumstances, no family constitution is enforceable. Indeed, if it were known with certainty that generation t would find it impossible to comply with the constitution, generation $t-1$ would not comply either. The same would be true of generations $t-2$, $t-3$, etc. No self-enforcing constitution would then exist. It might, however, if there is a risk that some future generation will default, but nobody can tell with certainty which.

In such circumstances, grandparents will be left to their own devices. Given that current adults cannot expect any old-age support from their children, they must then save enough to meet at least their and their children's future subsistence requirements, $(1+n)(a_s/r)$.[7] Since there is not enough to keep parents and children alive, there are clearly no resources to invest in education.[8] Therefore, (4) is binding. Parents and children can survive without delivering themselves or their children into bonded labour only on condition that

$$\frac{1+r+n}{r}a_s + c_s n \leq W_2 + w_c n + \frac{\omega h_0}{r}. \tag{23}$$

Suppose that, in exchange for a child, somebody is willing to pay the parents a lump-sum payment, A. If parents cannot borrow in the ordinary way, A must be larger than the net current contribution that the child would otherwise make to the family budget,

$$w_c - c_s < A,$$

or there would be no point in giving a child away. If parents can borrow, A must satisfy

$$w_c - c_s + \frac{\omega h_0 - a_s}{r} < A. \tag{24}$$

In the most optimistic hypothesis, (24) may be taken to imply that the bond taker can borrow at an interest factor lower than r. If that is not the case, however, it implies that the child's labour is worth more to the bond taker than to an ordinary employer. This may mean that that a bond taker can get away with using the child for activities that are either illegal, or illegally carried out. The latter may consist of making the child work excessively long hours. The former will include physically dangerous, or morally objectionable

---

[6] Bales (1999) reports evidence of parents giving children away to buy consumer durables.

[7] This implies that they can buy assets or lend money. If they could only store durable goods, they would have to save at least $(1+n)a_s$.

[8] Edmonds and Sharma (2004) study the effects of debt bondage in the Terai region of Nepal, and find that children vulnerable to bondage are indeed less likely to attend school, have lower educational achievements if they do go to school, and are more likely to work even before being bonded, than children who are not.

activities. A bonded child is thus more likely than an ordinary working child to be engaging in what the international conventions classify as 'unconditional worst' forms of child labour.

Let B denote the number of children offered as bonds. Obviously

$$0 \le B \le n. \tag{25}$$

Since the present and the future consumption of unbonded family members is fixed at the subsistence level, both $u(a_0, a_1, a_2, a_3)$ and $U^*(c_1, c_2, y)$ are equal to zero. As there is nothing to maximize, B is then determined by the household budget constraint. Assuming that parents cannot borrow, the latter may now be written as

$$\frac{1+r}{r}a_s + \left(c_s - w_c + \frac{a_s - \omega h_0}{r}\right)(n - B) = W_2 + AB. \tag{26}$$

By the assumption that the family cannot survive if B is equal to zero, the first constraint in (25) will never be binding. If the second one is binding, survival requires

$$\frac{1+r}{r}a_s \le W_2 + An. \tag{27}$$

If (25) is not binding, the number of children bonded is given by

$$B = \frac{(1 + r + n)a_s + [(c_s - w_c)n - W_2]r - \omega h_0 n}{(A + c_s - w_c)r + a_s - \omega h_0}. \tag{28}$$

In the light of (28), B is clearly a decreasing function of A. That should not come as a surprise, because an increase in A is equivalent to a reduction in the interest rate implicitly charged by the bond taker for lending a given amount of money to the parents. The effect of an increase in w_c,

$$\frac{dB}{dw_c} = -\frac{(An + W_2)r - (1 + r)a_s}{(A + c_s - w_c)r + a_s - \omega h_0}r, \tag{29}$$

are negative if and only if (27) holds as inequality (non-positive if and only if it holds as an equation). Put another way, provided that the parents do not need to bond *all* their children in order to survive, B will decrease as w_c increases. This raises a difficult moral question.

Imagine that a firm opens a factory in an area where children are at risk of ending as bonded workers. If the factory pays adult workers more than the going wage, that will reduce the risk of both ordinary and bonded child labour because W_2 will increase. If the factory employs only child workers, however, and pays them more than the going wage, that will reduce the probability of bonded child labour, and increase that of ordinary child labour. Is that better or worse than the status quo?[9] Answering this question requires a strong value judgement. If the answer is that it is better, one is in effects saying that an increase in the number of children working is a price worth paying to prevent even only a small number of children being abused. If the answer is that it is worse, it means that one is not willing to pay the price.

[9] A specific instance of this dilemma is the spread throughout Latin America of *maquiladoras*, firms specialized in processing duty-free imports of semi-finished products (often garments destined for the North American or West European markets) prior to re-exportation. These firms are accused of imposing punishing work routines on their employees, often school-age children, but pay wages substantially higher than anything available in the area.

3

Fertility, Infant Mortality, and Gender

In this chapter, we deal with a number of questions relating to reproduction, infant mortality, and the position of women. The term 'gender' is used in its current sociological connotation alluding to the social implications of sex differences. Given the complexity of the points at issue, we retain at first the simplifying assumption that parents act as if they were one person, and that children belonging to the same family are treated the same. Then we distinguish between mother and father, and between boys and girls, to show how the woman's unique role in the generation of children may affect her claim on domestic resources.

3.1 REPRODUCTION AND SURVIVAL

This section is concerned with stages 1 and 0 of the domestic decision process. At stage 1, the number of live births b is already known, but the number n who will survive to school age, and the state of the world that they will face if they do, are not yet known. At this stage, parents allocate household resources between themselves and their children in the knowledge that this will affect the survival probability of the latter. At stage 0, there are no children, and the probability distribution of childbirth is conditioned by the reproductive behaviour of would-be parents. This part of the analysis resembles Cigno (1998). There, however, the number of births is determined by fiat, and stages 0 and 1 are consequently collapsed into one.

3.1.1 *Infant mortality*

Substituting the stage-2 choice of (c_2, h, m, s) into U_2 makes it a function, $v(n, \theta)$, of the number of surviving children, n, and of the economic environment,

$$\theta = (W_2, w_c, r, \omega)$$

that the household will face at stage 2.

The value to the parents of an extra child reaching school age is given by

$$v_n = [w_c - c_2 - Q(h, w_c, p_k)] u_{a_2} - m u_{a_3} + \beta U^*. \tag{1}$$

The first term on the right-hand side of this expression takes the sign of the net contribution that a child will make to the stage-2 family budget, $(w_c - c_2 - Q)$. The second term takes opposite sign to parental net transfers, m. The third is always positive. The sign of (1) is thus likely to be positive at low realizations of n, where the marginal utilities of stage-2 and stage-3 parental consumption, u_{a_2} and u_{a_3}, are small, negative at high ones. The turning point will occur at a lower n for poor than for well-off families.

The effect of the child wage rate on the value that parents attribute to n,

$$v_{w_c} = (1 - Q_{w_c})\, n u_{a_2}, \tag{2}$$

is positive if school-age children work, zero if they do not. That of the rate of remuneration of human capital,

$$v_\omega = \beta h n U_y^*, \tag{3}$$

is positive in any case.

Let us place ourselves at stage 1. The probability that a child will survive to stage 2 is affected by exogenous factors such as climate, biological inheritance, and government provision of sanitation, safe water, preventive medicine, etc. But it depends also on the amount of nutrition and health care, included in c_1, that a child receives from his parents at the present stage. For simplicity, we shall assume that there are only two possible outcomes, either every child that is born survives to school age ($n = b$), or none does ($n = 0$). The results do not change substantially if we attach a positive probability to all values of n between 0 and b as in Cigno (1998). Denoting the exogenous mortality-reducing factors by μ, we can then write $\pi(c_1, \mu)$, with $\pi(.,.)$ is increasing and concave, for the conditional probability that b children survive to school age. The expected number of school-age children is then $b\pi(c_1, \mu)$. Further assuming that parents have point expectations about the future realization of θ,[1] the expected value of $v(n, \theta)$ is

$$E(v(n; \theta)) = \pi(c_1, \mu)\, v(b, \theta) + [1 - \pi(c_1, \mu)]\, v(0, \theta). \tag{4}$$

We argued in the last chapter that assetless parents will find it difficult to borrow against their children's future earnings. If that is true at stage 2 of the decision process, where n is known, it will be true all the more at stage 1, where n is uncertain. Realistically assuming that stage-1 parental earnings are low for life-cycle reasons, and that any bequests will not be forthcoming until stage 2 (in other words, that the grandparents are still alive), parents are also unlikely to be able to buy assets, or lend money. The stage-1 budget constraint is then

$$a_1 + p_1 c_1 b + \phi(b) = W_1, \tag{5}$$

---

[1] Recall that we made the same assumption at stage 2 about the realization of ω. Now, however, there is uncertainty about the realization of n.

where W_1 denotes current parental earnings, and p_1 the price of c_1. The term $\phi(b)$ may be interpreted as the difference between the opportunity-cost, increasing and convex in b, of parental time spent looking after b infants, and the income-equivalent of the pleasure, increasing and concave in b, of doing that. Therefore, $\phi(b)$ can be either positive or negative, and $\phi'(b)$ is likely to be negative at low realizations of b, when the pleasure of an extra child can be expected to outweigh the opportunity cost, positive at high realizations of b, when the opposite is true.

In view of (5), and of uncertainty over the realization of n, parents choose c_1 to maximize

$$E(U_1) = u_1(W_1 - p_1 c_1 b - \phi(b)) + E(v(n; \theta)), \qquad (6)$$

taking b and μ as given. As we are interested in what happens to children, we restrict our attention to families with positive b.

The first-order condition for (6) to be at a maximum,

$$-b p_1 u_1'(W_1 - W_1 - p_1 c_1 b - \phi(b)) + [v(b, \theta) - v(0, \theta)] \pi_{c_1}(c_1, \mu) = 0, \qquad (7)$$

tells us that parents raise c_1 to the point where the marginal utility of current parental consumption forgone equals the expected marginal utility of n. Assuming that parents will be happier, at stage 2, if all their children survive, than if none does,

$$v(b, \theta) > v(0, \theta). \qquad (8)$$

The second-order condition,

$$\Delta_1 \equiv b^2 p_1^2 u_1''(W_1 - p_1 c_1 b - \phi(b)) + [v(b, \theta) - v(0, \theta)] \pi_{c_1 c_1}(c_1, \mu) < 0, \qquad (9)$$

is then satisfied.

The marginal effect of the number of children born on the amount spent for each of them at the present stage is

$$\frac{\partial c_1}{\partial b} = \frac{\begin{aligned} p_1[u_1'(W_1 - p_1 c_1 b - \phi(b)) - (p_1 c_1 + \phi'(b)) u_1''(W_1 - p_1 c_1 b - \phi(b))] \\ -d(b, \theta) \pi_{c_1}(c_1, \mu) \end{aligned}}{\Delta_1}, \qquad (10)$$

where

$$d(b, \theta) \equiv v_n(b, \theta) - v_n(0, \theta).$$

Plausibly assuming that, at stage 2, the couple will appreciate an extra child more if none have survived, than if any positive number b has, we can take $d(b, \theta)$ to be positive. The first term of the numerator on the right-hand side of (10) is positive for sufficiently high realizations of b, but could otherwise be negative. The second right-hand side term is unambiguously negative. The relationship between c_1 and b is thus either decreasing throughout, or hump-shaped.

Let us see how c_1 is affected by the stage-1 exogenous variables. The marginal effect of parental income,

$$\frac{\partial c_1}{\partial W_1} = \frac{p_1 u_1''(W_1 - p_1 c_1 b - \phi(b))}{\Delta_1},$$
(11)

is clearly positive. That of the price of c_1,

$$\frac{\partial c_1}{\partial p_1} = \frac{u_1' - b c_1 p_1 u_1''(W_1 - p_1 c_1 b - \phi(b))}{\Delta_1} b,$$
(12)

is clearly negative.

The higher-stage exogenous variables also affect the choice of c_1. Since $v_{w_c}(0, \theta)$ and $v_\omega(0, \theta)$ are clearly zero, the effect of the child wage rate,

$$\frac{\partial c_1}{\partial w_c} = -\frac{v_{w_c}(b, \theta) \pi_{c_1}(c_1, \mu)}{\Delta_1},$$
(13)

and that of the rate at which human capital is remunerated in adult life,

$$\frac{\partial c_1}{\partial \omega} = -\frac{v_\omega(b, \theta) \pi_{c_1}(c_1, \mu)}{\Delta_1},$$
(14)

are both positive. Therefore, the expectation that their children will attract high wages, either at school age or in adult life, will induce parents to take better care of them, and reduce the probability that they will die in infancy.

The effect of mortality-reducing policies is given by

$$\frac{\partial c_1}{\partial \mu} = -\frac{[v(b, \theta) - v(0, \theta)] \pi_{c_1 \mu}(c_1, \mu)}{\Delta_1}.$$
(15)

The sign of $\pi_{c_1 \mu}$ tells us whether μ raises or lowers the marginal effect of c_1 on a child's survival probability. We say that μ and c_1 are gross complements if $\pi_{c_1 \mu}$ is positive, gross substitutes if $\pi_{c_1 \mu}$ is negative. In view of (8), public expenditure on health and sanitation will then crowd in parental expenditure for children's nutrition and health care if μ and c_1 are gross complements, crowd it out if they are gross substitutes.[2]

Let σ denote the rate at which children survive to adult age. Suppose, for a moment, that all families behave the same, so that $\sigma = \pi b$. The marginal effect of mortality-reducing policy is then

$$\frac{d\sigma}{d\mu} = \left(\pi_{c_1} \frac{\partial c_1}{\partial \mu} + \pi_\mu \right) b,$$
(16)

positive by definition. This is the sum of an indirect effect, $b \pi_{c_1}(\partial c_1 / \partial \mu)$ and a direct one, $b \pi_\mu$. If μ crowds in c_1, the indirect effect is positive. The overall

---

[2] Cigno and Pinal (2004) report local evidence that private and public mortality-reducing expenditures are complements. We are not aware of other empirical studies addressing the issue.

effect of the policy is then larger than the direct one. If μ crowds out c_1, by contrast, the indirect effect is negative, and the overall effect is smaller than the direct one. With heterogeneous families, the aggregate effect of the policy will depend on the distribution of personal characteristics, but is will still be true that the policy has a stronger aggregate effect if private and public mortality-reducing expenditures are gross complements, than if they are gross substitutes.

By way of example, consider a marshy area where half the children die in infancy, mostly of malaria. Suppose that a land reclamation programme gets rid of the marshes, and of the mosquitoes that inhabit them. By eliminating a major cause of infant death, that will raise the private return to spending on the nutrition and medical care of small children. At the same time, however, it will raise the number of mouths that have to be fed out of any given family budget. If parents do not change c_1, infant mortality in the area will fall, say to one in three. If the policy induces parents to raise c_1, infant mortality will fall further, say to one in four. If parents respond to the policy by reducing c_1, however, infant mortality will stay higher than one in three. For another example, suppose that the government starts to dispense a certain life-saving paediatric drug free of charge. Parents who would have bought the drug anyway will then spend less for this item. If they use the saving to buy more food and medical care for their children, that will reinforce the effect of the policy. If they use it for their own consumption, that will weaken it.

3.1.2 *Fertility*

Substituting the value of c_1 chosen at stage 1 into (6) makes the maximized value of $E(U_1)$ a function, $g(b; \Theta)$, of b and

$$\Theta = (W_1, p, p_1, \mu, \theta).$$

The value of an extra birth is then given by

$$g_b(b; \Theta) = -(p_1 c_1 + \phi'(b))u'_1(W_1 - p_1 c_1 b - \phi(b)) \qquad (17)$$

This expression may be positive at low realizations of b, when $\phi'(b)$ is negative, but will be negative at high ones, when $\phi'(b)$ is positive. The effect of μ on the value that parents attach to b,

$$g_\mu(b; \Theta) = [v(b, \theta) - v(0, \theta)]\, \pi_\mu(c_1, \mu), \qquad (18)$$

is positive in view of (8). The effects of the other elements of Θ have the obvious signs, negative that of p_1, positive those of W_1, W_2, w_c, and ω.

At stage 0 of the decision process, the number of live births b is still uncertain. Parents can now affect the probability of a high, b^H, or a low, b^L, outcome by choosing the level of birth control, denoted by c_0. Writing $\psi(c_0)$, where $\psi(.)$ is increasing and concave, for the conditional probability of b^L, the expected number of births is

$$\psi(c_0)b^L + [1 - \psi(c_0)b^H].$$

Assuming point expectations about the expected value of $g(b; \Theta)$ is

$$E(g(b; \Theta)) = \psi(c_0)g(b^L; \Theta) + [1 - \psi(c_0)]\, g(b^H; \Theta).$$

Let W_0 denote current parental earnings. Since the reasons for assuming zero saving apply at stage 0 with even greater force than at the stage 1, we shall write the current budget constraint as

$$a_0 + p_0 c_0 = W_0, \tag{19}$$

where p_0 denotes the marginal cost of birth control. This will consist of the monetary cost of any contraceptive devices and medical assistance used to reduce the probability of an extra birth or, in the case of traditional forms of birth control (*coitus interruptus*, abstinence, or abortion), of the income equivalent of the disutility of the practice itself.

The couple will choose c_0 to maximize

$$E(U_0) = u_0(W_0 - p_0 c_0) + E(g(b; \Theta)). \tag{20}$$

The first-order condition,

$$-p_{c_0} u_0' + g(b^L; \Theta)\psi'(c_0) = 0, \tag{21}$$

tells us that a couple raises the level of birth control to the point where the marginal cost equals the expected marginal benefit. Assuming

$$g(b^L; \Theta) > g(b^H; \Theta),$$

otherwise the couple would not practise birth control at all (and b would then be equal to the physiological maximum), the second-order condition,

$$\Delta_0 \equiv p_0^2 u_0''(W_0 - p_0 c_0) + [g(b^L; \Theta) - g(b^H; \Theta)]\, \psi''(c_0) < 0, \tag{22}$$

is satisfied.

Let us see how the level of birth control is affected by the stage-0 exogenous variables. Since

$$\frac{dc_0}{dW_0} = \frac{p_0 u_0''}{\Delta_0} \tag{23}$$

is clearly positive, a reduction in income will induce a reduction in birth control. That explains the apparent paradox that fertility is highest in the lowest strata of society. But it should be kept in mind that we are talking of the effect of stage-0 income (the income of a young couple without children), not of the present value of a couple's lifetime income stream. We should thus refrain from deducing that fertility and wealth (or permanent income) are positively correlated.

The effect of the marginal cost of birth control,

$$\frac{dc_0}{dp_0} = \frac{u'_0 - c_0 p_0 u''_0 (W_0 - p_0 c_0)}{\Delta_0} \tag{24}$$

is clearly negative. Notice that this is the sum of an income and a substitution effect. By reducing the private monetary cost and the unpleasantness of birth control, the free distribution of modern contraceptive devices would thus induce a higher level of birth control, and consequently reduce the fertility rate.

Let us now look at the effects of the higher-stage exogenous variables on the level of birth control. That of w_c,

$$\frac{\partial c_0}{\partial w_c} = -\frac{\pi(c_1, \mu) v_{w_c}(b, \theta)}{\Delta_0}, \tag{25}$$

is positive if the children who survive to school-age work, zero if they do not. That of ω,

$$\frac{\partial c_0}{\partial \omega} = -\frac{\pi(c_1, \mu) v_\omega(b, \theta)}{\Delta_0}, \tag{26}$$

are positive anyway. An increase in ω would thus discourage birth control, and raise aggregate fertility. An increase in w_c will discourage birth control only in families where school-age children work, but would still raise aggregate fertility. Since the probability that a school-age child will work is positively affected by the child wage rate, this prediction is consistent with the positive correlation between fertility and child labour that we usually find in the data.

The effect of the marginal cost of the good consumed by pre-school children,

$$\frac{\partial c_0}{\partial p_1} = -\frac{g_{p_1}(b^L; \Theta) \psi'(c_0)}{\Delta_0}, \tag{27}$$

is clearly positive. An increase in this cost would thus encourage birth control, and reduce aggregate fertility. The effect of mortality-reducing policy,

$$\frac{\partial c_0}{\partial \mu} = -\frac{g_\mu(b^L; \Theta) \psi'(c_0)}{\Delta_0}, \tag{28}$$

is positive too. Mortality-reducing policies have thus the effect of encouraging birth control, and reducing the fertility. Chapters 5 and 9 report evidence of this interesting cross effect.

It should be clear from the discussion in sections 1.2 and 1.3 that, if stage-2 decisions regarding school-age children are inefficient, stage-0 decisions regarding birth control will be inefficient too. If child labour is inefficiently high, fertility also will be inefficiently high. It is difficult to discriminate empirically between efficient and inefficient child labour, or between efficient and inefficient fertility, but there is evidence (see, again, Chapters 5 and 9) that fertility and child labour are positively correlated.

3.1.3 *The effects of capital markets and public pensions*

We have seen that not only education policy, but also public expenditure on sanitation and preventive medicine may have an effect on fertility, infant mortality, and child labour (Chapters 5 and 8 report the evidence). We have also seen that asset and credit markets affect fertility. We now consider two policies that may be useful for encouraging birth control.

As we saw in section 1.3, a rise in the interest rate, or the introduction of a public pension scheme, would reduce the fraction of the adult population for whom a self-enforcing family constitution exists. The same may be said of access to asset and credit markets by wider strata of society, or of the extension of an existing pension scheme to a higher proportion of the population (in developing countries, public pensions are often a privilege of civil servants, the police, and the armed forces). In this subsection, we use the theoretical apparatus developed so far to explain how pensions and interest rates affect reproductive decisions, and ultimately child labour. We shall look at the evidence in Chapter 9.

Let us go back to stage 2 of the decision process, when the number of school-age children is already known. Suppose that a public pension scheme exists, and consider the effect on infra-marginal players (compliers and go-it-aloners who do not switch strategy as a result of the change) of increasing either the pension contribution T or the market interest factor r. The budget constraint is now

$$a_2 + [c_2 + Q(h, w_c, p_k)] \, n + s = W_2 + w_c n - T. \tag{29}$$

Old-age consumption is given by

$$a_3 = rs - mn + Tr. \tag{30}$$

W_2 and m are obviously net of x in the case of compliers, gross in that of go-it-aloners. As people have no choice whether to participate in the pension scheme, the maximized value of U_2 is now a function of T too, $v(c_1; n, \theta, T)$.

The marginal valuation of n is again given by (1), but the marginal utilities of parental stage-2 and stage-1 consumption, u_{a_2} and u_{a_3}, are now functions of T. A change in T will then affect the stage-2 valuation of an extra birth,

$$v_{nT} = -[w_c - c_2 - Q(h, w_c, p_k)](u_{a_2 a_2} - r u_{a_2 a_3}) + m(u_{a_3 a_2} - r u_{a_3 a_3}). \tag{31}$$

The $(u_{a_2 a_2} - r u_{a_2 a_3})$ term is negative. The $(u_{a_3 a_2} - r u_{a_3 a_3})$ term is positive. But $[w_c - c_2 - Q(h)]$ and m can have any sign. Therefore, if children are a net charge on the family (w_c greater than the sum of c_2 and Q, and m greater than zero), the effect of T on the marginal valuation of n by infra-marginal compliers is then negative. Otherwise, it could be positive.

This has an important policy implication. If (31) is negative, an expansion of the public pension scheme will reduce the demand for children. The level of birth control will then rise. The latter may be true even if (31) is positive, because switchers will have fewer children,[3] and this could more than compensate for the increase in the fertility of infra-marginal players. The evidence reported in section 9.2 suggests that public pension coverage does indeed reduce fertility.

The child labour implications are quite obvious. A complier's demand for children is, at least in part, a demand for old-age consumption. Some compliers will not be rich or generous enough to support their children out of their own resources until these children reach adulthood, and will not be able to borrow against their children's future adult earnings. Their children will then have to support themselves by working while of school age. If the policy reduces the number of children born for old-age support purposes, child labour will then fall too.

The effect of an increase in the market rate of interest is more complicated. On the one hand, the increase will have a positive effect on the fertility on infra-marginal players. On the other, a number of persons who would have otherwise complied with a family constitution will now go it alone. Furthermore, as we saw in Chapter 2, an increase in the interest rate raises the probability that a school-age child will work. The overall effect of an interest rate rise is thus highly ambiguous. The empirical evidence reported in section 9.2 suggests that the effect has different sign in different countries.

3.2 GENDER ISSUES

Let us now distinguish between mothers and fathers, and between boys and girls. So far, we have assumed that the amount of human capital with which a person enters adult life is partly innate, and partly the product of educational investment. We now add that human capital may also increase with work experience in the course of adult life.[4] Since the cost of an infant includes the opportunity cost of parental time, this additional consideration establishes a link between domestic division of labour and educational investment. The analysis that follows is broadly based on Cigno (1991).

3.2.1 *Domestic division of labour*

Let w_f denote the father's, and w_m the mother's wage rate. In a developing country context, it seems reasonable to suppose that school-age children tend to look after themselves. Parental time is thus essentially required for the care of pre-school children. Drastically simplifying the technology of child care, we shall also assume that a pre-school child requires a fixed amount of maternal time t_0 around the date of birth, and a fixed amount t of either parent's time

---

[3] Not necessarily zero as in the simpler model of section 1.3, because go-it-aloners may now have children for altruistic reasons.

[4] Alternatively and equivalently, we could assume that labour experience reduces the rate at which human capital depreciates with the passage of time.

after that. Past the initial period when the mother is indispensable, the father's time is thus a perfect substitute for the mother's. Let t_i denote the amount of time, other than t_0, that parent i ($i = f, m$) devotes to each child, so that

$$t = t_f + t_m.$$

The opportunity-cost of a child is then given by

$$p = t_f w_f + [t_0 + (t - t_f)] \, w_m. \tag{32}$$

Let us now suppose that work experience augments human capital at a constant rate α. The latter may reflect not only learning by doing, but also seniority rules at the place of employment. Denoting parent i's stage-1 work experience by L_i, we can then write

$$w_i = (h_i + \alpha L_i)\omega. \tag{33}$$

By using the same value of α and ω for both sexes, we are implicitly saying that there is no sex discrimination. That may be far from the truth, but allows us to isolate the effects of domestic division of labour from those of other, more obvious, factors.

Normalizing the stage-1 time endowment of an adult to unity, the father's stage-1 work experience is

$$L_f = 1 - b t_f,$$

and the mother's

$$L_m = 1 - (t_0 + t_m) \, b.$$

Suppose that parents allocate their time to children so as to minimize the total opportunity cost.[5] Realistically, the amount of maternal time absorbed by a child round about the time of birth will be less than twice the amount of additional parental time that the child will optimally absorb before reaching school age,

$$t_0 < 2t.$$

Let us also assume that b is not so large, that the mother could not look after all her children single handed,[6]

$$(t_0 + t) \, b \leq 1.$$

---

[5] We shall see that this is not necessarily the case if the solution is bargained.
[6] That may not be true if b is very large.

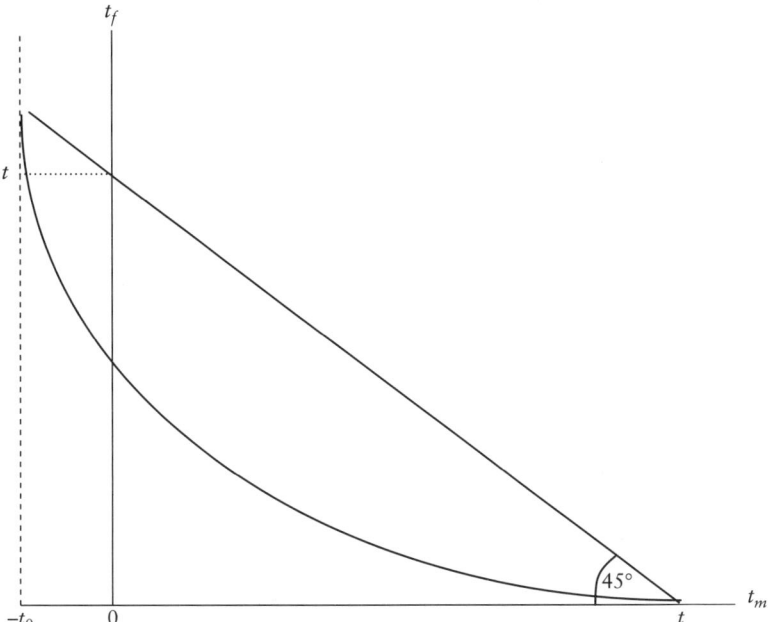

Figure 3.1. *Domestic division of labour*

    The cost-minimizing allocation of parental time is illustrated in Fig. 3.1. The straight lines with absolute slope equal to unity are isoquants. The convex-to-the-origin curves are isocosts. The latter have absolute slope,

$$-\frac{dt_f}{dt_m} = \frac{h_m + [1 - b(t_0 + 2t_m)]\,\alpha}{h_f + (1 - 2bt_f)\alpha},\tag{34}$$

decreasing as t_m is substituted for t_f. Cost is minimized at a corner, where either t_f or t_m is equal to zero.[7]

    Consider first the case where mother and father entered adult life with the same amount of human capital,

$$h_m = h_f = h.$$

In that case, cost is minimized at point $(t, 0)$ of Fig. 3.1, where the mother specializes fully in child rearing. The mother's initial stock of human capital

---

[7] The same would be true if the father's time were highly, rather than perfectly, substitutable for the mother's (i.e. so long as the isocosts were more convex than the isoquants, but not necessarily linear).

would have to be strictly higher than the father's,

$$h_m \geq h_f + \alpha b t_0, \tag{35}$$

for the cost-minimizing allocation to be at the opposite corner, $(0, t)$. Cost minimization would then require that the father take over the care of the children entirely after the initial period when the mother's presence is indispensable. In the first case, the mother would then reach stage 2 with a lower wage rate than the father (and the gap will increase with the number of children), even though they started from the same base. In the second, the mother's initial advantage would be reinforced. If h_m were higher than h_f, but not high enough to satisfy (35), the mother would still end up with a lower wage rate than the father's.

3.2.2   *Implications for fertility and infant mortality*

It is sometimes assumed that mothers are either genetically predisposed to love their children more than fathers, or become 'addicted' to their children over the initial period when the child is the mother's exclusive responsibility. That may or may not be true, but interests may diverge even if the spouses have exactly the same attitude towards children. We have seen that the mother's wage rate is negatively affected by fertility in any case, while the father's may or may not. If domestic decisions are bargained, and the parent with the higher income has the higher bargaining power, this will obviously reflect in the reproduction strategy, and in the domestic division of labour.

Let a_j^i denote i's consumption at stage j ($i = f, m, j = 2, 3$). At stage 2, when children no longer require parental supervision,[8] i's utility will be given by

$$U_2^i = U_2\left(a_2^i\right) + U_3\left(a_3^i\right) + \beta U^*(c_2, y)\, n. \tag{36}$$

As the term $U^*(c_2, y)n$ is the same for both spouses, school-age children are a kind of local public good. Notice that we are attributing the same preferences to both parents.

The stage-2 budget constraint may now be written as

$$a_2^f + a_2^m + [c_2 + Q(h, w_c, p_k) - w_c]\, n + s = W_f + W_m, \tag{37}$$

where W_i is defined as the sum of the wages and net transfers accruing at this stage to partner i. Having normalized to unity the amount of time available to each partner at each decision stage,

$$W_f = [h_f + (3 - b t_f)\alpha]\, \omega + m_f \tag{38}$$

---

[8] Or so we have assumed, but the argument does not change if we say that they absorb much less time than at stage 1.

and

$$W_m = [h_m + (3 - (t_0 + t_m)\, b)\alpha]\, \omega + m_m, \tag{39}$$

where m_i is the net transfer that partner i receives from her own parents (see section 2.2).

Suppose that a plan $\left(a_2^f, a_2^m, a_3^f, a_3^m, c_2, h, s\right)$, satisfying (37), has somehow been chosen. Substituting into (36), we can then write

$$U_2^i = v^i(n;\, W_f,\, W_m),$$

where $v^i(.)$ is i's stage-1 valuation function. If the planned $\left(a_j^f, a_j^f\right)$ is the same as the planned (a_2^m, a_3^m), the valuation is the same for f and m. We can then dispense with the i superscript, and proceed as in section 1.1. If not, parents will value n differently despite the fact that they have exactly the same preferences.

At stage 1, when children use parental time, the expected utility of parent i will then be given by

$$E\left(U_1^i\right) = u_1\left(a_1^i\right) + bv^i(c_1, n;\, W_f,\, W_m)\pi(c_1, \mu). \tag{40}$$

The household budget constraint is now

$$a_1^f + a_1^m + \left[t_f w_f + (t_0 + (t - t_f))\, w_m + c_1 p_1\right] b = w_f + w_m. \tag{41}$$

where

$$w_f = [h_f + (2 - bt_f)\alpha]\, \omega \tag{42}$$

and

$$w_m = [h_m + (2 - (t_0 + t - t_f)\, b)\alpha]\, \omega. \tag{43}$$

Notice that not only the two wage rates, but also the cost of a child now depend on the allocation of parental time.

Let us now move to stage 0. Again supposing that a plan $\left(a_1^f, a_1^m, c_1\right)$, satisfying (41), has somehow been decided, we can write

$$E\left(U_1^i\right) = g^i(b;\, h_f, h_m, m_f, m_m),$$

where $g^i(.)$ is i's stage-0 valuation function. Parents with exactly the same preferences may thus differ in their valuation of the number of births either because they have different valuation functions, or because the planned a_1^f differs from the planned a_1^m.

At this stage, i's expected utility is given by

$$E\left(U_0^i\right) = u_0\left(a_0^i\right) + \psi(c_0)\, g^i\left(b^L; h_f, h_m, m_f, m_m\right)\psi(\xi) + [1 - \psi(c_0)]\, g(b^H; \Theta),$$

$$(44)$$

and the household budget constraint by

$$a_0^f + a_0^m + p_0 c_0 = (h_f + h_m)\omega. \tag{45}$$

Notice that the marginal cost of birth control, p_{c_0}, is assumed to be the same for both partners. This may be far from the truth.[9] Even it it is true, however, and despite the assumption that mother and father have exactly the same preferences, the solution favoured by the mother may still be different from the one favoured by the father. Let us see in which way.

3.2.3 *Birth control and personal endowments*

In general, the level of birth control at stage 0, and the allocation of time and expenditure at stages 1 and 2, will depend on the decisions of the marriage partners, and on the random factors that affect fertility and child survival. The question is how the partners make their decisions. We consider first the possibility that decisions are the outcome of a Nash-bargaining equilibrium, and that the bargaining takes place *before* the wedding. If the negotiation is successful, the partners agree on a contingent allocation of domestic resources and distribution of family income. The stage-2 allocation is then determined by the number of children who actually reach school age, and the stage-1 allocation by the number of children who are actually born.

Let R_i be i's reserve utility, that is to say, his or her utility in the best alternative to the prospected wedding. Whether the best alternative is singlehood or marriage with someone else, R_i will depend positively on i's endowments. We may thus write

$$R^i = R(h_i, m_i), \tag{46}$$

where $R(.,.)$ is an increasing function. Notice that R^i depends on h_i and m_i, rather than on i's total income $h_i w_i + m_i$, because w_i may itself depend on h_i and m_i.

The Nash-bargaining equilibrium maximizes

$$\Omega = \left(E\left(U_0^f\right) - R\left(h_f, m_f\right)\right)\left(E\left(U_0^m\right) - R\left(h_m, m_m\right)\right), \tag{47}$$

---

[9] Unless the father totally internalizes the mother's sufferings, the disutility of abortion will in fact accrue primarily to the mother.

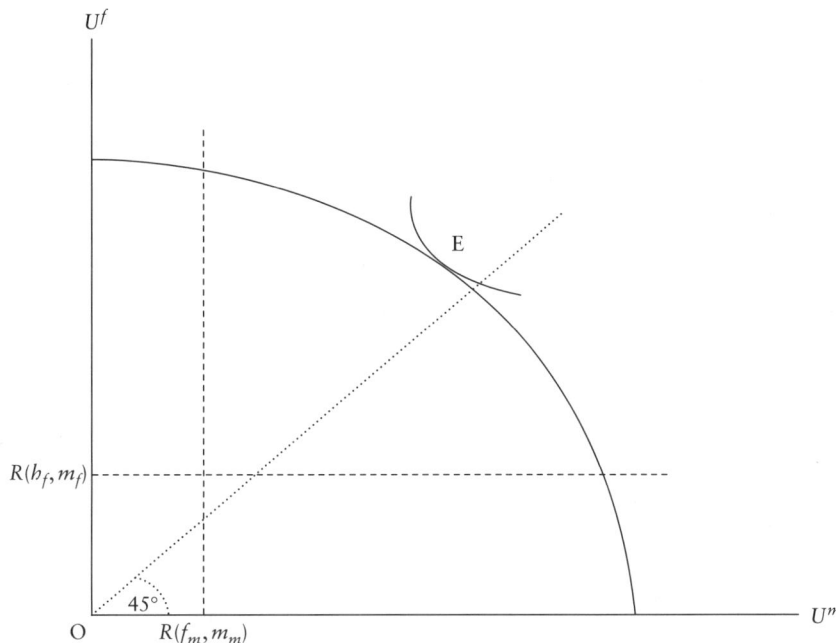

Figure 3.2. *The Nash-bargaining equilibrium*

subject to the utility-possibility frontier,

$$F\left(E\left(U_0^f\right), E\left(U_0^m\right)\right) \leq 0. \tag{48}$$

The implicit function $F(.,.)$ is obtained by maximizing the stage-0 expected utility of either partner, subject to (45), and (44) for $i = f, m$.

The solution is illustrated in Fig. 3.2. The concave-to-the-origin curve, symmetrical around the 45° line, represents the utility-possibility frontier. The hyperbola with asymptotes $(R(h_m, m_m), 0)$ and $(0, R(h_f, m_f))$ is the profile of (47) for a given value of Ω. Equilibrium is reached at point E. The position of this point clearly depends on that of the *threat point*, with coordinates $(R(h_m, m_m), R(h_f, m_f))$. The higher $R(h_i, m_i)$, the higher the equilibrium level of $E\left(U_0^i\right)$. Since a Nash-bargaining equilibrium is a point on the utility-possibility frontier, it is always efficient. We have seen, however, that efficiency requires division of labour, and that the division of labour has a negative effect on the earning capacity of the parent who specializes in the care of children. Since that exposes the child carer to the risk of opportunistic bargaining when the child care season is over, a Nash-bargaining equilibrium will be forthcoming only if the partner who specializes in income production can credibly commit to the agreed contingent plan.

In a developing country context, where children are an important source of old-age support, a not fully satisfactory marriage may nonetheless be better than no marriage. A wedding might then take place even in the absence of a credible commitment to a contingent plan. If it does, however, prudence will lead each partner to retain control over his or her own time and income, and to allocate these factors so as to maximize his or her own utility given the allocation chosen by the spouse. The outcome will be a Cournot–Nash, rather than a Nash-bargaining, equilibrium. As is generally the case with non-cooperative equilibria, the domestic allocation of resources will then be inefficient. The main source of inefficiency, in the present context, is that neither partner wants to specialize in child rearing as far as would be efficient, because that would reduce the amount of income under his or her control. As in the Nash-bargaining case, the equilibrium utility of partner i will then increase with h_i and m_i.

Cross-sectional data often show a negative correlation between fertility and the mother's education, and between the latter and the amount of consumption allotted to each child.[10] That is true also of the empirical studies reported in the following chapters. The correlation between fertility and mother's education is typically explained by saying that more-educated mothers are better capable of using modern contraception; the one between fertility and the amount of consumption allotted to each child by saying that more-educated mothers are better able to exercise an 'advocacy' role on their children's behalf. The first argument implies that contraception is restricted essentially by the mother's ignorance, the second that mothers are more caring than fathers.

Neither of these arguments is necessary to generate the correlations that we find in the data. If c_0 increases with h_m, as both the Nash-bargaining and the Cournot–Nash approaches suggest, we can expect to find a negative correlation between realized fertility and mother's education. Indeed, we do (see Chapters 5 and 9). On the other hand, at the high fertility levels that characterize developing countries, c_1 in highly likely to be a decreasing function of b in view of (10). We can thus explain a positive correlation between the amount of goods consumed by pre-school children, and the mother's education, without recourse to an advocacy role of mothers, or to the assumption that the effective use of contraceptive technology depends primarily on the woman's education.

Our line of reasoning bears some similarity to Eswaran (2002). There too, fertility and the allocation of resources are modelled as a Nash-bargaining equilibrium, but the bargaining is assumed to occur—as in Manser and Brown (1980), and McElroy and Horney (1981)—*after* the wedding has taken place.[11] The model predicts, as in our case, that fertility will be lower if women have

---

[10] See, for example, Haddad and Hoddinott (1994), Hoddinott and Haddad (1995).

[11] In contrast with those classical articles, Eswaran does not allow for the possibility of divorce if bargaining fails. As in Lundberg and Pollak (1996), the assumption is instead that the couple will stay together, and behave non-cooperatively. Thinking of America rather developing countries, Bergstrom (1996) vividly describes this as a case of 'harsh words and burnt toast'.

the upper hand, but this result is driven by the assumption that fertility has a negative effect on the mother's health. This is very different from our argument that, if pre-marital bargaining is impeded by insufficient commitment, the woman will favour a lower fertility level than the man because children reduce her share of consumption in the non-cooperative equilibrium. Adding Eswaran's very plausible assumption that fertility has a negative effect on the mother's health would only strengthen our predictions.

3.2.4 Feeding and educating girls

We have seen that the stock of human capital with which a woman enters adult life is less likely to bring a high monetary reward than that of a man. Anticipating that, parents may be unwilling to spend on the education of a daughter as much as they do for the education of a son. They will invest in a girl's human capital only if an affordable level of educational expenditure will bring her human capital to a level where it is likely to be put to good use in any prospective marriage deal. A reason why a girl does not get an education might then be that her native talent, h_0, is low. Another might be that her parents cannot borrow, and are not rich enough to educate all their children irrespective of sex out of their own stage-2 resources.

Given that the benefit a woman gets from marriage increases with her reserve utility, and that her reserve utility increases with both h_m and m_m, yet another possible explanation why a girl does not get an education might be that parents serve a daughter's interests better by giving her a dowry, equal to the discounted value of m_m. There is ample evidence to the effect that the size of the dowry—and legal or customary restrictions on its destination, such that it should be returned to the family of origin in the event of divorce—strengthens the position of a married woman in a traditional society.

There are thus circumstances where parents will be willing to pay only for the education of their male children. Notice that we have not assumed sex discrimination on the part of either parents or employers. Discrimination may well exist and be rampant for cultural or religious reasons, but it is not necessary to explain a gender bias in education. An assumption of opposite direction is that the woman's human capital is prized by her suitors either for its consumption value (social prestige, pleasant conversation), or for its use in the education of offspring. The former is likely to be relevant only for the higher strata of society, but the latter could well apply also further down the social scale.[12] Whichever the reason for prizing a woman's human capital independently of its labour market value, if education raises a woman's chances of a good marriage match, that will tend to redress the gender bias in school attendance.

---

[12] Evidence of a tutorial role of educated mothers is reported in Behrman et al. (1999).

Another gender effect comes to the fore if we drop the simplifying assumption that all births occur at the same time. If births are sufficiently staggered, a family will in fact include at the same time both school-age and pre-school children. That being the case, parents may find it optimal to allocate the time of a school-age child to the care of a pre-school sibling. If the human capital of women is judged to be less valuable than that of men for the reasons we have discussed, girls rather boys will then tend to be given the task of looking after younger brothers and sisters. Notice that we have not assumed a natural predisposition on the part of girls for this task. If we did, that would only strengthen the argument. There is some empirical evidence that the mother's educational level is negatively correlated with the school attendance of daughters.[13] If girls are more likely than boys to be lumbered with the care of younger siblings, this correlation is easily explained by the fact that a better-educated woman is more likely to be employed outside the home.

In some developing countries, there are more males than females. In view of the fact that the probability of a female birth is the same as that of a male birth, and that, given the same treatment, a girl's chance of survival is at least as good as a boy's, this may be taken as evidence that a number of girls are either suppressed at birth, or given less food and medical care than boys in the critical early stages of life.[14] This odious form of selectivity is explainable by the same kind of arguments that we used to explain a gender bias in education. Where a woman attracts a lower wage than a man of the same age and ability, or a young woman requires a dowry to make a satisfactory marriage match, poor parents with a large number of babies of both sexes may choose to get rid of some of the girls, either before or after they reach school age. [15] Notice that this last argument rests on the fact, recognized in our analysis, that couples do not have perfect control over their fertility. Were that not so, it would not make sense to talk of parents having 'too many' children.

[13] See, for example, Basu (1993).   [14] See Klasen (1996).

[15] In such a situation, the probability that a girl will live to school age increases if she can be sold or 'bonded' (see section 2.4).

4

International Trade

In the previous two chapters, we examined household responses to given prices, wages, and interest rates. Basu and Van (1998), reviewed in Chapter 1, and Baland and Robinson (2000), mentioned in Chapter 2, take the analysis a little further by postulating a domestic demand for labour, and looking for a partial equilibrium in the domestic labour market. This implies that the labour market is somehow insulated from the rest of the domestic and world economy. An alternative is to postulate that the prices of traded goods are internationally determined like with the interest rate, and that the returns to non-traded factors reflect comparative factor endowments. In an increasingly globalized economy, that may be not far from the truth.

Figs. 4.1 and 4.2, drawn from Cigno, Rosati, and Guarcello (2002), give us a broad-brush picture of the correlation between child labour and trade. Child labour is measured as the labour participation rate of persons aged 10 to 14 in Fig. 4.1, and as the primary school non-enrolment rate in Fig. 4.2.[1] In either figure, trade is measured as the ratio of imports plus exports to GDP. The data refer to all developing countries for the years 1980, 1990, 1995, and 1998. It is clear from the diagrams that both measures of child labour are negatively correlated with trade. It is also clear that the correlation is not very high (the interpolating line is shown just as a guide to the eye, and should not be taken to imply a causal relationship).

It is interesting to note that the dispersion around the interpolating line tends to decrease as trade increases. In other words, countries with little international exposure differ more widely with regard to child labour than countries well integrated in the global economy. Those with trade up to 20 per cent of GDP, for example, have labour participation rates for 10–14-year-olds ranging from little over zero to more than 55 per cent, and primary school non-attendance rates ranging between zero and 80 per cent. By contrast, in countries with trade equal to more than 40 per cent of GDP, both measures of child labour range between little over zero and little over a quarter of the relevant age group. That trade makes countries more alike is hardly surprising. That trading countries should have less child labour than autarchic ones is not so obvious. In this chapter we review the relevant theory, and then look at the econometric evidence.

---

[1] Both are in a sense underestimates, because they miss out either the bottom or the top end of the relevant age range. The latter also contains an element of overestimate in that some of the primary-school-age children not attending school may not be working.

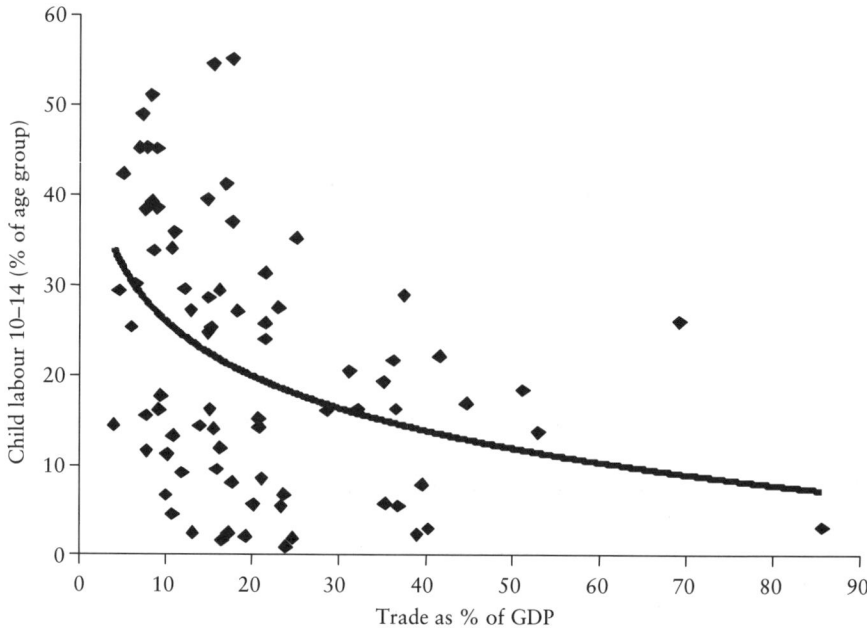

Figure 4.1. *Correlation between trade and child labour*

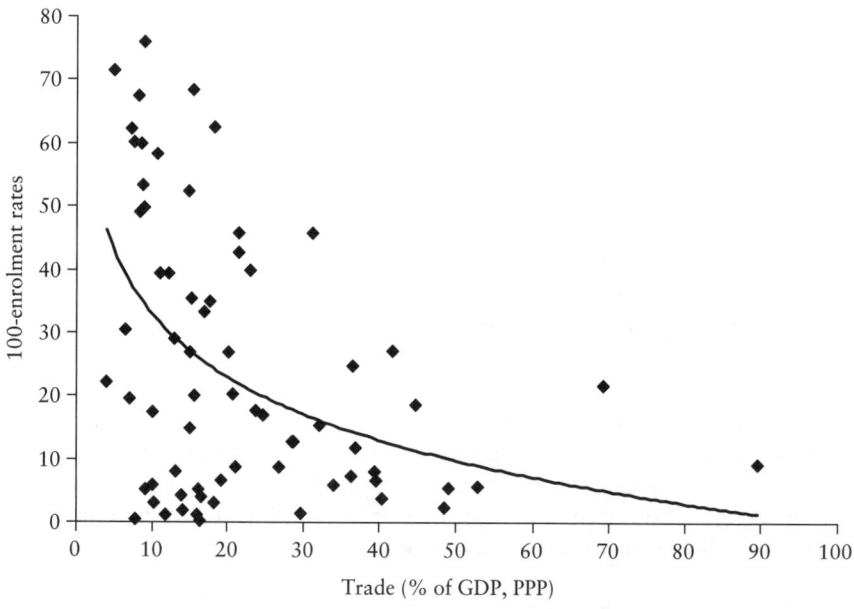

Figure 4.2. *Correlation between primary school non-attendance and trade*

4.1 THEORY

Standard trade theory tells us that, if a country opens itself to trade, it will specialize to some extent in the production of the good that makes intensive use of its comparatively abundant non-traded factor. As the relative price of the good will fall from its autarchy level, the relative price of the non-tradable factor will rise for the Stolper–Samuelson theorem. The benefits of trade will thus accrue to the comparatively more abundant non-traded factor. Comparative-statics further tell us that an increase in a trading country's endowment of a non-tradable factor may either raise or lower the price of that factor, depending on whether the factor is used intensively in the exporting or in the import-competing sector.[2]

In traditional classroom accounts of trade theory, the non-tradable factors of production are capital and labour. Participation in international trade is thus predicted to bring about an increase in the wage rate relative to the rental price of capital if the country in question has a comparatively large endowment of labour, a reduction if the country has a comparatively large endowment of capital. Wood (1994) points out, however, that financial capital is highly mobile, and that physical capital (hence, technology) follows financial capital with only a short lag. If any factor other than land and natural resources is sluggish in moving from one country to another, it is labour. Since the skill composition of a country's stock of workers (as distinct from the flow of new workers) takes a long time to change, trade will then affect the relative wage rates of workers with different skill levels. Thus reformulated, trade theory leads us to expect that, if a country opens itself to trade, the skilled wage rate will rise relative to the unskilled wage rate if the country has a comparative abundance of skilled workers, fall if it has a comparative abundance of unskilled ones. In the first case, the skill premium will rise, in the second it will fall. It also leads us to expect that, if the number of skilled workers of a trading country with a comparative abundance of unskilled workers increases, the skill premium will increase too.

We saw in Chapter 2 that child labour decreases if the marginal return to education increases. Since the marginal return to education is directly proportional to the rate of remuneration of human capital, a rise in the skill premium can then be expected to reduce child labour. We also saw, however, that if parents cannot borrow against their children's expected adult earnings, educational costs must be met out of the household's current earnings and assets. If that is the case, 'absolute' wage rates are important too. If the unskilled wage rate rises relative to the price of consumption goods, as well as relative to the

---

[2] In the first case, we cannot rule out the possibility that the country's welfare will fall, because the favourable effect of the factor increase through an expansion in output potential could be outweighed by the adverse effect through a deterioration in the terms of trade. In the second case, by contrast, that possibility ('immiserizing growth') can be definitely ruled out.

skilled wage rate, that will then have an ambiguous effect on child labour. On the one hand, it will raise the skill premium, and thus increase the incentive to send children to school rather than to work. On the other, it will tighten the budget constraints of the households from which child workers are most likely to come, namely households where the adult members are unskilled. In general, however, trade theory can only tell us what happens to relative, not absolute wage rates.

Policy also matters. As we saw in Chapter 2, if educational costs must be met out of the household's current earnings and assets, lump-sum income redistribution would reduce child labour, because it would relax the liquidity constraint on educational investment in the households where it is tighter. Redistribution through a progressive income tax would have an ambiguous effect, however, because it would reduce the skill premium, hence the marginal return to education. Free or subsidized education, by contrast, is doubly beneficial because it not only lowers the marginal cost to parents of sending their children to school, and thus raises the private marginal return to education, but also relaxes the liquidity constraint in the poor households, where it is more likely to be binding. As we saw in Chapter 3, public expenditure on sanitation and preventive medicine reduces both fertility and infant mortality. If it reduces fertility more than it reduces infant mortality,[3] there will be fewer school-age children, and the probability that any of them works will fall. There will then be fewer child labourers. If their number falls more than the number of school-age children, the child labour participation rate will fall too.

4.2 EVIDENCE

The evidence coming from developed countries appears to support Wood's hypothesis that trade is driven by the comparative skill endowments. Krugman (1995) reports that wage inequality in developed countries has increased over the globalization process. This is consistent with the idea that trade raises the skill premium in countries with a comparative abundance of skilled labour. Cross-country evidence reported in Wood (1998) does not reject the hypothesis that the rise in the relative demand for skilled labour in developed countries over recent decades was caused by falling trade barriers, in particular by import penetration of goods manufactured in developing countries.

What about developing countries? Nobody appears to be particularly interested in the effect of trade on wage inequality in those countries. A number of authors do, however, worry about the effect trade has on child labour and education. Using longitudinal data from Vietnam, a country with a relatively well-educated labour force, Edmonds and Pavcnik (2001) find that exposure to trade reduces child labour. Using cross-country data, Wood and Ridao-Cano

---

[3] In other words, if the country has undergone what demographers call the 'demographic transition'.

(1999) find that exposure to international trade tends to increase differences in school enrolment rates between developing countries with more, and developing countries with less well-educated labour forces. Three other cross-country studies, Shelbourne (2001), Cigno, Rosati, and Guarcello (2002), and Edmonds and Pavcnik (2004), find a negative association between trade and child labour.

4.2.1 *Child labour in an international perspective*

In this section, we look in somewhat greater detail at Cigno, Rosati, and Guarcello (2002), and then compare their results with those of Edmonds and Pavcnik (2005). The data used in both studies include the *World Development Indicators* relating to all developing countries. Cigno et al. draw on this source to construct a 'global panel' including data for the years 1980, 1990, 1995, and 1998, and supplement it with information on the presence of obstacles to free trade provided by Sachs and Warner (1995). Edmonds and Pavcnik use only the 1995 *World Development Indicators*, but supplement them with the information on bilateral trade flows contained in the *World Trade Analyzer*.

Child labour may be measured alternatively as the labour participation rate of children aged 10 to 14, or as the primary school non-attendance rate. In one respect, this measure is an overestimate, because it includes also children not involved in child labour. In another respect, however, both measures are underestimates, because they exclude either the top or the bottom end of the relevant age range.

Actual exposure to international trade is represented by the trade ratio (imports plus exports, divided by GDP). As an alternative to actual trade exposure, one may use information on the presence of obstacles to trade. Sachs and Warner (1995) define a country as 'closed' if any of the following circumstances applies:

1. average tariffs higher than 40 per cent,
2. non-tariff barriers covering more than 40 per cent of imports,
3. socialist economic system,
4. state monopoly of major exports,
5. black market premium in excess of 20 per cent.

Rodriguez and Rodrik (2000) criticize the way in which this definition of closedness is actually implemented by Sachs and Warner, on the grounds that the fourth hurdle is set up on the basis of World Bank data on African economies undergoing a structural adjustment programme between 1987 and 1991. That is clearly restrictive. They question the fifth hurdle, too, because it also reflects domestic factors unrelated to trade such as political corruption and bureaucratic inefficiency. The criticism is valid if the Sachs–Warner categorization of countries into open and closed is used to explain economic growth (that is indeed the purpose for which it was originally devised), but not if it is used to explain the effect of trade-induced wage changes on child labour. If the aim is to capture the effect of skill endowments on the domestic wage rate structure, it is actually desirable to take account not only of the presence of barriers to trade, but also of other possible price distortions.

Skill endowments may be represented by the share of the population aged 25–65 that completed only primary education, and that which completed at least secondary education. According to the World Bank Development Indicators (1980–98), the former ranges between 0.9 and 92 per cent of the age group, the latter between 0.1 and 59 per cent. Most developing countries have a comparative abundance of workers who did not even finish primary education. A substantial minority, however, have a comparative abundance of workers with completed primary education. A much smaller one may have a comparative abundance of workers with completed secondary education. None has a comparative abundance of workers with higher than secondary education (those reside mostly in the developed world). With trade controlled for, the coefficients of these skill endowment variables tell us how the dependent variable would be affected by an increase in the number of educated workers. With skill endowment variables controlled for, the coefficient of the trade variable tells us how exposure to international trade affects countries with different comparative advantages.

Income is measured as per capita GDP in constant PPP units. Health policy is represented by the share of public health expenditure in GDP. It would have been desirable also to control for income distribution, but consistent statistics (across years and countries) are just not available. It would have also been desirable to control for current educational policy. That was not possible either, however, because the only available proxy for educational policy, educational expenditure, is a very close correlate of the dependent variable (number of children working, or number of children not attending primary school). Health expenditure is thus the only policy indicator explicitly considered. Since public expenditure must satisfy the government budget constraint, however, the government ability to raise revenue increases with aggregate income. As well as a serving as a proxy for average household income, per capita GDP may thus be taken to be a proxy for public expenditure on items other than health.

Cigno et al. use fixed-effect ordinary least squares to estimate the effects of skill endowments, income, policy, and either the trade ratio or the Sachs–Warner index, on either the child participation rate or the primary school non-attendance rate, in their global panel (descriptive statistics are reported in Table 4.1). Edmonds and Pavcnik use two-stage least squares to estimate the effect of income and the trade ratio on child labour participation in the year 1995. Therefore, they do not exploit the time-series information,[4] do not use alternative measures of child labour and trade exposure, and do not control for

---

[4] They renounce using the panel information on the grounds that time variation may have more to do with data construction than with actual behaviour.

Table 4.1. *Descriptive statistics for the variables used in the regressions*

Variable	Mean	Stand. deviat.	Min.	Max.
Child labour	18.567	16.180	0	70.89
Trade	32.200	48.685	0	570.87
Open	0.426	0.495	0	1
GDP	3,361.12	3,594.67	343.7	24,200
Health expenditure	2.409	1.437	0.0001	7.76
100-enrol. rate	22.257	22.289	0.100	85.5
Primary education	0.179	0.153	0.009	0.918
Secondary education	0.108	0.115	0.001	0.589

either policy or skill endowments. On the other hand, they use instrumental-variable methods to control for possible endogeneity of income and trade. Income is instrumented with lagged income and investment. Trade is instrumented with information on bilateral trade flows taken from the *World Trade Analyzer*, and on bilateral geographic characteristics taken from Rose (2002).

4.2.2 *The effect of trade*

Table 4.2 reports the Cigno et al. estimates obtained using the trade ratio as an explanatory variable. The left-hand panel shows the effects of the independent variables on the 10–14 labour participation rate, the right-hand panel those on the primary non-enrolment rate. If skill endowments are not held constant (first column of either panel), trade raises the 10–14 labour participation rate, but has no significant effect on the primary school non-attendance rate. If skill endowments are held constant (columns 2 and 3), trade has no significant effect on either measure of child labour.

Since the effect of trade exposure on the incidence of child labour is supposed to come through relative wage rate changes, it may be argued that this effect is not captured by the share of trade in national income (a centrally planned economy could conceivably increment its external trade without any change in internal prices). The estimates obtained using the Sachs–Warner index in place of the trade ratio are reported in Table 4.3. They show that absence of obstacles to trade has somewhat more favourable effects, where child labour is concerned, than actual trade. Trade openness does in fact reduce child labour no matter whether the latter is measured by the 10–14 labour participation rate (left-hand panel) or by the primary non-enrolment rate (right-hand panel). In the first case, the effect is statistically very significant even when skill endowments are held constant.

Table 4.2. *Estimates using the trade ratio as a measure of openness*

	Dependent variable					
	Child labour			100-enrolment rate		
Trade	0.065 (2.34)*	0.05 (1.65)	0.031 (1.1)	0.063 (1.37)	0.037 (0.78)	0.02 (0.42)
GDP	−0.003 (8.57)**	−0.002 (4.71)**	−0.001 (2.89)**	−0.003 (5.05)**	−0.001 (2.01)*	−0.001 (0.86)
Health expend.	−3.202 (5.05)**	−2.036 (2.60)*	−2.136 (2.92)**	−3.882 (2.95)**	−1 (0.74)	−1.214 (0.91)
Primary educ.		−17.775 (2.57)*	−8.004 (1.18)		−42.77 (3.83)**	−34.788 (3.00)**
Secondary educ.			−43.291 (4.75)**			−37.173 (2.09)*
Constant	31.441 (17.67)**	28.581 (13.78)**	29.735 (15.28)**	36.286 (10.68)**	30.95 (8.89)**	31.591 (9.19)**
Observations	211	147	147	142	102	102
R-squared	0.41	0.41	0.49	0.26	0.33	0.36

Note: Absolute value of *t*-statistics in parentheses; *significant at 5%; **significant at 1%.

Table 4.3. *Estimates using the Sachs–Warner measure of openness*

	Dependent variable					
	Child labour			100-enrolment rate		
Open	−10.243 (5.47)**	−7.664 (3.74)**	−6.999 (3.64)**	−7.128 (1.86)	−2.077 (0.58)	−1.293 (0.37)
GDP	−0.002 (7.39)**	−0.001 (5.22)**	−0.001 (2.89)**	−0.002 (4.28)**	−0.001 (2.04)*	−0.0003 (0.63)
Health expend.	−2.881 (4.03)**	−2.198 (2.80)**	−2.474 (3.35)**	−4.436 (2.94)**	−1.315 (0.95)	−1.389 (1.02)
Primary educ.		−13.049 (1.87)	−3.086 (0.45)		−43.612 (3.73)**	−35.673 (2.96)**
Secondary educ.			−43.505 (4.35)**			−40.63 (2.16)*
Constant	35.955 (18.36)**	32.165 (14.37)**	33.307 (15.75)**	41.921 (10.58)**	32.225 (8.46)**	32.64 (8.74)**
Observations	166	136	136	116	94	94
R-squared	0.49	0.44	0.51	0.3	0.31	0.35

Note: Absolute value of *t*-statistics in parentheses; *significant at 5%; **significant at 1%.

These estimates tell us that, other things being equal, international competition leads to lower or, at worst, the same level of child labour. It is interesting that the more optimistic scenario is associated with trade openness, which takes into account the conditions under which trade takes place, rather than with the volume of trade. Since the beneficial effects of trade exposure are supposed to come through relative price changes, it is in fact not irrelevant whether internal prices are subject to government control or free to adjust to international prices, and whether foreign trade is distorted by quotas and state monopolies or not.

Controlling for the endogeneity of actual trade, Edmonds and Pavcnik (2004) find that the effect of actual trade on child labour remains negative, but becomes smaller (the elasticity falls from -0.67 to -0.38). When the endogeneity of income (the effect of child labour on income) is also taken into account, however, the effect of actual trade on child labour becomes stronger (the elasticity increases to -0.68). This is consistent with the finding of Cigno, Rosati, and Guarcello (2002) that the (clearly exogenous) Sachs–Warner index has a more negative, and statistically more significant, child labour effect than the (possibly endogenous) trade ratio.

4.2.3 *The effects of policy and skill endowments*

The estimated coefficients of the skill endowment variables reported in Tables 4.2 and 4.3 show the effects of increasing the proportion of the total workforce that achieved a certain educational level (primary only, secondary or higher) holding all the other variables constant. It would have been desirable to introduce interaction terms showing how the effect of trade volume or openness is modified by the presence of a more or less skilled labour force, but data limitations did not permit such refinements. Given, however, that more than 40 per cent of countries are classified as open by the Sachs–Warner criterion, and even those classified as closed have a certain amount of trade exposure, the findings are compatible with the proposition that trade increases the skill premium in countries with a comparative abundance of educated workers.

If skill endowments are not controlled for, the share of public health expenditure in GDP significantly reduces child labour, no matter how the latter is measured. Controlling for skill endowments reduces the statistical significance of health policy, but the effect of the policy remains nonetheless highly significant if child labour is measured by the 10–14 labour participation rate. This finding is coherent with the proposition that educational investments are affected not only by education policies, but also by public health.

The coefficient of per capita GDP reflects the effect of relaxing the liquidity constraint on the education investment decisions of the average household. As already pointed out, however, it may also pick up the effect of public expenditure on items other than health. A rise in per capita GDP reduces child labour, but the effect is statistically insignificant if the latter is measured by the primary school non-enrolment rate, and the proportion of workers with secondary or higher education is taken into account (possibly because per capita income is positively correlated with the share of the adult population that achieved a secondary or higher education diploma). This is consistent with the proposition that growth (an increase in real per capita income) may not be the answer to the problem of child labour.

4.3 DOES GLOBALIZATION INCREASE
CHILD LABOUR?

We started this chapter by saying that increasing globalization justifies modelling child labour in an open economy setting. The findings we have reported prompt a comment on the popular view that globalization is, if not the main cause of child labour, at least an aggravating factor of child labour. That view is largely founded on reports of children engaged in sewing footballs or knotting carpets for foreign markets, but does not take account of the fact that the alternative could be much worse. It also ignores the fact that the bulk of child labour is in agriculture, or in the informal sector, and that much of the output of these sectors is not traded internationally. Indeed, child labour is negatively associated with international trade.

The theory and evidence outlined in this chapter help us to understand why this may be so. As the estimates reported in Table 4.2 show, trade volume has a positive or insignificant effect on child labour. Table 4.3 makes it clear that child labour is lower where internal prices and the exchange rate are not distorted. Both tables show the importance of initial conditions and domestic policies. These findings suggest that pulling down trade barriers in countries with comparatively large endowments of educated workers raises the incentive for parents to send their children to school. By contrast, pulling down trade barriers in countries with a comparatively large endowment of uneducated workers can make the problem worse, because it reduces the incentive to send children to school.

There may thus be some truth in the proposition that globalization raises the incidence of child labour, but only in those countries with too little human capital to participate in international trade as anything other than suppliers of products with no formal education content. Elsewhere, by contrast, participation in international trade may be conducive to lower child labour. Figs. 4.3 to 4.5 present the same kind of information provided in Fig. 4.1 separately for each continent, except that the data are now averaged over the four years of observation to highlight national differences. A negative correlation between trade and child labour is still apparent, but it is clear that the countries with a much lower, or much higher, share of educated workers stand apart from the rest. The story would not change much if we also broke down by continent the information contained in Fig. 4.2.

In Asia (Fig. 4.3), Bhutan and Nepal have five times the participation rate of countries with a similar or higher volume of trade, but a better-educated workforce, like China, India, and Sri Lanka. In Africa (Fig. 4.4), Algeria, Egypt, and Morocco have much lower participation rates than less well educated, but otherwise comparable, sub-Saharan countries. Among the large Latin American countries, Brazil has nearly four times the participation rate of better-educated Argentina despite the similarity in volume of trade (Fig. 4.5). Among the small ones, Guatemala has more than eight times the participation

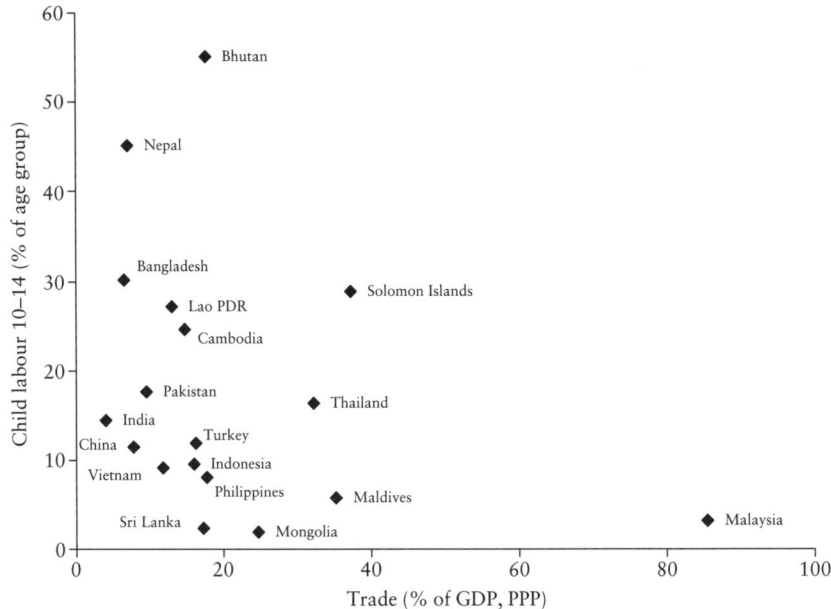

Figure 4.3. *Correlation between trade and child labour (Asia)*

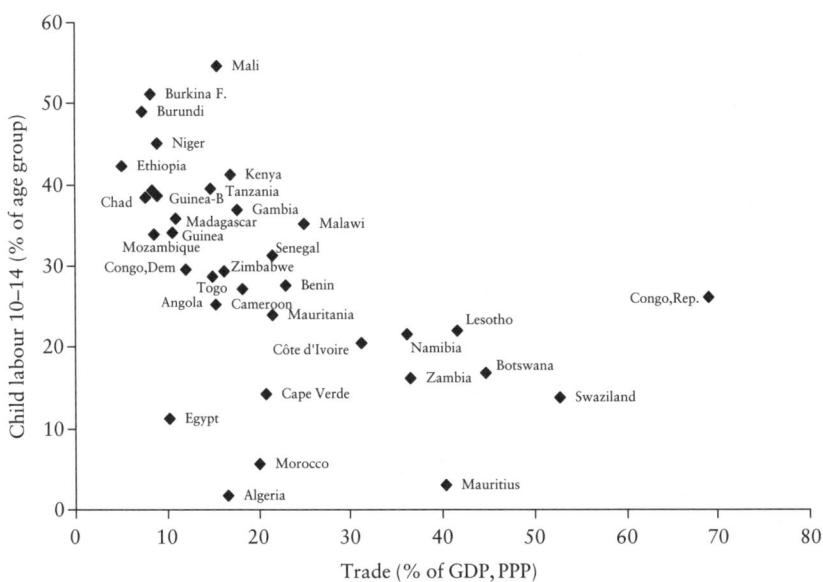

Figure 4.4. *Correlation between trade and child labour (Africa)*

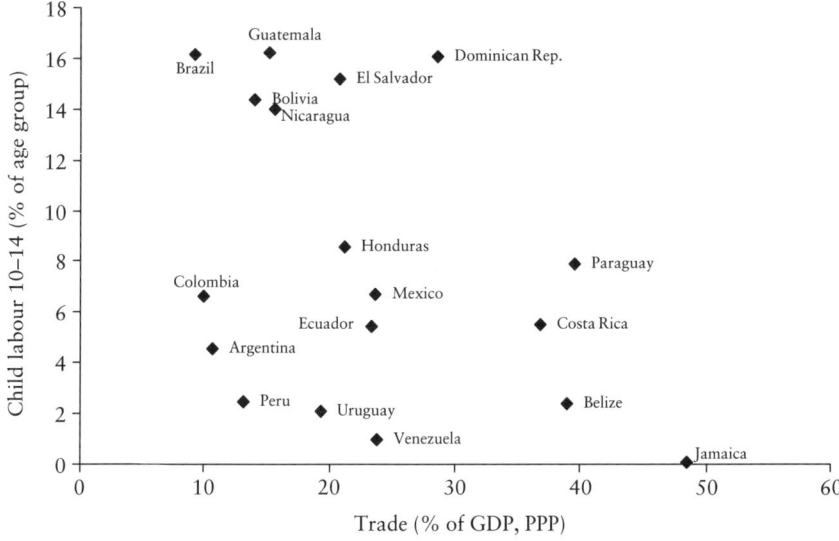

Figure 4.5. *Correlation between trade and child labour (Latin America)*

rate of better-educated Uruguay. All these examples refer to countries where trade accounts for no more than 20 per cent of GDP. Above that mark, as we have already pointed out, the differences between countries with similar trade volumes get much smaller.

It thus looks *as if* countries self-select into world trade with a view to what this will do for their child labour. But that interpretation is probably far fetched. A more plausible one is that countries with a largely uneducated workforce find it difficult to participate in the globalization process. The latter does in fact mean more than increasing trade. By facilitating the coordination of dispersed production activities, falling transport costs and advances in information technology are favouring the segmentation of production processes and the location of different segments of the same process in different countries. The growing literature on this new aspect of international trade emphasizes the effects of market size on the international division of labour.

Duranton (1998) adds an extra dimension to the discussion by pointing out that, since the output of different segments of the same production process must ultimately be combined into a final good, the extent to which these different segments can be carried out in different countries is limited by the ability of different workforces to produce intermediate goods that will prove mutually compatible. As this means, in large measure, ability to deliver goods in time, and of the right quality, the compatibility requirement is clearly easier to satisfy if the workforces available in the different countries have similar educational levels. That is consistent with the observed growth in intra-industry trade, and with the fact that this trade has so far occurred mainly among countries at similar stages of development.

This argument points to a trade-off between comparative advantage, which privileges trade with unequals, and compatibility, which favours trade with equals. Tension between the two considerations may lead to complex dynamics, with a phase in which international trade is driven primarily by differences in relative factor endowments, and one in which workforces with similar characteristics form integrated production systems that tend to uncouple from the rest of the world economy. The danger of the latter for the developing countries with the wrong initial conditions is that, instead of increasing wage inequalities within countries, which provide the stimulus for educational investment, international trade could end up increasing inequalities between countries. Evidence of that is reported in Krugman and Venables (1995).

The emergence of clubs of developed countries speaking only to one another faces developing countries with a largely uneducated workforce with the risk of exclusion from trade and economic integration with the developed world. The danger is most obvious for the African continent, where only 15 workers out of 100, compared with more than 31 in the developing world as a whole, have at least primary education, but also for those Asian countries where less than 2 per cent of the workforce reaches that level of education. Where initial conditions are so unfavourable, exposure to international trade by countries should be preceded by vigorous educational policies aimed at increasing the proportion of educated workers in the country's total labour force, and accompanied by health, education, and distribution policies aimed at making it feasible and profitable for parents to invest in their children's education, rather than in mere reproduction (see the theoretical discussion at the end of section 3.1).[5]

4.4 INTERNATIONAL LABOUR STANDARDS

We have deliberately left out trade sanctions against countries that use child labour, because this requires a separate discussion. The argument in favour of such sanctions is that countries applying lower labour standards than the rest of the world give themselves an unfair trade advantage. The argument against is that the cost of labour is one of the factors determining a country's comparative advantage, and that preventing poor countries from using their comparative advantages is nothing but protectionism. And protectionism hurts consumers in the country that practises it, as well as producers in the country against which it is used.

Using an extended version of the model outlined in section 1.1, Basu (1999) shows that the effects of a ban on imports with a child labour content differ according to whether it is imposed on just one country or worldwide, and

---

[5] See also Strulik (2003) on the dynamic effects of a public education programme on fertility and growth.

whether capital is fixed or mobile. Take first the case of a ban on imports from a particular country. If firms in this country cannot easily relocate abroad, workers in this country will be better off (shutting off the demand for child labour will raise the adult wage rate above subsistence level). If firms are perfectly mobile, however, they will flee the country subject to the ban. Workers in this country are then likely to be worse off as a result of the ban. Take next the case of an internationally agreed ban on imports with a child labour content from any country. As it applies to all countries without distinction, the ban does not cause capital flight. In the countries that formerly used child labour, workers will be better off because adult wage rates will rise above subsistence. In countries that never used child labour, workers will also be better off because they will no longer suffer unfair competition from abroad. The author thus concludes that a multilaterally imposed and universally applied ban on child labour is preferable to a unilaterally imposed and idiosyncratically applied one.

This theoretical argument in favour of a multilateral ban must be taken with caution. First, because it arises from a model based on very particular assumptions. We have seen that, if individuals have a more conventional utility function, and markets are imperfect, simply banning child labour could make both parents and children worse off. Secondly, because the argument presupposes instant adjustment. As we pointed out in section 1.1, if firms using child labour do not change their production processes very quickly in response to a ban on child labour, households will continue to supply child labour in order to survive (and the government will close its eyes in order to prevent mass starvation). Thirdly, because a ban on imports with a child labour input is equivalent to a lump-sum monetary sanction on the exporting countries, and will thus make poor countries even poorer. In the absence of compensatory measures, and given that child labour supply is negatively related to lump-sum income, it is doubtful whether trade sanctions would have the desired effect, or would be effectively enforced. Basu's plea for multilateral action is thus fine on condition that it includes not only a ban on goods produced with child labour, but also compensation for countries that give up using child labour.

5

Child Labour, Education, Nutrition, and Fertility in Rural India

With this chapter, we begin the presentation of a series of country-specific empirical studies aimed at testing and illustrating the theory developed in earlier chapters. The present one provides a test of the theoretical edifice as a whole. Subsequent chapters will deal with the effects of specific policies, and go deeper into the issue of causality. The data used here come from the Human Development of India (HDI) survey. The econometric analysis revises and extends Cigno and Rosati (2002).

5.1 DATA DESCRIPTION

HDI is a multi-purpose sample survey of rural households carried out in 1994 by the National Council of Applied Economic Research (NCAER) of New Delhi. A two-stage stratified and partially self-weighting design was used to sample a total of 34,398 households spread over 1,765 villages and 195 districts in 16 states. Two separate rounds of interviews were carried out. One elicited economic information from an adult male. The other obtained information about (i) the household's current demographic composition, (ii) its fertility and mortality history, (iii) the educational level of each adult, (iii) the height and weight of each child, and (iv) whether the child attends school, from an adult female. The sample is representative of the rural population at national and state level, and at the level of selected population groups for the states drawn.

Table 5.1 shows that school enrolment in rural India is relatively high. About 65 per cent of children in the 6–16 age range attend school, but the enrolment rate of males is 15 percentage points higher than that of females. The same table tells us that about 15 per cent of children are engaged in either paid or unpaid work. But work and school attendance are neither exclusive nor exhaustive descriptions of children's activities. A majority of children do either one or the other, a few do both, many apparently do neither. It is important to note that less than 7 per cent of the age group work outside the household, and only about half of that receive wages in money or in kind.

Directly or indirectly, the great majority of working children are employed by their own parents, helping in the family farm or in the family business, helping friends and neighbours on a reciprocity basis, or performing domestic chores.

Table 5.1. *Child labour participation (by sector) and school enrolment rates, by sex (%)*

Type of activity	Sex		
	Male	Female	All
Agricultural	5.19	4.49	4.86
Non-agricultural	2.29	1.66	1.99
Household	5.27	10.45	7.7
Total participation	12.75	16.6	14.55
School enrolment	71.53	56.94	64.69

Table 5.2. *Work/study status of children by sex (%)*

Work/study status	Sex		
	Male	Female	All
Work only	7.9	13.28	10.42
Neither work nor study	20.57	29.78	24.90
Study only	66.7	53.7	60.50
Work and study	4.9	3.3	4.10

While sex differences are not particularly relevant where outside employment is concerned, the participation rate of girls in household work is twice as large as that of boys. By contrast, there are more boys than girls reported not working. The imbalance is reflected partly in the fact that more of the boys go to school, but partly in the fact that more of them apparently do nothing.

We have rearranged children in four mutually exclusive and exhaustive categories: work only, study only, work and study, neither work nor study. Table 5.2 shows that over 60 per cent of the children study only. The second largest category, 25 per cent of the total, is that of children reported doing nothing. The rest work only (about 10 per cent), or attend school and work at the same time (less than 5 per cent). The large proportion of reportedly idle children is a source of concern.[1] It may be that all of these children are really sitting at home doing nothing. But, it may also be that some of them are actually engaged in the very kind of work the ILO is concerned about (see the Introduction to this book), and that their parents understandably do not wish this to be known. In the worst of all possible hypotheses, some of these children may be reported present and doing well, but have actually been bonded or sold to pay for family debts.

Table 5.3 shows how the allocation of children to our four work/study categories varies with household income. The probability that a child will study,

[1] For a detailed analysis, see Biggeri et al. (2003).

Table 5.3. *Work/study status of children by household income*

Work/study status	Income quintile				
	1	2	3	4	5
Work only	12.24	12.31	11.93	9.38	6.26
Neither work nor study	31.55	29.65	26.06	20.76	16.42
Study only	52.19	53.86	57.43	66.04	73.27
Work and study	4.03	4.19	4.59	3.82	4.04

Table 5.4. *Work/study status of children by age*

Years of age	Work/study status			
	Work only	Neither work nor study	Study only	Work and study
6	4.77	47.62	45.32	2.30
7	3.96	27.29	65.11	3.64
8	4.98	23.78	66.43	4.81
9	4.98	16.39	73.10	5.53
10	7.29	20.51	67.15	5.05
11	6.66	15.31	72.69	5.34
12	9.36	21.06	64.12	5.46
13	12.35	20.43	63.04	4.19
14	16.02	23.24	56.44	4.30
15	21.31	25.16	51.11	2.42
16	30.49	26.23	41.01	2.28

full or part time, rises with household income. Conversely, the probability that a child works full time falls as income rises. Coherently with either of our tentative explanations, the same is true of reportedly idle children.

Table 5.4 shows that the proportion of children who work only rises with age, while the proportion of children working and studying at the same time has a U-shaped profile. This indicates that some children enter the labour force initially without leaving school, but tend to leave education as they get into their teens. The proportion of children reported doing nothing is highest among those aged 6, suggesting a mere delay in starting school, but remains substantial even at higher ages (over a quarter of those aged 15–16).

Up to the age of 12, the survey also gives the child's height and weight.

Tables 5.5 and 5.6 show, separately for boys and girls, how an anthropometric indicator of nutritional status, the body mass index (BMI, calculated dividing weight by height squared), varies with the child's work/study status. In addition to showing nutritional status, BMI is a predictor of the child's probability of

Table 5.5. *Body mass by age and work/study status (boys)*

Work/study status	Years of age						
	6	7	8	9	10	11	12
Work only	15.74	15.30	15.02	14.41	15.64	15.39	16.13
Study only	14.87	14.88	15.19	14.99	15.26	15.41	15.54
Work and study	14.50	14.35	14.62	14.70	14.83	15.36	15.53
Neither work nor study	15.20	14.99	15.16	15.39	15.41	15.24	15.91

Table 5.6. *Body mass by age and work/study status (girls)*

Work/study status	Years of age						
	6	7	8	9	10	11	12
Work only	15.30	15.64	14.79	15.11	15.24	15.04	15.49
Study only	14.82	14.66	14.78	14.71	14.85	15.08	15.63
Work and study	14.77	14.43	15.05	13.95	14.64	15.02	15.43
Neither work nor study	14.80	15.75	14.91	15.09	15.05	15.41	15.40

survival to (and, more generally, health status in) subsequent stages of life.[2] Fogel points out that weight and height enter separately into the determination of a person's survival probability, and that the same weight/height ratio could thus be associated with different survival rates. Indeed, Waaler (1984) and Fogel (1993) report evidence that the relationship between survival and BMI has a reverse-U shape. But the data they use concern only adults in developed countries. In view of the fact our data concern only children, and that practically all of them are undernourished by Western standards, it may reasonably be assumed that we only observe the upward-sloping branch of the curve.

Looking at the raw data, we cannot say that working children fare worse than children attending school. Reportedly idle children appear to be fed only slightly worse than children working only. Children working and attending school at the same time fare worst of all. Working girls up to the age of 10, and working boys up to the age of 7, have higher BMI than their contemporaries attending school. At higher ages, there is no clear pattern. Of course, body mass reflects not only nutrition, but also the ratio of muscle to fat. Since a child born with more muscle is more likely to be selected for work activities than one with less muscle (Dasgupta 1997), and given that the ratio of muscle to fat increases with physical exertion, it could be that working children tend to have higher BMI simply because they are constitutionally stronger. Given that a working child needs more food to maintain any given body weight, however, it seems unlikely that, of two children of the same sex, age, and body mass, the one

[2] See, for example, de Onis and Habicht (1996), Klasen (1996).

who works is getting less nutrition than the one who does not. In Chapter 7, we shall use data from rural Vietnam and Guatemala to investigate the effect of work on future health.

Summing up, the data show that child work is an important phenomenon, particularly if we count as work also the domestic chores carried out mostly by girls. Almost as important is the phenomenon of children reported doing nothing. Working children appear to fare better, in terms of current nutrition, than children who study. As children who study will enter adult life with a larger stock of human capital, there is an obvious trade-off between present and future consumption. For children who combine work with study, the size of this trade-off will depend on the extent to which work reduces educational achievement, but HDI is silent on the subject, and evidence from other countries (e.g. Psacharopoulos 1997, Patrinos and Psacharopoulos 1997) is somewhat discordant.

5.2 FROM THEORY TO DATA

We now refer back to the theory developed in earlier chapters of the present book, and adapt it to the data provided by the HDI survey. The theoretical chapters portray parental decisions as a three-stage process (see Fig. 2.1). Since the survey shows that most of the premature mortality occurs before the age of 5, we identify the interval between stages 1 and 2, when parents take actions affecting infant mortality, with the first five years in a child's life. Given that school begins at the age of 6, we identify the interval between stages 2 and 3 with the subsequent eleven years in the child's life.

In Chapters 2 and 3, we reasoned as if all children were born simultaneously. That is a convenient simplification, because it implies that, at any given date, all children in the family have the same age. As this is not true in practice, however, an important consideration to be kept in mind in moving from theory to data is that decision stages may overlap. This implies that reproductive decisions will take into account the number of children of different ages who are already there, hence that decisions concerning the treatment of any particular child may be affected by the presence of elder or younger siblings. It also implies that higher-stage decisions may be affected by exogenous variables that, in the theoretical analysis, figure only at lower-stage decisions. For example, decisions concerning a school-age child may be influenced by policies that, in the theory, affect only the survival probability of pre-school children.

The data tell us whether a school-age child works or studies, but not for how many days in the year, and how many hours in the day. Rather than explaining how much time a child in that age group spends in each of these activities, we shall thus aim to explain the probability that the child will study only, work only, work and study, or do neither. The theory explains the choice of the last alternative with the existence of fixed costs. The survey contains

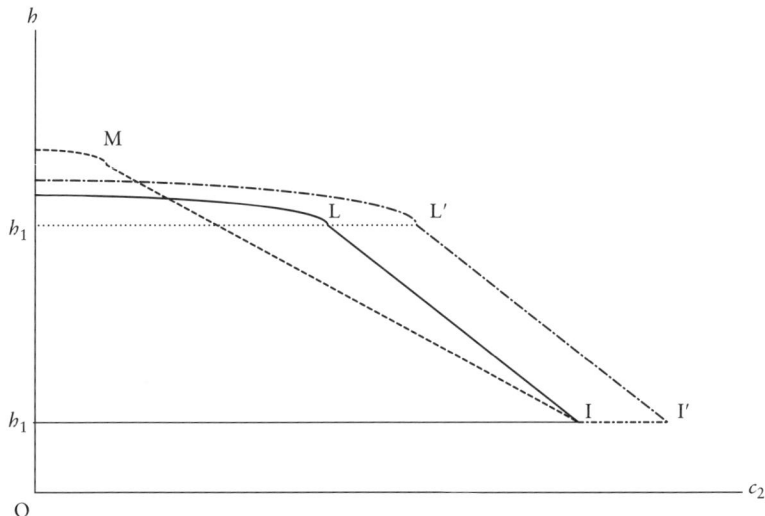

Figure 5.1. *The effect of a rise in full household income or in the opportunity cost of a child's time on the shape of the domestic production frontier*

some information about access to education (the presence, or otherwise, of a school in the village), but not about access to work.

In the present context, it seems reasonable to assume that parents have neither access to credit, nor significant assets they can readily sell. The solution is thus a point on the domestic production frontier. The kinked curve through points **I** and **L** in Fig. 5.1 represents this frontier for a given configuration of parameters. If the solution is at point **I**, the child works only. If it is a point between **I** and **L**, the child works and studies. If it is at or above point **L**, the child studies only. We shall use this diagram to illustrate the effects of some parameter changes.

A lump-sum increase in the household's full income would shift the frontier outwards, without changing the position of h_0 and h_1. The new frontier would then look like the kinked curve through points **I'** and **L'**. As we do not have the indifference map, we do not know on which point of the domestic frontier the solution will fall, either before or after the parameter change. We can talk, however, about the probability that the solution will be in one segment or other of the frontier. In this case, the probability of a study-only solution ($h \geq h_1$) increases, and that of a work-and-study ($h_0 < h < h_1$) or work-only ($h = h_0$) solution decreases.

Now suppose that the marginal opportunity cost of the child's time rises, but this change is compensated by a lump-sum tax calculated to maintain the household's full income constant. The new frontier will look like the kinked curve through points **I** and **M**. Notice that h_1 has moved upwards, because parents economize on the child's time, and that the linear segment of the frontier has become less steep, because q has increased (see Chapter 2). In this case, the

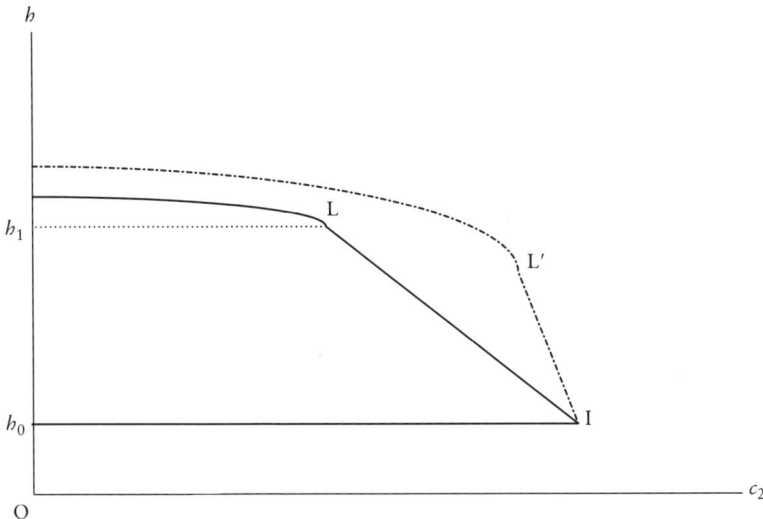

Figure 5.2. *The effect of a rise in the marginal return to education on the shape of the domestic production frontier*

probability of a work-and-study solution $(h \geq h_1)$ increases, and that of a study-only or work-only solution decreases.

Finally consider the effect of a rise in the marginal return to education. In Fig. 5.2, the original frontier is again represented by the kinked curve through the kinked curve through I and L. The new frontier looks like the kinked curve through I and L′, everywhere steeper than the one through I and L. The probability of studying only will rise, that of working and studying at the same time or working only decreases.

5.3 ESTIMATES AND DATA

We shall report estimates of reduced-form equations predicting the effects of a number of independent variables on:

(i) fertility,
(ii) time use of school-age children,
(iii) educational expenditure,
(iv) the nutritional status of pre-school and school-age children.

Fertility is defined as the probability of an extra birth in the two years preceding the interview (two rather than one, because there is a certain margin of error in the recording of the exact date of birth of each child, and also because it gives us more observations). As already mentioned, time use means the probability of working, attending school, doing both, or doing neither. In the absence of direct information on the amount of consumption allocated to children, and given that the body mass index is a stock measure, reflecting the cumulative effects of past food consumption, we use the BMI of school-age children as a proxy for both their current, and their pre-school consumption (since height and weight information is available only for children aged up to 12, school age is redefined for BMI calculation purposes as 6–12). In the theoretical analysis, the consumption of these children was defined to include also private medical expenditure. As we do not have information about that, health status is outside the scope of the present study. We shall deal with that in Chapter 7.

Table 5.7 provides descriptive statistics for the main explanatory variables. These reflect, as closely as data permit, those figuring in the theory, plus a number of variables aimed at controlling for the child's, the mother's, and the father's personal characteristics. The mother's characteristics include age and education. The father's include education, religion, and caste (the latter is a dummy taking value 1 if he is low caste or a member of scheduled tribes, 0 otherwise). In addition to those listed, there is a dummy for each state, necessary to control for geographical heterogeneity in a country as vast as India. We do not have information on credit and insurance availability. Family composition is represented by the number of children (by age bracket where significant), and the total number of family members. Since fertility is endogenous, the number of children aged 0–5 should be treated as endogenous too, but we disregard the problem on the grounds that the flow is small relative to the stock.

The survey provides a measure of household income gross of land rent, defined as the money value of own production, plus outside earnings by all household members, including children. This is obviously a measure of actual, not full (potential), household income. The survey includes also an expert-group classification of households by poverty level (taking values from 1 for least poor, to 4 for poorest) that reflects natural breaks in the income distribution. In preliminary trials, this categorical variable outperformed the continuous income variable in all the estimates. That is hardly surprising. First, because the continuous variable includes the amount of income earned or produced by the children, and is thus obviously endogenous. Secondly, because it is well known that measures of income in developing countries, especially at the lower end of the income distribution, contain significant measurement errors. We shall thus use the poverty class as a negative proxy for full household income. Assuming that a child's income contribution is unlikely to change the poverty status of a household, this can be expected to minimize endogeneity biases, as well as measurement errors.

Land size refers to the amount of land farmed, not owned. The survey provides some wage information about working children, but this concerns only the very small number who work outside the household, and is also incomplete. We thus assume that the opportunity cost of a child's time reflects the marginal productivity of labour on the family farm. That is less than satisfactory, because not all children work on the land, but is probably the best one can do in the circumstances. With family composition controlled for, land size is

Table 5.7. *Descriptive statistics for the variables employed in the regressions*

Variable	Mean	Std. dev.	Min.	Max.
Child is female	0.44	0.49	0	1
Child's age	10.80	3.03	6	16
Child's age squared	12.60	67.00	36	256
Poverty	2.60	0.98	1	4
Land tenure	0.29	0.45	0	1
Land size	2.23	1.44	1	5
Household income	25,139	19,259	677	99,000
No. of household members	7.16	3.01	2	19
No. of children	3.82	1.57	0	12
No. of children aged 6–16	3.01	1.50	1	10
No. of children aged 0–5	0.92	1.15	0	10
Type of school available	1.60	0.95	0	3
Father is Hindu	0.83	0.38	0	1
Father is Muslim	0.11	0.31	0	1
Father is Christian	0.02	0.15	0	1
Father is other	0.04	0.19	0	1
Father has less than primary education	0.53	0.49	0	1
Father has primary education	0.28	0.45	0	1
Father has middle education	0.13	0.34	0	1
Father has secondary or higher education	0.06	0.38	0	1
Mother's age	34.80	5.83	18	49
Mother has less than primary education	0.75	0.42	0	1
Mother has primary education	0.18	0.39	0	1
Mother has middle or higher education	0.03	0.21	0	1
Village survival rate to the age of 6	0.90	0.06	0.62	0.99

thus a proxy for the marginal productivity of child labour. As we do not have a control for the fixed cost of access to work, however, land size may pick up also the effects of a reduction in the fixed cost of access to work (the more land a family owns or rents, the less likely that a child will have to travel far to go to work, and the less likely also that he or she will have to bear search costs).

The land tenure variable takes value 1 if land is owned, 0 otherwise. With poverty and the quantity of land controlled for, land ownership implies that the family does not pay land rent. To the extent that it affects only a fixed cost, land tenure is then another proxy for full household income. Its effects should thus be the opposite of those of poverty (but, owning land may affect family status also in other ways).

The village survival rate to the age of 6 may be taken to represent parental perceptions of the probability that a child with the average personal characteristics survives to the age of 6, given the average amount of nutrition observed in the village. We are thus saying that parental actions cause a dispersion of individual survival probabilities around the village mean. Assuming that individual decisions have negligible effects on the village-level aggregate, we take the latter to be exogenous.[3] Since differences in village survival rates reflect, among other factors, also public provision of health and sanitation, the village survival rate may be expected to pick up the effects of mortality-reducing policies. The probability of premature death is concentrated in the first five years of a person's life, but is still significantly higher than zero when the person reaches the age of 16. Since the probability of death (and the positive correlated probability of serious illness) of young adults affects the marginal return to education, the village survival rate proxies for both μ and ω (see Chapters 2 and 3).

The type of school available is a categorical variable taking value 0 if there is no school in the village where the child lives, 1 if there is only a primary school, 2 if there is a primary and a middle school, 3 if there is also a high school. An increase in the value of this variable may thus mean either that there is a school where previously there was none, or that a higher-grade school has been added. The first change reduces the cost of access to primary education. The second would reduce the cost of access to the higher-grade school, but also increase the marginal return to attending primary school.

5.3.1   *Time use*

Cigno and Rosati (2002) estimate a multinomial logit model for the probability that a school-age child works only, works and studies, or studies only (the latter is taken as the reference state). Children reported doing nothing, a quarter of the age group, are excluded from the sample. Here, by contrast, we present estimates of an instrumental-variable bivariate probit model of the probability that a school-age child will study, and of the probability that he or she will work, obtained using the whole of the sample. We then calculate the marginal effects of the explanatory variables on the probability that a child will work only, study only, do both, or do neither (be 'idle'), from the estimated regression coefficients. This procedure will allow us to gain some insight into why some school-age children appear to be idle.

---

[3] To check the validity of this assumption, we tried replacing the village-level with the district-level survival rate. The results did not change to any significant extent.

Table 5.8. *Time use of school-age children (bivariate probit estimate)*

	Work		School	
	Coeff.	z	Coeff.	z
Child is female	0.14	8.30	−0.49	−34.9
Child's age	−0.08	−3.9	0.79	45.2
Child's age squared	0.01	7.8	−0.04	−47.4
Poverty	0.45	17.8	−0.76	−35.2
Land tenure	−0.28	−10.8	0.37	17.4
Land size	0.04	6.3	−0.07	−13.3
Caste	−0.09	−4.9	0.22	14.2
No. of children aged 0–5	0.10	0.7	−0.14	−15.3
No. of children aged 6–16	0.04	4.8	−0.03	−4.8
No. of household members	−0.03	−5.9	0.07	17.5
Type of school available	−0.003	−0.3	0.04	4.6
Village survival rate	−0.62	−4.3	0.48	3.9
Mother has primary education	−0.37	−12.0	0.58	22.2
Mother has middle or higher education	−0.65	−0.780	0.56	10.0
Father is Muslim	−0.08	−1.4	−0.16	−3.1
Father is Christian	0.15	2.5	−0.55	−10.2
Father is other	−0.28	−2.6	−0.17	−2.1
Constant	0.68	3.3	−5.50	−31.7

Since the probability that a household falls in one or other of the poverty categories (see last section) may be endogenous with respect to the decision to make a child work, we instrument poverty with the education and sector of activity of the household head, and with five indices of village development (relating to the percentage of irrigated area, and to the presence of various types of infrastructure, NGO schemes, etc.) provided in the same survey. As none of these variables has a direct effect on the probability of either working or attending school, the choice of instrumental variables appears to be appropriate.

Table 5.8 shows the estimated coefficients and z-statistics of the explanatory variables (other than the state dummies). Consistently with the considerations made in Chapter 3, we find that a girl is more likely to work, and less likely to attend school, than a boy with the same family characteristics. The finding that the existence of siblings in either age group has the effect of reducing the probability that a school-age child will attend school, and of raising the probability that he or she will work, tells us that not only pre-school but also school-age children are a net charge on the family (in the sense in which this expression is used in Chapter 2).

The probability that a child works is higher, and the probability that he or she attends school lower, if the mother has primary education, than if she has none. If the mother has more than primary education, this has a positive effect on the probability that the child will attend school, but no significant effect on the probability that he or she will work. As pointed out in Chapter 3, this may be because, on the one hand, better-educated mothers are likely to have more weight in household decision making, but on the other are also more likely to work outside the home, and thus to have their children (particularly female) substituting for them in the performance of household chores. The father's education (omitted from the final estimates) is not significant.

We also find that a child is more likely to work, and less likely to attend school, if the father is of lower or no caste. As income is controlled for, this suggests either that caste discrimination persists despite valiant government efforts to eradicate it, or that the culture associated with each caste still has an influence on parental behaviour (poor, but relatively well educated, Brahmins are a common occurrence). The same may be said about religion. Compared with the father being Hindu (the reference state), a child is significantly more likely to work, and less likely to attend school, if the father is Christian. If the father is either Muslim, or anything other than Christian, this significantly reduces the probability that a child will attend school, but also the probability that the child will work. In other words, it makes it more likely that the child will be (reported) doing nothing.

Rather than dwelling on the effects of the remaining variables, we now go on to comment on the marginal effects of these variables, which more readily lend themselves to an economic interpretation. Where the explanatory variable is continuous, the marginal effect is computed as a derivative. Where the explanatory variable is dichotomous or categorical, the marginal effect is calculated by difference for a finite change. Table 5.9 reports the marginal effects of the explanatory variables for which it makes sense to carry out such calculations, starting with the proxies for full household income.

Poverty is found to have a positive marginal effect on the probability that a child works only, and on the probability that a child works and studies at the same time. By contrast, it has a negative marginal effect on the probability that a child studies only, and on the probability that a child does nothing. The same is true, with the signs changed, of land ownership. It must be remembered, however, that we are talking of the effects of large finite changes of the explanatory variable (in the case of poverty, of going down a whole step, in the case of tenure, from having to pay rent on all the land worked, to not paying any rent at all). In other words, the effects of the full-income proxies reported in Table 5.9 are not marginal at all. The effects of a truly marginal change in full household income on the probability that a child studies only, or does nothing, are thus substantial, but its effects on the probability that a child works only, or works and studies at the same time, are very small indeed. This has the important policy implication that (lump-sum) income redistribution would increase school attendance, but the additional students would come primarily from the ranks of previously idle children. The number of children working, full or part time, would be scarcely affected. Since the incidence of the fixed costs of access

Table 5.9. *Marginal effects of the explanatory variables on the probability of working only, studying only, doing both, and doing neither*

	Work only	Work and study	Study only	Do nothing
Child is female	0.035	−8.010	−0.158	0.133
Child's age	−0.044	0.029	0.244	−0.229
Child's age squared	0.002	−0.001	−0.012	−0.011
Poverty	0.082	0.005	−0.282	0.194
Land tenure	−0.043	−0.008	0.135	−0.084
Land size	0.007	0.000	−0.025	0.017
No. of children aged 0–5	0.008	−0.006	−0.045	0.043
No. of children aged 6–16	0.005	0.002	−0.014	0.007
No. of household members	−0.006	0.001	0.025	−0.020
Type of school available	−0.002	0.001	0.012	−0.012
Village survival rate	−0.083	−0.033	0.200	−0.084

to education and work obviously decreases as income increases, the finding that poverty and land tenure have a substantial effect on the probability that a child does nothing is consistent with the theoretical predictions of Chapter 2.

Land size has a negative marginal effect on the probability that a child studies only, and a positive one on the probability that a child works only or is reported doing nothing. The effect on the probability that a child combines work with study is positive but very small. Since the quantity of land farmed is a proxy for the opportunity cost of the child's time, the estimated marginal effects on the probability that the child studies full time or combines work with study are consistent with the theoretical prediction (section 5.2) that an increase in that opportunity cost reduces the probability of a study-only solution, and increases that of a work-and-study one. The finding of a positive marginal effect on the probability that the child works full time appears to contradict the theoretical prediction that an increase in the opportunity cost of the child's time reduces the probability a of a work-only solution. Since, as already remarked, land size may pick up the effect of the fixed cost of access to work (not controlled for), however, the positive effect of a reduction in this access cost associated with an increase in the amount of land available could well outweigh the negative effect of the increase in the opportunity cost of the child's time, and thus explain why the marginal effect of land size on the probability of working full time is positive, and the marginal effect on the probability of combining work with study is small. If land size picks up the effect of the fixed cost of access to work, however, it is doubly strange that it should raise the probability of being idle. One cannot but wonder whether a child reported as neither working nor attending school really is idle (see the discussion in Chapter 2).

One more child aged 6–15 reduces the probability that other school-age children will study only, and increases not only the probability that they will work, full or part time, but also the probability that they will reportedly do nothing. Leaving aside the last effect, this is consistent with the theory for the case where school-age children make a negative net contribution to the family budget. The last effect strengthens the suspicion that a 'no' answer to the question whether a child works, and to the question whether a child studies, might not necessarily imply that the child does nothing. A possibility is that the parents effectively gave the child away (see the last section of Chapter 2).

The marginal effects of the number of children aged 0–5 are similar to those of the number of children aged 6–15. Since pre-school children cannot be other than a net cost, that is as one would have expected. The only difference between these effects and those of the number of children in the higher age group is that one more pre-school child has a negative effect also on the probability that school-age children work and study at the same time. This may mean that a number of school-age children, particularly females, who would have otherwise combined school attendance with the performance of domestic chores, in particular with the care of younger siblings, will now find time only for the latter.

School availability has a positive marginal effect on the probability of studying full or part time, and a negative one on the probability of either working only, or doing nothing. As the effects on both the probability of working only, and the probability of combining work with study, are very small, these findings indicate that the additional students will come mostly out of the ranks of children otherwise reportedly doing nothing (as in the case of an increase in full income). Given that a higher value of the type-of-school variable may mean either that a school has been built in a village where previously there was none, or that a higher-grade school has been added to the existing lower-grade ones, this variable picks up not only the effects of a reduction in the fixed cost of access to education, but also those of an increase in the expected rate of remuneration of adult human capital, hence in the expected marginal return to education. Under the assumption that parents cannot borrow, and have no assets to sell, we predicted in section 5.2 that a rise in the marginal return to education would raise the probability of a study-only solution relative to a work-and-study one, and the probability of a work-and-study solution relative to a work-only one. But we also know from Chapter 2 that a reduction in the fixed cost of access to education would increase that of a study-only solution (the predicted effect on the probability of a work-and-study solution is ambiguous). The empirical findings are thus consistent with the hypothesis that parents cannot dissave.

The village survival rate is found to have a strong positive effect on the probability of studying only, and smaller negative ones on the probability of anything else. Since this variable has a positive effect on the expected rate of return to adult human capital, its estimated effects on the time allocation of school-age children are consistent with the theory. But this variable is also a proxy for policies that increase the survival probability of pre-school children. Since, in the sample, families include children in both age groups, it is difficult to disentangle the two sets of effects. To the extent that they can be attributed to an increase in the marginal return to education, however, the estimated effects of the village survival rate are consistent with the empirical findings about the effects of the type of school available.

5.3.2 *Educational expenditure*

Given that educational expenditure is incurred only by parents who choose to send their children to school, the effects of the exogenous variables on this form of expenditure are estimated by Heckman's two-stage procedure. The results are reported in Table 5.10. The significance of the selectivity parameter, *lambda*, confirms the appropriateness of the estimation strategy.

The first-stage (probit) results are consistent with the time-allocation predictions of the bivariate probit (see Table 5.8). At the second stage of the estimation procedure, it seemed appropriate to replace the child's age with the

Table 5.10. *Educational expenditure (Heckman selection model)*

	Coeff.	z	Probit Coeff.	z
Child is female	−0.04	−3.0	−0.18	−14.0
Child's age			0.27	16.8
Child's age squared			−0.1	−18.0
No. of children aged 0–5	−0.03	−3.6	−0.06	−6.8
No. of children aged 6–16	−0.03	−4.5	0.01	0.9
No. of household members	0.01	3.4	0.03	7.4
Poverty	−0.17	−8.8	−0.28	−15.3
Land size	0.003	0.5	−0.01	−3.1
Type of school available	0.01	0.7	0.02	3.2
Class attended	0.18	14.1		
Village survival rate	0.28	3.48	0.31	2.7
Land tenure	0.10	5.1	−0.15	8.1
Mother has primary education	0.03	1.05	0.12	6.0
Mother has middle or higher education	0.17	4.8	−0.06	−1.5
Caste	0.04	2.6	0.08	5.5
Constant	4.39	30.8	−2.01	−13.2
Rho	0.29			
Sigma	1.06			
Lambda	0.31			

school grade, which reflects not only age, but also other factors (aptitude for study, morbidity history, etc.). These estimates show that the level of educational expenditure undertaken by the parents for a child attending school is lower if the child is female, and rises with the grade of school attended. They also show a positive effect of land tenure, and a negative effect of poverty. Coherently with the theory, full income thus raises the amount spent on a child that goes to school, as well as the probability that he or she will do so.

The estimated effects of village survival rate, land size, and type of school available are all positive, but the last two are insignificant. The positive effect of the village survival rate confirms that this variable acts as a proxy for the expected rate of remuneration of adult human capital. Land size raises the marginal product of child labour, and may thus be expected to have a negative effect on the educational expenditures of families where children work and study at the same time. Since only a small minority of children combine work with study, however, it is not surprising that this effect should be statistically insignificant. School availability reduces the fixed cost of access to education, and raises the marginal return to education. One might thus have expected it to have a significant effect, but the village survival rate possibly takes significance away from it.

5.3.3 *Nutrition and anthropometry*

The BMI equation is estimated by ordinary least squares. The results reported in Table 5.11 are entirely consistent with the theory. The number of siblings (the age distribution is insignificant) has a negative effect, confirming that children of any age have a net cost.

Poverty is found to have a negative effect, land ownership to have a positive one. This implies that children born to low-income families will consume less at each stage, and have thus a lower probability of surviving to the next stage, than children born to higher-income families (see Chapter 3).

Land size has a positive effect. Since this variable is a proxy for the opportunity-cost of the child's time, this is clearly a cross-substitution effect. School availability also has a positive effect. Since this variable picks up both the effect of a reduction in fixed access costs, and the effect of an increase in the marginal return to education, there are income and cross-substitution effects pulling in opposite directions. The finding suggests that the income effect predominates.

The village survival rate has a positive effect too. The theory predicts (see Chapter 3) that mortality-reducing public expenditure may either crowd in or crowd out parental expenditure on pre-school children. Since the BMI of school-age children reflects not only current, but also previous food intake, the finding suggests crowding-in. But the theory does not permit us to say whether private and public expenditures are complements or substitutes (see Chapter 3).

Table 5.11. *Body mass of school-age children*

	Coeff.	t
Child's sex	−0.18	−3.21
Child's age	−0.61	−4.25
Child's age squared	0.04	4.97
Mother's age	0.13	2.63
Mother's age squared	0.00	−2.43
Poverty	−0.11	−3.16
Land tenure	0.10	1.52
Land size	0.11	5.23
No. of children	−0.06	−2.88
No. of household members	0.02	2.22
Type of school available	0.08	2.54
Village survival rate	1.00	2.02

Table 5.12. *Probability of a birth in the last two years (probit estimates)*

	Coeff.	z
Children work only	0.41	9.33
Mother's age	−0.05	−4.06
Mother's age squared	0.00	2.28
Caste	−0.06	−2.92
Land tenure	−0.09	−2.90
Poverty	0.22	14.79
Father has no education	−0.04	−0.64
Father has primary education	−0.06	−1.07
Father has secondary education	−0.08	−1.42
Father is Muslim	0.16	1.81
Father is Christian	0.49	5.04
Father is other	−0.09	−0.80
Birth order	−0.24	−23.63

5.3.4 *Fertility*

Table 5.12 shows the estimates of a probit model for the probability of an extra birth. As usual in this type of estimate,[4] the probability of a birth increases with the mother's age up to a point, and then decreases.

The explanatory variables include, in addition to those used for the other estimates, also birth parity (hence, the number of children already born), and the proportion of school-age children in the family who work only. The latter proxies for the probability that the economic environment (parental

[4] See, for example, Atella and Rosati (2000).

income and assets, marginal product of child labour, returns to education, etc.) facing the household when the newborn child reaches school age will be such that the child will work only. In conjunction with birth parity, it thus makes the proxies for the marginal product of child labour (land size and family composition) redundant.

Birth parity has a negative effect (the larger the number of children, the lower the demand for extra ones). Consistently with the theoretical prediction (see Chapter 3) that the expectation of a higher child wage rate would induce couples to reduce the level of birth control, the proportion of school-age children that work only has a positive and highly significant effect on the probability of an extra birth.

The mother's education is not significant, and was omitted in the final estimates. This may be due to the fact that birth parity picks up the effects of the variables, including the opportunity cost of the mother's time, that affect the demand for completed fertility. To check that, we estimated an equation with completed fertility (approximated, for any given age of the mother, by the total number of births to the date of the interview) instead of the probability of an extra birth on the left-hand side, and obviously without birth parity on the right-hand side, and found that the mother's education is significantly negative (the effects of the other explanatory variables retain their signs). The father's education has a significantly negative effect on the probability of an extra birth, thus throwing doubt on the common assumption that only the mother's education matters.

Poverty has a positive effect on the probability of an extra birth, land tenure a negative one. Therefore, full household income encourages fertility as the theory predicts (see Chapter 3). This belies the commonly held view that low-income families have many children *because* they have low income. Fertility decisions depend on the whole economic environment, not just on one dimension of it.

5.4 DISCUSSION

The empirical findings reported in the present chapter show a high degree of consonance between theory and data. As we did not go into the question of unobserved heterogeneity, we cannot yet claim to have unearthed causal relationships. We shall deal with that issue in the next four chapters, in particular in Chapter 9, which uses the same data as the present one. That notwithstanding, the indications provided by the present chapter are enough to make us confident that the decision-theoretical analysis of Chapters 2 and 3 has put us on the right track. We now go on to discuss the policy implications of some of our empirical findings. For expositional convenience, we shall argue as if causality had already been established, but our earlier remarks should make it clear that, at the present stage, we can only be entitled to talk of statistical association.

We have found that a marginal increase in full household income—proxied by the poverty class (suitably instrumented to take care of endogeneity), and land ownership—raises substantially the probability that a child in the relevant age range will attend school, and reduces substantially the probability that he or she will be reported doing nothing, but has little effect on the probability that the child will either work and study, or work only.[5] We have also found that it raises the nutritional status of children, and the amount spent on a child's education conditional on attending school. This helps explain why the raw data show that child labour participation decreases more slowly, as household income increases, than the share of 'idle' children, and that it remains high even in households of the top income quintile (see Table 5.3). Since, for any given number of births, the number of school-age children increases with nutrition, an implication of these findings is that income redistribution is not a very effective way of reducing the child labour participation rate, even less of reducing the absolute number of child workers. On the other hand, income redistribution has a number of desirable effects. It reduces inequality. It reduces the number of children reported as neither working nor attending school, and thus at risk of being sold or bonded. It improves the nutritional status of children, and thus presumably reduces morbidity and premature mortality. Last but not least, it increases the amount of time and money invested in education.

Land size is found to have a negative marginal effect on the probability that a child studies only, and a positive one on the probability that the child works only, or combines work with study. The effect on the amount that parents spend on a child's education, conditional on the child attending school, is not significant. These findings require careful explanation. With family composition controlled for, the amount of land farmed by the family is a proxy for the marginal product of child labour. With poverty and land tenure controlled for, an increase in land size is thus equivalent to an increase in the child wage rate, accompanied by a lump-sum tax such that full household income remains constant. Redistributing land without redistributing income would thus have the effect of lowering the marginal rate of return to education in families that, before the policy, had little or no land, and of raising it in families that, before the policy, had a lot of land. The policy would then raise child labour participation in the families that receive land, and lower it in those that have land taken from them. Since most of the children are in the first category of families, aggregate child labour participation would then rise. For the same reason, aggregate infant mortality would fall. Child labour would thus rise not only as a proportion of the number of school-age children, but also in absolute terms.

Historically, however, land redistribution has been accompanied by some measure of full-income redistribution in the same direction. In the history of

---

[5] There is an argument, however, that this could be the effect of, in some sense, averaging over different income groups. Edmonds (2005) uses a non-parametric decomposition to estimate the effect of an increase in household income (proxied by per capita expenditure) on child labour in Vietnam. The paper finds that the effect is very strong in very poor households, much weaker in less poor ones. If the estimation procedure does not account for this non-linearity, the effect of income could be underestimated.

land reform, land has in fact been confiscated from large land owners and given to landless peasants with little or no compensation for the former, and little or no charge for the latter. In child labour terms, this policy will have been less detrimental than pure land redistribution, but it is hard to believe that it was actually beneficial. In rural India, where full household income appears to have little effect on the probability that a child works, it would make little difference whether land were redistributed with or without compensatory income transfers.

Let us now move on to the effects of education and health policies, staring with the former. As theory and common sense led us to expect, we found that building a school in a village where previously there was none, or building a higher-grade school were previously there was only a lower-grade one, has a positive marginal effect on the probability of either studying only or working and studying at the same time, and a negative one on the probability of either working only or doing nothing. This is consistent with the earlier findings of Rosenzweig and Everson (1977), Rosenzweig and Schultz (1982), and Rosenzweig and Wolpin (1982). It would thus appear that the policy could be a useful tool not only for encouraging school attendance, and reducing the number of children at risk of being sold or bonded, but also for reducing child labour participation and infant mortality. We further discovered that school provision is positively associated with the nutritional status of school-age children, hence that it may reduce mortality at all stages, and thus raise the marginal return to education. Since the policy also appears to affect school attendance by reducing the fixed cost of access to education, and given that this cost is more important for families with lower full income, the policy is likely to be good also from an equity point of view.

The effects of health policy are also consistent with the theory, but somewhat less obvious than those of education policy. Mortality-reducing public expenditure, proxied by the village survival rate, appears to have a positive effect on the BMI of school-age children. This result, predicted by the theory, implies that this form of public expenditure crowds in parental expenditure on their children's nutrition (see Chapter 3). The policy is found to have also a strongly positive effect on the probability that a child studies full time. Therefore, mortality-reducing public expenditure has beneficial implications for education and child labour,[6] as well as morbidity and mortality. On the other hand, however, the policy encourages fertility.

The finding that an additional birth is more probable if the new child is expected to work full time when he or she reaches school age, and that this effect is highly significant, suggests that the demand for an extra child is, to a large extent, a demand for an extra pair of arms. In the light of the theoretical analysis of Chapters 2 and 3, this suggests that a substantial number of parents (*a*) are too poor to attach much weight to altruistic considerations, and (*b*) have

---

[6] Recall that we found the same effect, at cross-country level, in Chapter 4.

neither access to credit, not assets to sell. Proposition (*a*) is consistent with the observation that only 4 per cent of school-age children combine work with study, while as many as a quarter do nothing. In the light of the theory, it is also a symptom that, for a large number of households, the fixed costs of access to education and work are high in relation to full income. Proposition (*b*) is consistent with other indications that parents behave in the way predicted by the theory in the no-dissaving case.

6

Child Labour Effects of Access to Basic Utilities

Evidence from Five Countries

In the theoretical analysis of Chapters 2 and 3, the availability or otherwise of a number of facilities was subsumed in the parameters of the cost functions (of human capital, and of the good consumed by pre-school children), and of the probability distribution of survival. Access to such utilities may well have important effects on the allocation of household resources. The effects of educational and health facilities were examined in Chapter 5. Anecdotal evidence on road infrastructure suggests that good roads raise school attendance. In the present chapter, we report the results of a study by Guarcello, Lyon, and Rosati (2003) on the effects of electricity and piped water.

Lack of piped water may raise the opportunity cost of time spent studying, as children are needed to fetch water, or to help pay for the cost of purchasing water. The same may be said about lack of electricity, as children are needed to collect wood.

The paper investigates the link between child labour and access to water and electricity in five countries: El Salvador, Ghana, Guatemala, Morocco, and Yemen. As Table 6.1 shows, a significant proportion of the population

Table 6.1. *Water and electricity access, by country and residence*[a]

Country	Households with water access			Households with electricity access		
	Rural	Urban	Total	Rural	Urban	Total
El Salvador	40.4	81.0	64.3	70.8	97.3	86.4
Ghana	22.1	84.2	44.8	19.6	78.1	41.1
Guatemala	53.7	88.1	68.7	57.3	93.7	73.1
Morocco	36.9	—	36.9	17.3	—	17.3
Yemen	22.8	81.6	38.1	23.4	89.1	40.5

[a] See Appendix 6.1 for questions upon which the access indicators are based.

Source: UCW calculations based on Ghana: *Ghana Living Standard Measurement Survey*, 1998–9; Yemen: *National Poverty Survey*, 1999; Guatemala: *Encuesta de condiciones de vida* (ENCOVI), 2000; El Salvador: *Enquesta de hogares de propósitos múltiples* (EHPM) 2001; Morocco: *Living Standard Measurement Survey*, 1998–9.

of these countries lacks, particular in rural areas, adequate access to water and electricity. The investigation uses data sets from recent national household surveys containing detailed information both on children's activities and on basic services access. The data sets used are listed in Appendix 6.1.

6.1 CHILD ACTIVITY STATUS

Two alternative definitions of working children are used. The first classifies as workers all children aged between 7 and 14 who carry out an economic activity for at least one hour a day. The second includes in the number of working children also those performing household chores for at least twenty-eight hours a week. As data on hours spent on household chores are available only for El Salvador and Guatemala, the extended

Table 6.2 shows the proportion of children who, according to these definitions, work only, work and study, study only, or do nothing, in the five countries. The proportion of children involved full time in economic activities ranges from 10 per cent in Morocco to 2 per cent in El Salvador, and rates of full-time school attendance from 76 per cent in Morocco to 51 per cent in Yemen. The proportion of children combining school and economic activity varies from 12 per cent in Guatemala to just 1 per cent in Morocco.

All these countries feature a significant proportion of children absent from both school and work. More than one in three children in Ghana and Yemen, and almost one in five in El Salvador and Guatemala, fall into this category. In Morocco, 15 per cent of the 7–14 age group are reported doing nothing. Some of these reportedly 'idle' children may be engaged in unreported work.[1] Others may perform household chores—including water or fuel collection—that allow other household members to engage in productive activities.[2]

As international labour standards make exceptions for household chores performed in a child's own household, these activities are normally excluded from estimates of child labour. Since they can interfere with school and leisure, however, they also merit consideration. As shown in Table 6.3, the inclusion of household chores raises the participation rate, and reduces the incidence of children reportedly neither working nor attending school. The effect is particularly strong in El Salvador, where including household chores raises the

[1] Parents may falsely report their children as not working because (at best) children are forbidden work, or (at worst) because their children are engaged in illegal or dangerous activities. Alternatively, parents may misinterpret the survey question, and report a child as idle because he or she was not working at the time of the interview, although he or she may work in other periods.

[2] A recent study of the phenomenon of 'idle' children (UCW Project, 'The Puzzle of Apparently Idle Children: Evidence for Six Countries', Oct. 2003) provides evidence suggesting that children can be absent from both school and external work because they are needed to perform household chores, because of their health, or because they are unable to find work after leaving school. But the study indicates that a large proportion of children not in school or economic activity do not fall into any of these categories. In Guatemala, one of the countries considered in the present chapter, the 'unexplained' portion of idle children is 70%.

Table 6.2. *Child activity status (excluding household chores), by sex and country*

Country	Activity status	Male %	Male No.[a]	Female %	Female No.[a]	Total[b] %	Total[b] No.[a]
El Salvador	Working[c] and not attending school	3.3	25.1	1.3	10.0	2.3	35.1
	Attending school and not working	73.3	564.2	77.4	585.7	75.3	1,150.0
	Working and attending school	6.7	51.9	2.9	22.0	4.8	73.9
	Not working and not attending school	16.7	128.7	18.3	138.7	17.5	267.4
Ghana	Working[c] and not attending school	9.3	282	9.7	287	9.5	569
	Attending school and not working	46.8	1,427	46.9	1,384	46.8	2,811
	Working and attending school	6.5	199	5.5	163	6.03	362
	Not working and not attending school	37.4	1,140	37.94	1,121	37.67	2,261
Guatemala	Working[c] and not attending school	9.5	123	5.9	72	7.7	195
	Attending school and not working	60.9	790	64.1	787	62.4	1,577
	Working and attending school	16.4	212	8.1	99	12.3	311
	Not working and not attending school	13.3	172	22	270	17.5	442
Morocco	Working[c] and not attending school	11.0	297.5	8.6	231	9.8	528.5
	Attending school and not working	80.9	2,198.2	70.3	1,877.8	75.6	4,075.9
	Working and attending school	1.8	49.9	0.8	20.87	1.3	70.7
	Not working and not attending school	8.1	220.5	21.1	563.1	14.5	783.6
Yemen	Working[c] and not attending school	5.0	140.8	10.8	284.8	7.9	425.6
	Attending school and not working	62.6	1,749.3	38.4	1,011.3	50.9	2,760.5
	Working and attending school	6.3	175.2	2.0	51.5	4.2	226.6
	Not working and not attending school	26.1	728.1	48.8	1,283.1	37.1	2,011.2

[a] Numbers expressed in thousands.
[b] Totals may not add up due to rounding.
[c] Economically active children.

Source: UCW calculations based on Ghana: *Ghana Living Standard Measurement Survey,* 1999; Guatemala: *Encuesta de condiciones de vida* (ENCOVI), 2000; El Salvador: *Enquesta de hogares de propósitos múltiples* (EHPM) 2001; Morocco: *Labour Force Survey,* 1998; Yemen: *National Poverty Survey,* 1998–9.

Table 6.3. *Child activity status (including household chores), by sex and country*

Country	Activity status	Male		Female		Total[b]	
		%	No.[a]	%	No.[a]	%	No.[a]
El Salvador	Working[c] and not attending school	13.4	103	11.0	83	12.2	186
	Attending school and not working	44.0	340	54.0	407	49.0	747
	Working and attending school	36.0	276	26.0	200	31.2	476
	Not working, not attending school	7.0	51	9.0	65	8.0	116
Guatemala	Working[c] and not attending school	10.8	140	11.6	142	11.18	282
	Attending school and not working	57.8	751	53.9	662	55.9	1,413
	Working and attending school	19.4	252	18.3	224	18.6	476
	Not working, not attending school	12.0	156	16.3	200	14.2	356

[a] Numbers expressed in thousands.
[b] Totals may not add up due to rounding.
[c] Economically active children and children performing household chores for at 28 hours per week, eliminating the overlapping category doing both.

Source: UCW calculations based on Guatemala: *Encuesta de condiciones de vida* (ENCOVI), 2000; El Salvador: *Enquesta de hogares de propósitos múltiples* (EHPM) 2001.

participation rate from 7 to 43 per cent, and reduces the proportion of childen reported idle from 18 to 8 per cent.

6.2 THE EFFECT OF ACCESS TO WATER AND ELECTRICITY

As Fig. 6.1 and 6.2 and Tables 6.4 and 6.5 show, children's activity status in the five countries varies dramatically according to whether the household does or does not have access to water and electricity. With the exception of Guatemala, where the survey does not specify it, access to water is intended to mean that the household has piped drinking water. With the exception of Guatemala and Morocco, where the surveys ask about connection to the electricity network, electricity access refers to the source of lighting for the dwelling. Details of the questions used in the survey and precise definitions of the variables used in the estimates and tabulations are given in Appendix 6.1.

In all five countries, the percentage of children working only is much higher, and the rate of full-time school attendance much lower, among children from households without access to water or electricity. With the exception of Guatemala, the rate of full-time child involvement in work, for example, is more than three times higher in households without, than in households with, water access. In all five countries, a much higher proportion of children from households not served by water and electricity are also reportedly 'idle'. In

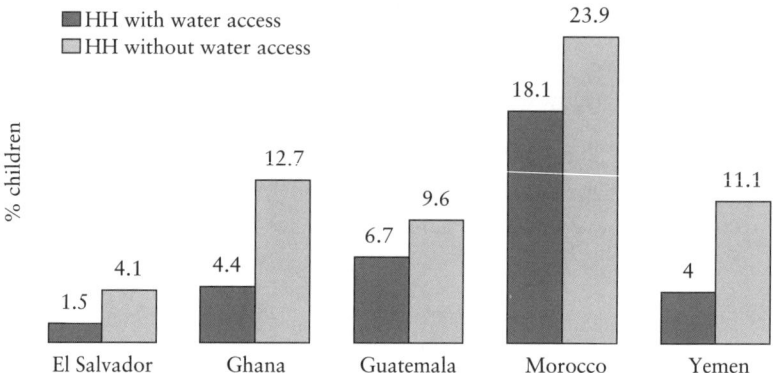

Figure 6.1. *Rate of involvement in economic activity only, by household water access*

Source: UCW calculations based on Ghana: *Ghana Living Standard Measurement Survey*, 1998–9; Yemen: *National Poverty Survey*, 1999; Guatemala: *Encuesta de Condiciones de Vida* (ENCOVI), 2000; El Salvador: *Enquesta de hogares de propósitos múltiples* (EHPM) 2001; Morocco: *Living Standard Measurement Survey*, 1998–9

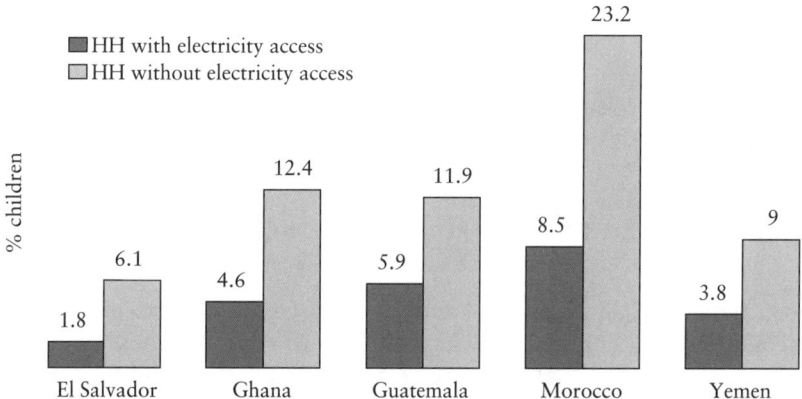

Figure 6.2. *Rate of involvement in economic activity only, by household electricity access*

Source: UCW calculations based on Ghana: *Ghana Living Standard Measurement Survey*, 1998–99. Yemen: *National Poverty Survey*, 1999. Guatemala: *Encuesta de condiciones de vida* (ENCOVI), 2000. El Salvador: *Enquesta de Hogares de Propósitos Múltiples* (EHPM) 2001. Morocco: *Living Standard Measurement Survey*, 1998–99.

general, the variation in children's activity status by water/electricity access is higher among girls than boys, and higher in rural compared to urban areas.

Similar patterns prevail in El Salvador and Guatemala also when household chores are counted as work (Tables A6.2.3–A6.2.4, Appendix 6.2).

Table 6.4. *Child activity status (excluding household chores) by water access, sex, and country*[a]

Country	Activity status	Households with water access			Households without water access		
		Male	Female	Total	Male	Female	Total
El Salvador	Working[b] and not attending school	1.9	1.1	1.5	6.1	2.1	4.1
	Attending school and not working	83.1	86.3	84.7	67.4	73.4	70.4
	Working and attending school	6.3	3.4	4.9	9.2	3.0	6.1
	Not working and not attending school	8.6	9.2	8.9	17.3	21.5	19.3
Ghana	Working[b] and not attending school	2.8	5.9	4.4	13.0	12.4	12.7
	Attending school and not working	66.8	63.8	65.2	34.9	35.0	35.0
	Working and attending school	3.1	3.4	3.3	8.5	6.9	7.7
	Not working and not attending school	27.3	26.9	27.1	43.6	45.8	44.6
Guatemala	Working[b] and not attending school	7.8	5.5	6.7	12.8	6.4	9.6
	Attending school and not working	65.9	68.2	67.0	51.1	57.1	54.1
	Working and attending school	15.1	9.3	12.3	18.9	6.0	12.3
	Not working and not attending school	11.3	17.0	14.0	17.2	30.5	24.0
Morocco	Working[b] and not attending school	15.9	20.3	18.1	23.2	24.6	23.9
	Attending school and not working	63.2	38.6	51.1	66.4	41.1	54.3
	Working and attending school	2.3	0.7	1.5	2.4	0.8	1.6
	Not working and not attending school	18.6	40.4	29.4	8.1	33.5	20.2
Yemen	Working[b] and not attending school	3.0	5.1	4.0	6.7	15.8	11.1
	Attending school and not working	79.7	65.0	72.5	61.7	28.3	45.6
	Working and attending school	4.9	1.7	3.3	8.3	2.5	5.5
	Not working and not attending school	12.4	28.3	20.2	23.3	53.4	37.8

[a] See Appendix 6.1 for questions upon which the access indicators are based.
[b] Economically active children.

Source: UCW calculations based on Ghana: *Ghana Living Standard Measurement Survey*, 1998–9; Yemen: *National Poverty Survey*, 1999; Guatemala: *Encuesta de condiciones de vida* (ENCOVI), 2000; El Salvador: *Enquesta de hogares de propósitos múltiples* (EHPM) 2001; Morocco: *Living Standard Measurement Survey*, 1998–9.

Table 6.5. *Child activity status (excluding household chores) by electricity access, sex, and country*[a]

Country	Activity status	Households with electricity access			Households without electricity access		
		Male	Female	Total	Male	Female	Total
El Salvador	Working[b] and not attending school	2.3	1.3	1.8	9.5	2.5	6.1
	Attending school and not working	81.4	84.7	83.0	56.0	63.1	59.4
	Working and attending school	6.8	3.3	5.0	10.8	2.9	7.0
	Not working and not attending school	9.5	10.7	10.1	23.7	31.5	27.4
Ghana	Working[b] and not attending school	3.8	5.4	4.6	12.2	12.5	12.4
	Attending school and not working	66.4	65.0	65.7	35.7	35.0	35.4
	Working and attending school	5.0	4.7	4.8	7.4	6.0	6.7
	Not working and not attending school	24.8	24.8	24.8	44.7	46.6	45.6
Guatemala	Working[b] and not attending school	6.9	4.8	5.9	15.7	8.1	11.9
	Attending school and not working	67.3	71.0	69.1	45.4	49.2	47.4
	Working and attending school	15.3	8.7	12.2	18.9	6.6	12.7
	Not working and not attending school	10.5	15.5	12.9	20.0	36.0	28.1
Morocco	Working[b] and not attending school	9.9	6.9	8.5	21.3	25.1	23.2
	Attending school and not working	77.5	66.2	72	63.8	36.4	50.6
	Working and attending school	2.9	3.2	3	2.2	0.5	1.4
	Not working and not attending school	9.7	23.7	16.5	12.6	37.9	24.9
Yemen	Working[b] and not attending school	2.4	5.5	3.8	9.0	9.0	9.0
	Attending school and not working	65.4	50.4	59.0	40.8	20.2	32.5
	Working and attending school	1.5	2.3	1.9	5.3	1.3	3.7
	Not working and not attending school	30.6	41.7	35.3	44.9	69.5	54.8

[a] See detailed table in Appendix 6.2 for disaggregation by both residence and sex.
[b] Economically Active Children.

Source: UCW calculations based on the following surveys. Ghana: *Ghana Living Standard Measurement Survey, 1998–9*; Yemen: *National Poverty Survey, 1999*; Guatemala: *Encuesta de condiciones de vida* (ENCOVI), 2000; El Salvador: *Enquesta de hogares de propósitos múltiples* (EHPM) 2001; Morocco: *Living Standard Measurement Survey, 1998–9.*

For example, school attendance rates in El Salvador and Guatemala decrease from 85 per cent and 79 per cent, respectively, for households with access to water, to 72 per cent and 66 per cent, respectively, for households without water access.

There is, therefore, a strong correlation between water/electricity access and the activities of children. But is there also a causal link? Disentangling the causal relationship is not straightforward. The observation, for example, that households without water access are less likely to send their children to school is not sufficient to establish a causal relationship, because a household without water access may have a set of characteristics (observable and unobservable) that makes them more likely to send their children to work. The next three sections deal with the issue.

6.3 ECONOMETRIC METHODOLOGY

The econometrics are set out in detail in the Appendix to this book. Here, we limit ourselves to outlining the estimation procedure, and summarizing the results. The main econometric problem in estimating the effects of access to basic services is the potential endogeneity of such variables. Guarcello, Lyon, and Rosati (2003) estimate the probability ('propensity score') that a household with characteristics X has access to water or electricity. In each case, specification of the propensity score is achieved by checking whether the balancing property of the estimated probability is satisfied. Since access to water and electricity is likely to be different for urban and rural households, the propensity score is computed separately for the two areas of residence. The estimated distributions of the propensity scores are shown in Appendix 6.3.

The distributions of the propensity scores for 'treated' and 'non-treated' groups of households overlap to a large extent for El Salvador (rural areas) and Guatemala (rural and urban areas) in the case of water access, and for Morocco (rural areas) in the case of electricity access. This indicates that the characteristics of the two groups of households that have and do not have access to water (electricity) do not differ in a significant way. In the other cases, however, the 'treated' and 'non-treated' groups of households overlap much less, and the estimates are consequently more sensitive to model specification.

Average treatment effects (ATT) are computed using a nearest-neighbour-matching estimator. The results are shown in Tables 6.6 and 6.7. Access to water in rural areas appears to raise school attendance and lower both child participation and the number of children reported doing nothing. The effects are somewhat differentiated by country, but have a similar pattern. In urban areas, the pattern is less well defined than in rural areas, and the effects are not always significant.

Access to electricity has broadly similar effects. It significantly increases the proportion of children in school (El Salvador, Ghana, Morocco), and significantly reduces the proportion of economically active children (Morocco) and idle children (El Salvador, Ghana, and Morocco). With the exception of Guatemala, the pattern is again less well defined in urban than in rural areas.

Table 6.6. *Average treatment effects for water access (results from matching procedure using water access as the treatment variable)*

Country	Outcome variable[b]	Urban				Rural			
		Treated	Control	ATT	t	Treated	Control	ATT	t
El Salvador	Children attending school	1,122	627	0.055	2.87	2,887	570	0.028	1.028
	Children working[a]	1,122	627	−0.016	−1.131	2,887	570	−0.027	−1.397
	Working[b] and not attending school	1,122	627	−0.007	−0.885	2,887	570	−0.015	−1.12
	Attending school and not working	1,122	627	0.004	0.316	2,887	570	−0.026	−1.55
	Working and attending school	1,122	627	0.05	2.347	2,887	570	0.053	1.795
	Not working and not attending school	1,122	627	−0.047	−3.244	2,887	570	−0.026	−1.55
Ghana	Children attending school	876	174	0.043	0.658	400	319	0.068	1.772
	Children working[a]	876	174	−0.096	−1.937	400	319	−0.088	−3.002
	Working[b] and not attending school	876	174	−0.023	−0.693	400	319	−0.04	−1.754
	Attending school and not working	876	174	−0.073	−1.938	400	319	−0.048	−2.543
	Working and attending school	876	174	0.109	1.63	400	319	0.144	3.875
	Not working and not attending school	876	174	−0.029	−0.47	400	319	−0.028	−0.748
Guatemala	Children attending school	1,516	171	−0.059	−1.411	1,263	611	0.065	2.784
	Children working[(a)]	1,516	171	0.078	1.295	1,263	611	0.015	0.74
	Working[b] and not attending school	1,516	171	−0.027	−1	1,263	611	0.001	0.06
	Attending school and not working	1,516	171	0.112	1.776	1,263	611	0.014	0.874
	Working and attending school	1,516	171	−0.032	−0.91	1,263	611	0.051	2.084
	Not working and not attending school	1,516	171	−0.052	−0.961	1,263	611	−0.066	−3.272
Morocco	Children attending school	—	—	—	—	726	404	−0.021	0.032
	Children working[a]	—	—	—	—	726	404	−0.053	0.027
	Working[b] and not attending school	—	—	—	—	726	404	−0.046	0.025
	Attending school and not working	—	—	—	—	726	404	−0.007	0.006
	Working and attending school	—	—	—	—	726	404	−0.015	0.032
	Not working and not attending school	—	—	—	—	726	404	0.067	0.026

a Economically active.
b The outcome variable is the proportion of children in each household involved in the reported activities.

Source: UCW calculations based on the following surveys. Ghana: *Ghana Living Standard Measurement Survey*, 1998–9; Yemen: *National Poverty Survey*, 1999; Guatemala: *Encuesta de condiciones de vida* (ENCOVI), 2000; El Salvador: *Enquesta de hogares de propósitos múltiples* (EHPM) 2001; Morocco: *Living Standard Measurement Survey*, 1998–9.

Table 6.7. *Average treatment effects for electricity access (results from matching procedure using water access as the treatment variable)*

Country	Outcome variable[b]	Urban				Rural			
		Treated	Control	ATT	t	Treated	Control	ATT	t
El Salvador	Children attending school	3,598	125	0.011	0.09	1,928	478	0.082	2.662
	Children working[a]	3,598	125	0.006	0.076	1,928	478	−0.029	−1.347
	Working[b] and not attending school	3,598	125	−0.013	−0.186	1,928	478	−0.01	−0.748
	Attending school and not working	3,598	125	0.08	0.639	1,928	478	0.108	3.249
	Working and attending school	3,598	125	−0.073	−0.971	1,928	478	−0.028	−1.345
	Not working and not attending school	3,598	125	−0.016	−0.168	1,928	478	−0.075	−2.943
Ghana	Children attending school	847	763	0.079	1.229	395	287	0.107	2.926
	Children working[a]	847	163	−0.041	−0.868	395	287	−0.05	−1.708
	Working[b] and not attending school	847	163	−0.031	−0.951	395	287	−0.031	−1.386
	Attending school and not working	847	163	0.067	1.035	395	287	0.119	3.282
	Working and attending school	847	163	−0.01	−0.298	395	287	−0.019	−0.946
	Not working and not attending school	847	163	−0.066	−1.062	395	287	−0.077	−2.197
Guatemala	Children attending school	1,283	541	0.165	5.775	1,557	140	0.168	1.887
	Children working[a]	1,283	541	0.022	0.912	1,557	140	−0.059	−0.958
	Working[b] and not attending school	1,283	541	−0.028	−1.541	1,557	140	−0.027	−0.554
	Attending school and not working	1,283	541	0.116	3.929	1,557	140	0.2	2.255
	Working and attending school	1,283	541	0.05	2.727	1,557	140	−0.032	−0.729
	Not working and not attending school	1,283	541	−0.131	−5.151	1,557	140	−0.141	−1.727
Morocco	Children attending school	—	—	—	—	393	361	0.189	4.859
	Children working[a]	—	—	—	—	393	361	−0.115	−3.797
	Working[b] and not attending school	—	—	—	—	393	361	−0.12	−3.926
	Attending school and not working	—	—	—	—	393	361	0.183	4.631
	Working and attending school	—	—	—	—	393	361	0.005	0.688
	Not working and not attending school	—	—	—	—	393	361	−0.069	−2.145

a Economically active.
b The outcome variable is the proportion of children in each household involved in the reported activities

Source: UCW calculations based on the following surveys. Ghana: *Ghana Living Standard Measurement Survey*, 1998–9; Yemen: *National Poverty Survey*, 1999; Guatemala: *Encuesta de condiciones de vida* (ENCOVI), 2000; El Salvador: *Enquesta de hogares de propósitos múltiples* (EHPM) 2001; Morocco: *Living Standard Measurement Survey*, 1998-99.

These results should be taken with caution because of the potential endogeneity arising from the existence of unobserved variables not taken into account in the estimation. We shall deal with the issue in the next section.

6.4 THE EFFECTS OF ACCESS TO WATER AND ELECTRICITY ON CHILDREN'S SCHOOL ATTENDANCE AND LABOUR SUPPLY: A BIVARIATE ANALYSIS

The distribution of the propensity scores for 'treated' and 'non-treated' groups of households (see Appendix 6.3) makes us confident that, under the unconfoundedness assumption, the use of a regression model does not imply that the estimation of treatment effects relies on extrapolation. Because of similar covariates' distributions for the treatment and control groups, model-based sensitivity should also be very limited. This allows us to draw causal inferences from a regression model.

As in Chapter 5, the effects of the explanatory variables are estimated by fitting a bivariate probit model of the probability of work and the probability of school attendance that takes into account the simultaneity of the decisions through the correlation of the error terms. The marginal effects are then calculated from the estimated coefficients of the probit model. Given that the results obtained with the propensity scores indicated clearly that rural and urban areas are not homogeneous, the estimates are carried out separately for the two areas.

Besides access to water and electricity, the list of explanatory variables includes the household's and the child's characteristics. These characteristics include the sex and age of the child, the income or expenditure of the household, the household's size and age composition, the education of the parents. Where available, other relevant variables such as the occurrence of shocks, availability of schools, presence of living parents, etc. are also included. The effects are very similar to those estimated in the last section (the full set of results is presented in Appendix 6.5).

Table 6.8 presents the marginal effects. Those of access to water and electricity are well defined, and relatively large, for almost all countries. Access to water in urban areas tends to increase the number of children that attend school only. This is normally associated with a reduction in the number of children working, or reported doing nothing. The size of the effect varies from country to country. Access to water in urban areas is associated with an increase in the probability of attending school of between 2 (Ghana) and 10 (Yemen) percentage points. In El Salvador and Yemen increased water access reduces the number of 'idle' children more then the number of children who work. In the other countries it is the other way round.

Access to water in rural areas shows a similar pattern. It induces an increase in the number of children attending school, and a reduction in the number of children either working or reported doing nothing. Notice that the size of

Table 6.8a. *Bivariate probit model marginal effects of access to water*[a]

Country	Residence	Working[b], not attending school		Attending school, not working		Working and attending school		Not attending school, not working	
		dy/dx[c]	z	dy/dx[c]	z	dy/dx[c]	z	dy/dx[c]	z
El Salvador	Rural	−0.003	−1.36	0.054	4.71	0.003	1.34	−0.055	−5.06
	Urban	−0.004	−3.21	0.041	4.24	−0.007	−1.99	−0.03	—
Ghana	Rural	−0.077	−7.47	0.074	3.02	−0.035	−5.98	0.039	1.59
	Urban	−0.016	−2.13	0.019	0.68	−0.019	−2.25	0.016	0.61
Guatemala	Rural	−0.012	−1.99	0.035	2.43	0.003	0.32	−0.0262	−2.29
	Urban	−0.004	−0.67	0.016	0.73	−0.001	−0.1	−0.011	−0.73
Morocco	Rural	−0.184	−5.28	0.094	1.06	−0.013	−4.98	0.103	1.16
	Urban	—	—	—	—	—	—	—	—
Yemen[d]	Rural	0.002	—	0.014	—	0.006	—	−0.021	—
	Urban	−0.004	—	0.04	—	−0.001	—	−0.034	—

[a] See Appendix 6.4 for all control variables.
[b] Economically active children.
[c] dy/dx is for discrete change in dummy variable from 0 to 1;
[d] Simulated effects after bivariate probit.

Source: UCW calculations based on the following surveys. Ghana: *Ghana Living Standard Measurement Survey*, 1998–9; Yemen: *National Poverty Survey*, 1999; Guatemala: *Encuesta de condiciones de vida* (ENCOVI), 2000; El Salvador: *Enquesta de hogares de propósitos Multiples* (EHPM) 2001; Morocco: *Living Standard Measurement Survey*, 1998–9.

Table 6.8b. *Bivariate probit model marginal effects of access to electricity*[a]

Country	Residence	Working,[b] not attending school		Attending school, not working		Working and attending school		Not attending school, not working	
		dy/dx[c]	z	dy/dx[c]	z	dy/dx[c]	z	dy/dx[c]	z
El Salvador	Rural	−0.01	−3.83	0.084	6.27	−0.004	−1.26	−0.07	−5.55
	Urban	−0.006	−2.08	0.081	3.87	−0.004	−0.61	−0.072	—
Ghana	Rural	0.025	1.66	0.017	0.74	0.029	2.94	−0.071	−3.04
	Urban	−0.041	−3.96	0.145	4.93	−0.021	−2.44	−0.083	−2.98
Guatemala	Rural	−0.019	−3.06	0.075	4.82	0.031	3.42	−0.087	−7.02
	Urban	−0.024	−2.59	0.144	4.75	0.028	2.5	−0.149	−5.63
Morocco	Rural	−0.097	−4.36	0.188	5.43	0.002	0.46	−0.093	−3.24
	Urban	—	—	—	—	—	—	—	—
Yemen[d]	Rural	−0.02	—	0.07	—	0.001	—	−0.05	—
	Urban	−0.015	—	0.11	—	−0.01	—	−0.09	—

a See Appendix 6.4 for all control variables.
b Economically active children.
c dy/dx is for discrete change in dummy variable from 0 to 1.
d Simulated effects after bivariate probit.

Source: UCW calculations based on the following surveys. Ghana: *Ghana Living Standard Measurement Survey*, 1998–9; Yemen: *National Poverty Survey*, 1999; Guatemala: *Encuesta de condiciones de vida* (ENCOVI), 2000; El Salvador: *Enquesta de hogares de propósitos múltiples* (EHPM) 2001; Morocco: *Living Standard Measurement Survey*, 1998–9.

the effects is generally larger in rural than in urban areas. Access to electricity increases school attendance in both urban and rural areas, with the exception of rural Ghana. The increase in school attendance is associated with a reduction of the number both of children working and of children neither attending school nor involved in economic activity. The size of the effect ranges between 11 per cent in urban Yemen and 18 per cent in rural Morocco. As the distribution of the propensity scores for the treated group is somewhat different from that of the control group, the effect of access to electricity and children's activities must be treated with more caution than that of access to water.

These estimates make it clear that access to water and electricity is an important determinant of household decisions concerning child labour and education. How important depends on the country. Given that the available controls are not the same for each country, however, it is difficult to draw any conclusion about differences in the size of the effects.

It is also interesting to distinguish the effects of access to water and electricity by age of the child. The graphs reported in Appendix 6.6 show the simulated effect on children's activities of access to these utilities. Where school attendance is concerned, the effects of access to basic utilities are higher for relatively young and relatively old children. This seems to indicate that availability of water and electricity helps both to increase school enrolment at younger ages, and to reduce the drop-out rate at later ages. The effect on labour participation tends to be more negative for relatively older children. 'Idle' children seem particularly to benefit from access to basic services at a young age. At the lower end of the age range, the increase in enrolment seems therefore to be due to children being released from full-time household chores (or to formerly 'idle' children being brought into the education system). At the upper end, access to water and electricity appears to help retain in the school system children that would have otherwise dropped out to join the labour market.

6.5 CAUSALITY

As already mentioned, the presence of unobservables influencing both the decision relative to children's activities and the presence of a certain facility could invalidate the causal interpretation of the estimated relationship. Were we talking of schools, for example, parents with a stronger interest in education could decide to live in an area served by a good school, or lobby for the improvement of the one that exists in the area where they live. The problem seems less serious where basic facilities like electricity and piped water are concerned. The methodology employed for the sensitivity analysis is briefly outlined in the Appendix to the book. The results for El Salvador and Guatemala[3] reported in Appendix 6.7 of the present chapter confirm the robustness of the results with respect to the possible presence of unobservables correlated both with

---

[3] For the other countries, see Guarcello, Lyon, and Rosati (2003).

children's activities and with access to the utility. We can thus be reasonably confident that the estimated relations are causal.

The finding of a strong causal link between access to water and electricty has the obvious policy implication that governments concerned about child labour and school attendance should attach a high priority to these basic facilities, as well as to the provision of schools and health (see previous chapter). Taken together with the findings reported in the last chapter, it also shows that there is no single remedy for child labour. The search for a miracle cure may thus prove vain as well as expensive.

Appendix 6.1 Surveys, and questions used to define variables for access to water and electricity

Question used to define access to water

	Ghana		Yemen		Guatemala		El Salvador		Morocco[a]
	What is the source of drinking water for your household?		What is the source of drinking water for your household?		What is the main source of water used by the household?		What is the source of drinking water for your household?		What is the main source of drinking water in the 'DOUAR'?
1	Indoor plumbing	1	Public net	1	Pipe (network) inside the dwelling	1	Pipe inside the dwelling	1	Public network
2	Inside standpipe	2	Cooperative net	2	Pipe, outside the dwelling but within the property	2	Pipe outside the dwelling but inside the property	2	Well
3	Water vendor	3	Private net	3	Pipe from a public well	3	Neighbour's pipe	3	Lake, river, spring
4	Water truck/tanker service	4	Well inside the dwelling	4	Public or private well	4	Fountain or public stream	4	Hill dam
5	Neighbouring household	5	Well outside the dwelling	5	River, lake, stream	5	Cooperative stream	5	Water truck
6	Private outside standpipe/tap	6	Spring	6	Water truck	6	Water truck	6	Other
7	Public standpipe	7	Covered pond	7	Rainwater	7	Private or cooperative well	
8	Well with pump	8	An open pond	8	Other (specify)	8	Lake, river, spring	
9	Well without pump	9	Dam	9			Other (specify)	
10	River, lake, spring, pond	10	Other					
11	Rainwater							
12	Other							

[a] Question applied to the rural questionnaire.

Note: In bold positive response used to define the variable 'access to water'.

Source: Ghana: *Ghana Living Standard Measurement Survey*, 1998–9; Yemen: *National Poverty Survey*, 1999; Guatemala: *Encuesta de condiciones de vida* (ENCOVI), 2000; El Salvador: *Enquesta de hogares de propósitos múltiples* (EHPM) 2001; Morocco: *Living Standard Measurement Survey*, 1998–9.

Question used to define access to electricity

Ghana		Yemen		Guatemala		El Salvador		Morocco[a]	
What is the main source of lighting for your dwelling?		What is the main source of lighting in the house?		This dwelling is connected to: An electrical energy distribution system?		What is the main source of lighting in this house?		Is there any electricity in this 'DOUAR'?	
Electricity (mains)	1	Public net	1	Yes 1, No 2		Electricity	1	Yes 1, No 2	
Generator	2	Cooperation net	2			Neighbour's electricity connection	2		
Kerosene, gas, lamp	3	Private net	3			Kerosene (gas)	3		
Candles/torches (flashlights)	4	Household private generator	4			Candle	4		
		Kerosene (gas)	5			Other	5		
		Gasoline torch	6						
		Other (specify)	7						

[a] Question applied to the rural questionnaire.

Note: In bold positive response used to define the variable 'access to electricity'.

Source: Ghana: *Ghana Living Standard Measurement Survey*, 1998–9; Yemen: National Poverty Survey, 1999; Guatemala: *Encuesta de condiciones de vida* (ENCOVI), 2000; El Salvador: *Enquesta de hogares de propósitos múltiples* (EHPM) 2001; Morocco: *Living Standard Measurement Survey*, 1998–9.

Appendix 6.2 Detailed descriptive statistics

Table A6.2.1. Child activity status by water availability, sex, residence, and country[a] (%)

Country	Activity status	Households with water access									Households without water access								
		Male			Female			Total			Male			Female			Total		
		Urban	Rural	Total	Urban	Rural	Total	Urban	Rural	Total	Urban	Rural	Total	Urban	Rural	Total	Urban	Rural	Total
El Salvador	Working[b] not attending school	0.7	4.7	1.9	0.7	1.9	1.1	0.7	3.3	1.5	3.9	6.9	6.1	1.9	2.1	2.1	2.9	4.5	4.1
	Attending school not working	88.2	71.6	83.1	88.4	81.6	86.3	88.3	76.5	84.7	75.5	64.6	67.4	76.9	72.2	73.4	76.2	68.4	70.4
	Working and attending school	4.0	11.6	6.3	3.2	3.8	3.4	3.6	7.8	4.9	5.6	10.5	9.2	4.9	2.3	3.0	5.3	6.4	6.1
	Not working not attending school	7.1	12.1	8.6	7.7	12.7	9.2	7.4	12.4	8.9	15.0	18.0	17.3	16.2	23.4	21.5	15.6	20.7	19.3
Ghana	Working[b] not attending school	2.0	4.6	2.8	4.5	8.7	5.9	3.3	6.7	4.4	4.9	13.9	13.0	7.2	13.0	12.4	6.1	13.5	12.7
	Attending school not working	72.1	55.3	66.8	68.6	54.1	63.8	70.3	54.7	65.2	46.8	33.6	34.9	49.5	33.1	35.0	48.2	33.4	35.0
	Working and attending school	3.5	2.2	3.1	2.2	5.7	3.4	2.9	4.1	3.3	7.8	8.6	8.5	7.0	6.9	6.9	7.4	7.8	7.7
	Not working not attending school	22.4	37.9	27.3	24.6	31.5	26.9	23.5	34.5	27.1	40.5	43.9	43.6	36.3	47.0	45.8	38.3	45.4	44.6
Guatemala	Working[b] not attending school	4.1	10.9	7.8	3.0	7.7	5.5	3.6	9.4	6.7	5.4	14.0	12.8	9.2	5.9	6.4	7.5	10.0	9.6
	Attending school not working	74.7	58.4	65.9	77.5	60.2	68.2	76.0	59.3	67.0	68.6	48.3	51.1	60.6	56.4	57.1	64.2	52.3	54.1
	Working and attending school	10.4	19.0	15.1	7.9	10.5	9.3	9.2	15.0	12.3	7.8	20.7	18.9	6.0	6.0	6.0	6.8	13.3	12.3
	Not working not attending school	10.8	11.7	11.3	11.6	21.7	17.0	11.2	16.4	14.0	18.2	17.0	17.2	24.2	31.8	30.5	21.5	24.4	24.0

Country	Category	Values
Morocco	Working[b] not attending school	— 15.9 15.9 — 18.1 18.1 — 23.2 23.2 — 24.6 24.6 — 23.9 23.9
	Attending school not working	— 63.2 63.2 — 51.1 51.1 — 66.4 66.4 — 41.1 41.1 — 54.3 54.3
	Working and attending school	— 2.3 2.3 — 1.5 1.5 — 2.4 2.4 — 0.8 0.8 — 1.6 1.6
	Not working not attending school	— 18.6 18.6 — 29.4 29.4 — 8.1 8.1 — 33.5 33.5 — 20.2 20.2
Yemen	Working[b] not attending school	1.2 4.9 3.0 0.5 7.4 4.0 3.4 7.0 6.7 3.8 16.9 15.8 3.6 11.7 11.1
	Attending school not working	87.0 71.9 79.7 84.2 65.0 85.6 72.5 75.4 60.5 61.7 62.9 25.3 28.3 69.2 43.6 45.6
	Working and attending school	2.4 7.5 4.9 0.5 2.9 1.7 1.4 5.3 3.3 3.9 8.7 8.3 1.5 2.6 2.5 2.7 5.8 5.5
	Not working not attending school	9.4 15.7 12.4 14.9 42.9 28.3 12.1 28.9 20.2 17.4 23.8 23.3 31.8 55.2 53.4 24.6 38.9 37.8

[a] See Appendix 6.1 for questions upon which the access indicators are based.
[b] Economically active children.

Source: UCW calculations based on Ghana: *Ghana Living Standard Measurement Survey*, 1998–9; Yemen: *National Poverty Survey*, 1999; Guatemala: *Encuesta de condiciones de vida* (ENCOVI), 2000; El Salvador: *Enquesta de hogares de propósitos múltiples* (EHPM) 2001; Morocco: *Living Standard Measurement Survey*, 1998–9.

Table A6.2.2. Child activity status by electricity access, sex, residence, and country[a] (%)

Country	Activity status	Households with electricity									Households without electricity								
		Male			Female			Total			Male			Female			Total		
		Urban	Rural	Total	Urban	Rural	Total	Urban	Rural	Total	Urban	Rural	Total	Urban	Rural	Total	Urban	Rural	Total
El Salvador	Working[b] not attending school	1.1	4.3	2.3	0.9	1.8	1.3	1.0	3.1	1.8	8.4	9.6	9.5	1.8	2.5	2.5	5.2	6.3	6.1
	Attending school not working	87.0	72.7	81.4	86.9	81.5	84.7	86.9	77.1	83.0	53.2	56.4	56.0	64.0	63.0	63.1	58.5	59.5	59.4
	Working and attending school	4.2	10.8	6.8	3.5	3.0	3.3	3.8	6.9	5.0	8.0	11.1	10.8	4.5	2.7	2.9	6.3	7.1	7.0
	Not working not attending school	7.8	12.2	9.5	8.7	13.7	10.7	8.2	12.9	10.1	30.4	22.9	23.7	29.7	31.8	31.5	30.1	27.1	27.4
Ghana	Working not[b] attending school	1.7	8.1	3.8	4.4	7.4	5.4	3.1	7.8	4.6	5.3	13.1	12.2	7.1	13.4	12.5	6.3	13.2	12.4
	Attending school not working	74.5	49.7	66.4	70.6	54.4	65.0	72.5	52.1	65.7	42.9	34.8	35.7	46.8	33.1	35.0	44.9	34.0	35.4
	Working and attending school	3.2	8.8	5.0	2.5	8.9	4.7	2.8	8.8	4.8	8.2	7.2	7.4	5.3	6.1	6.0	6.7	6.7	6.7
	Not working[b] not attending school	20.6	33.4	24.8	22.5	29.3	24.8	21.6	31.3	24.8	43.6	44.8	44.7	40.8	47.5	46.6	42.1	46.1	45.6
Guatemala	Working[b] not attending school	3.3	10.0	6.9	3.8	5.8	4.8	3.5	8.0	5.9	17.4	15.6	15.7	7.9	8.1	8.1	12.3	11.8	11.9
	Attending school not working	75.5	60.3	67.3	78.6	64.1	71.0	77.0	62.1	69.1	51.2	44.9	45.4	29.7	51.2	49.2	39.5	48.1	47.4

Working and attending school	10.0	19.8	15.3	7.4	9.9	8.7	15.2	12.2	11.1	19.6	18.9	9.3	6.4	6.6	10.1	13.0	12.7	
Not working[b] not attending school	11.2	9.9	10.5	10.3	20.2	15.5	10.7	14.7	12.9	20.4	19.9	20.0	53.0	34.3	36.0	38.1	27.1	28.1
Morocco Working[b] not attending school	—	9.9	—	6.9	—	8.5	—	—	—	21.3	21.3	—	25.1	25.1	—	23.2	23.2	
Attending school not working	—	77.5	—	66.2	—	72	—	—	—	63.8	63.8	—	36.4	36.4	—	50.6	50.6	
Working and attending school	—	2.9	—	3.2	—	3	—	—	—	2.2	2.2	—	0.5	0.5	—	1.4	1.4	
Not working[b] not attending school	—	9.7	—	23.7	—	16.5	—	—	—	12.6	12.6	—	37.9	37.9	—	24.9	24.9	
Yemen Working[b] not attending school	1.3	4.2	2.4	0.6	11.6	5.5	1.0	7.5	3.8	4.5	9.2	9.0	8.7	9.0	9.0	6.4	9.1	9.0
Attending school not working	68.1	61.3	65.4	57.9	41.1	50.4	64.0	52.2	59.0	44.1	40.6	40.8	20.3	20.2	20.2	33.1	32.5	32.5
Working and attending school	0.8	2.6	1.5	0.0	5.2	2.3	0.5	3.8	1.9	2.5	5.4	5.3	0.9	1.4	1.3	1.8	3.8	3.7
Not working not attending school	29.8	31.9	30.6	41.5	42.1	41.7	34.5	36.5	35.3	48.9	44.7	44.9	70.1	69.5	.58.7	54.5	54.8	

[a] See Appendix 6.1 for questions upon which the access indicators are based.
[b] Economically active children.

Source: UCW calculations based on Ghana: *Ghana Living Standard Measurement Survey, 1998–9*; Yemen: *National Poverty Survey, 1999*; Guatemala: *Encuesta de condiciones de vida* (ENCOVI), 2000; El Salvador: *Enquesta de hogares de propósitos múltiples* (EHPM) 2001; Morocco: *Living Standard Measurement Survey, 1998–9.*

Table A6.2.3. *Child activity status (including household chores) by water access, sex, and country*[a] *(%)*

Country	Activity status	Households with water access[b]			Households without water access[b]		
		Male	Female	Total	Male	Female	Total
El Salvador	Working and not attending school	10.39	8.85	9.63	18.05	14.34	16.2
	Attending school and not working	45.25	55.58	50.36	42.52	51.28	46.88
	Working and attending school	39.84	29.93	34.94	29.71	21.23	25.49
	Not working and not attending school	4.52	5.64	5.07	9.72	13.15	11.43
Guatemala	Working and not attending school	8.93	10.49	9.67	14.44	13.47	13.95
	Attending school and not working	63.12	58.99	61.16	47.43	45.15	46.27
	Working and attending school	17.81	18.46	18.12	22.55	17.9	20.19
	Not working not and attending school	10.14	12.07	11.06	15.58	23.48	19.58

[a] See Appendix 6.1 for questions upon which the access indicators are based.
[b] Economically active children.

Source: UCW calculations based on Ghana: *Ghana Living Standard Measurement Survey*, 1998–9; Yemen: *National Poverty Survey*, 1999; Guatemala: *Encuesta de condiciones de vida* (ENCOVI), 2000; El Salvador: *Enquesta de hogares de propósitos múltiples* (EHPM) 2001; Morocco: *Living Standard Measurement Survey*, 1998–9.

Table A6.2.4. *Child activity status (including household chores) by electricity access, sex, and country*[a]

Country	Activity status	Households with electricity access[b]			Households without electricity access[b]		
		Male	Female	Total	Male	Female	Total
El Salvador	Working and not attending school	10.98	9.55	10.27	24.8	18.5	21.78
	Attending school and not Working	45.98	55.78	50.87	35.73	44.22	39.81
	Working and attending school	37.75	28.38	33.08	26.9	16.84	22.07
	Not working and not attending school	5.29	6.28	5.79	12.56	20.43	16.35
Guatemala	Working and not attending school	7.72	9.14	8.4	18.17	16.83	17.49
	Attending school and not working	64.27	60.07	62.26	42.33	40.64	41.48
	Working and attending school	18.33	19.65	18.96	22.01	15.24	18.59
	Not working and not attending school	9.68	11.14	10.38	17.48	27.29	22.44

[a] See Appendix 6.1 for questions upon which the access indicators are based.
[b] Economically active children.

Source: UCW calculations based on Ghana: *Ghana Living Standard Measurement Survey*, 1998–9; Yemen: *National Poverty Survey*, 1999; Guatemala: *Encuesta de condiciones de vida* (ENCOVI), 2000; El Salvador: *Enquesta de bogares de propósitos múltiples* (EHPM) 2001; Morocco: *Living Standard Measurement Survey*, 1998–9.

Appendix 6.3 Comparison of distributions of propensity Scores for treated and control groups

A6.3.1 *Propensity scores comparison for water access*

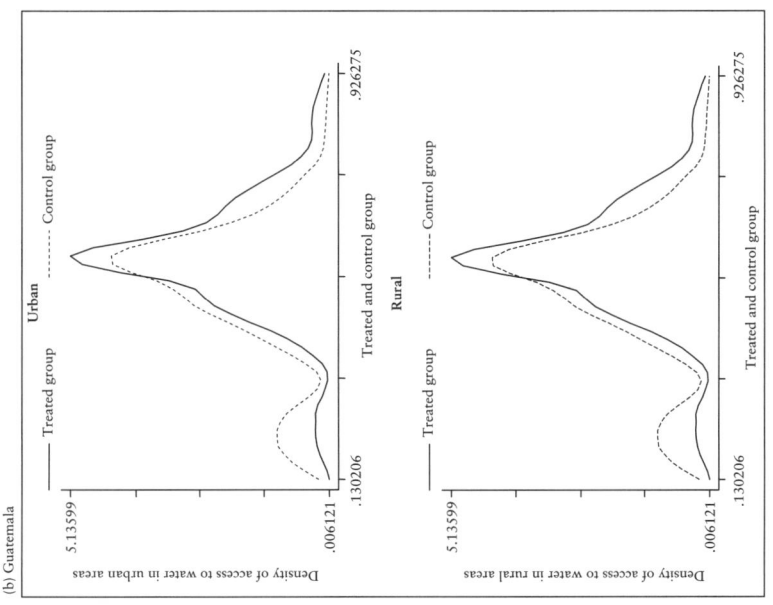

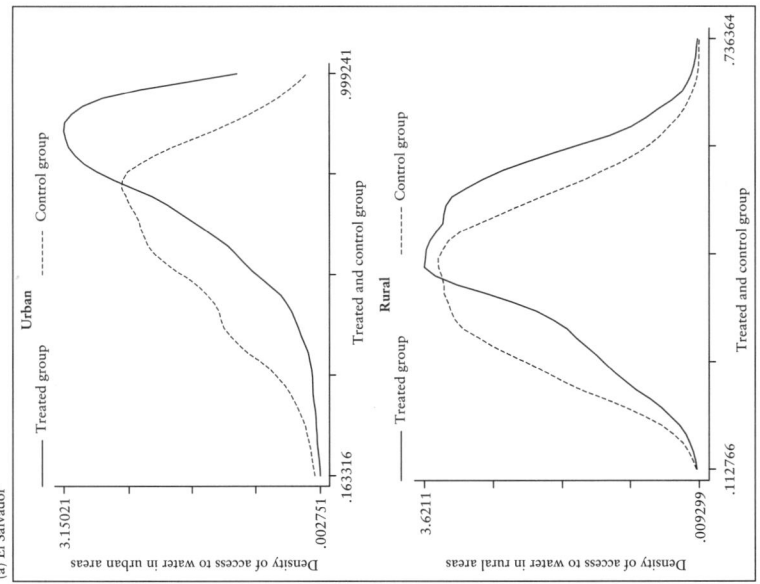

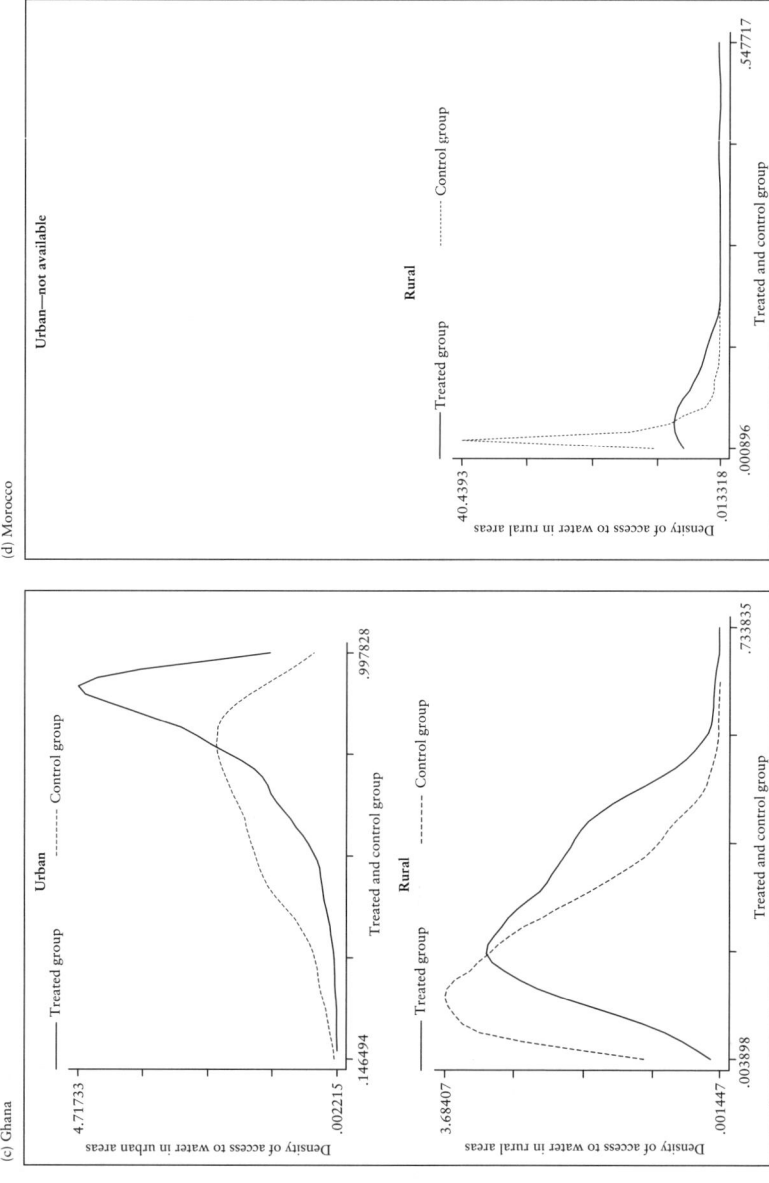

(c) Ghana

Urban

Treated group ——— Control group

Density of access to water in urban areas

4.71733

.002215 .146494 .997828

Treated and control group

Rural

Treated group ——— Control group

Density of access to water in rural areas

3.68407

.001447 .003898 .733835

Treated and control group

(d) Morocco

Urban—not available

Rural

Treated group ——— Control group

Density of access to water in rural areas

40.4393

.013318 .000896 .547717

Treated and control group

6.3.2   *Propensity scores comparison for electricity access*

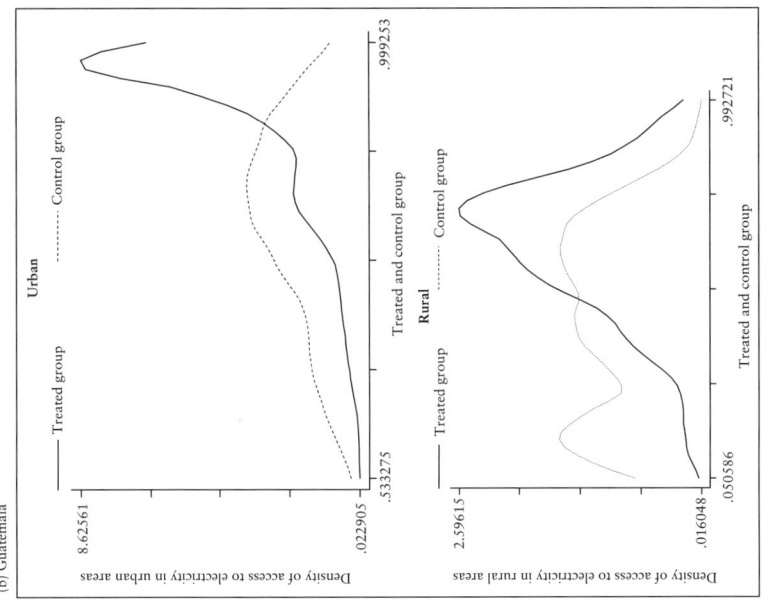

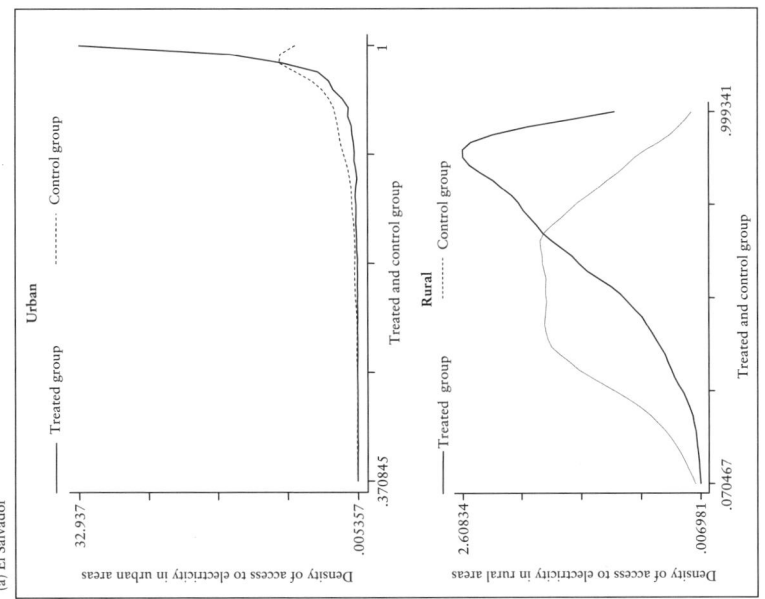

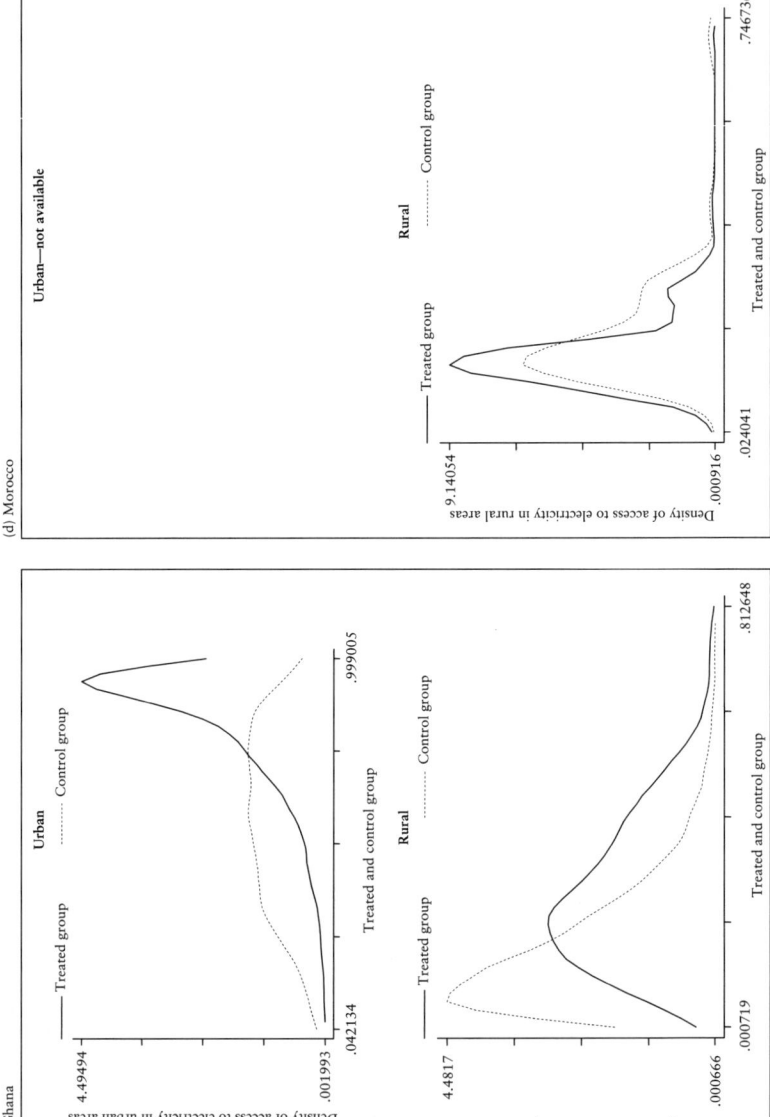

(c) Ghana

(d) Morocco

Appendix 6.4 Definition of variables

Child activities

Employment	1 if individual currently works, 0 otherwise
School attendance	1 if individual currently attends school, 0 otherwise
Work only	1 if individual currently works and does not attend school
Study only	1 if individual currently attends school and does not work
Work and study	1 if individual currently works and attends school
Neither	1 if individual currently neither works nor attends school

Access to basic services

Water	1 if household has access to public network, 0 otherwise
Electricity	1 if household has access to public network, 0 otherwise

Other variables

Female	1 if female, 0 otherwise
Household expenditures	logarithm of per capita household expenditure
Insurance	1 if at least one member of the household has medical insurance, 0 otherwise
Credit	1 if a household is credit rationed, 0 otherwise

Father's education

Fed_None	1 if he has no completed education, 0 otherwise
Fed_Primary	1 if he has completed primary education, 0 otherwise

Mother's education

Mother_None	1 if she has no completed education, 0 otherwise
Mother_Primary	1 if she has completed primary education, 0 otherwise (Secondary or higher education is the comparison group)

Shocks

Collective	1 if a household reported experiencing at least a collective shock, 0 otherwise
Individual	1 if a household reported experiencing at least an idiosyncratic shock, 0 otherwise

---

Appendix 6.5 Marginal effects calculated from bivariate probit estimates

Table A6.5.1. *El Salvador: marginal effects in urban area after bivariate probit regression*

Variable	Work only dy/dx	z	Study only dy/dx	z	Work and study dy/dx	z	Idle dy/dx	z
Female[a]	−0.0026	−3.33	0.0185	2.47	−0.0089	−3.36	−0.0069	—
Child age	−0.0080	−4.58	0.1963	18.54	0.0124	2.96	−0.2007	—
Child age squared	0.0005	5.24	−0.0098	−17.47	−0.0001	−0.68	0.0095	—
Age of household head	−0.0001	−2.47	0.0012	3.37	−0.0001	−1.11	−0.0010	—
Household size	−0.0003	−0.31	0.0051	0.52	−0.0001	−0.03	−0.0047	—
Number of children aged 0–5	0.0008	0.73	−0.0149	−1.33	0.0000	0.01	0.0141	—
Number of children aged 6–17	0.0010	1.04	−0.0131	−1.27	0.0017	0.49	0.0104	—
Number of adults	−0.0007	−0.71	0.0086	0.88	−0.0011	−0.33	−0.0069	—
Household expenditure	−0.0051	−5.21	0.0955	12.52	−0.0003	−0.11	−0.0901	—
Household head not educated[a]	0.0157	3.74	−0.1466	−6.44	0.0180	2.32	0.1129	—
Household head with primary education[a]	0.0059	4.63	−0.0749	−6.82	0.0108	2.80	0.0582	—
Household head self-employed[a]	0.0073	4.86	−0.0516	−5.14	0.0223	5.13	0.0221	—
Household head in other employ[a]	0.0066	1.70	−0.0664	−2.48	0.0095	0.99	0.0503	—
Household head unemployed[a]	−0.0004	−0.35	−0.0098	−0.84	−0.0044	−1.14	0.0145	—
Access to water [a]	−0.0038	−3.21	0.0410	4.24	−0.0069	−1.99	−0.0303	—
Access to electricity[a]	−0.0057	−2.08	0.0807	3.87	−0.0035	−0.61	−0.0715	—
region 1[a]	−0.0003	−0.33	0.0228	2.24	0.0062	1.31	−0.0286	—
region 2[a]	0.0034	2.36	−0.0133	−1.19	0.0157	2.85	−0.0057	—
region 3[a]	0.0012	0.87	0.0008	0.07	0.0073	1.35	−0.0093	—
region 4[a]	0.0003	0.24	0.0275	2.61	0.0172	2.74	−0.0449	—

[a] *dy/dx* is for discrete change of dummy variable from 0 to 1.

Table A6.5.2. *El Salvador: marginal effects in rural area after bivariate probit regression*

Variable	Work only		Study only		Work and study		Idle	
	dy/dx	z	dy/dx	z	dy/dx	z	dy/dx	z
Female[a]	−0.0330	−10.11	0.0620	5.34	−0.0464	−10.73	0.0174	1.63
Child age	−0.0101	−2.51	0.3672	24.06	0.0342	8.26	−0.3913	−25.61
Child age squared	0.0009	4.43	−0.0185	−21.23	−0.0011	−5.48	0.0187	22.54
Age of household head	0.0001	0.90	−0.0007	−1.26	0.00004	0.31	0.0006	1.09
Household size	−0.0055	−2.13	0.0413	2.59	−0.0031	−0.94	−0.0327	−2.12
Number of children aged 0–5	0.0089	3.08	−0.0625	−3.61	0.0056	1.54	0.0480	2.85
Number of children aged 6–17	0.0071	2.72	−0.0478	−2.94	0.0048	1.45	0.0360	2.33
Number of adults	0.0019	0.79	−0.0344	−2.24	−0.0017	−0.54	0.0342	2.33
Household expenditure	−0.0077	−4.38	0.1140	11.15	0.0033	1.54	−0.1096	−10.96
Household head not educated[a]	0.0166	2.07	−0.1409	−3.35	0.0054	0.61	0.1189	2.93
Household head with primary education[a]	0.0091	1.44	−0.0889	−2.32	0.0023	0.28	0.0775	2.10
Household head self-employed[a]	0.0101	4.06	0.0287	2.13	0.0213	5.78	−0.0601	−4.78
Household head in other employ[a]	−0.0041	−0.86	0.0335	1.09	−0.0024	−0.35	−0.0270	−0.94
Household head unemployed[a]	−0.0072	−2.84	0.0272	1.68	−0.0079	−2.43	−0.0121	−0.78
Access to water [a]	−0.0026	−1.36	0.0543	4.71	0.0034	1.34	−0.0552	−5.06
Access to electricity[a]	−0.0101	−3.83	0.0836	6.27	−0.0036	−1.26	−0.0699	−5.55
region 1[a]	−0.0009	−0.35	−0.0629	−3.77	−0.0089	−2.95	0.0727	4.57
region 2[a]	−0.0008	−0.28	−0.0073	−0.40	−0.0022	−0.62	0.0102	0.59
region 3[a]	−0.0001	−0.03	−0.0116	−0.66	−0.0017	−0.49	0.0134	0.80

[a] dy/dx is for discrete change of dummy variable from 0 to 1.

Table A6.5.3. *Morocco: marginal effects in rural area after bivariate probit regression*

Variables	Work only		Study only		Work and study		No activities	
	dy/dx	z	dy/dx	z	dy/dx	z	dy/dx	z
Female[a]	0.007	0.40	-0.275	-12.71	-0.027	-5.75	0.296	15.66
Household size	-0.022	-3.83	0.022	2.99	-0.001	-1.40	0.001	0.10
Child age	0.069	2.01	0.170	3.88	0.022	4.15	-0.261	-6.53
Child age squared	-0.001	-0.41	-0.011	-5.46	-0.001	-4.10	0.013	6.89
Household expenditures	-0.080	-2.88	0.102	2.68	-0.001	-0.48	-0.020	-0.62
Number of children aged 0–6	0.026	3.35	-0.031	-3.05	0.001	0.81	0.004	0.46
Number of children aged 7–15	0.013	1.80	-0.008	-0.79	0.001	1.27	-0.006	-0.75
Size of land holding	0.001	0.69	-0.002	-0.86	0.000	-0.21	0.001	0.49
Presence of primary school[a]	-0.068	-3.53	0.150	6.12	0.004	2.14	-0.087	-4.00
Average travel time to school	0.002	2.19	-0.001	-1.26	0.000	1.26	0.000	-0.58
Presence of public water network[a]	-0.192	-5.78	0.134	1.52	-0.007	-3.70	0.065	0.74
Presence of electricity[a]	-0.103	-4.50	0.190	5.40	0.001	0.36	-0.088	-3.02
Father's education	-0.054	-5.22	0.071	5.43	-0.001	-0.71	-0.016	-1.34
Mother's education	-0.074	-2.49	0.104	3.05	0.000	-0.14	-0.030	-0.90

[a] dy/dx is for a discreet change of dummy variable from 0 to 1.

Source: UCW calculations based on Morocco LSMS, 1998–9.

Table A6.5.4. *Ghana: marginal effects in urban area after bivariate probit regression*

Variable	Work only		Study only		Work and study		No activities	
	dy/dx	z	dy/dx	z	dy/dx	z	dy/dx	z
Female[a]	0.0054	1.06	−0.0436	−1.94	0.0001	0.02	0.0381	1.79
Household size	0.0050	2.85	−0.0354	−4.59	0.0008	0.47	0.0296	4.04
Number of children aged 0–6	0.0071	2.19	−0.0318	−2.19	0.0041	1.23	0.0206	1.50
Number of adults	0.0014	0.51	0.0043	0.35	0.0025	0.88	−0.0082	−0.69
Child age	0.0096	0.74	0.2438	4.53	0.0514	3.73	−0.3049	−5.94
Child age squared	−0.0004	−0.59	−0.0085	−3.35	−0.0018	−2.88	0.0106	4.41
Log of household expenditure	−0.0115	−2.17	0.1022	4.64	0.0014	0.26	−0.0922	−4.42
Father's education	−0.0007	−0.31	0.0183	1.91	0.0021	0.95	−0.0197	−2.17
Mother's education	−0.0010	−0.43	0.0393	3.74	0.0049	1.90	−0.0431	−4.33
Father not alive[a]	0.0063	0.83	−0.0205	−0.62	0.0049	0.62	0.0094	0.30
Mother not alive[a]	0.0129	1.71	−0.0825	−2.81	0.0025	0.36	0.0670	2.40
Access to water[a]	−0.0161	−2.13	0.0190	0.68	−0.0186	−2.25	0.0157	0.61
Access to electricity[a]	−0.0409	−3.96	0.1454	4.93	−0.0212	−2.44	−0.0833	−2.98

[a] dy/dx is for discrete change of dummy variable from 0 to 1.

Table A6.5.5. *Ghana: marginal effects in rural area after bivariate probit regression*

Variable	Work only		Study only		Work and study		No activities	
	dy/dx	z	dy/dx	z	dy/dx	z	dy/dx	z
Female[a]	−0.001	−0.16	−0.007	−0.46	−0.004	−0.71	0.012	0.78
Household size	0.003	1.12	−0.008	−1.66	−0.001	−0.32	0.006	1.12
Number of children aged 0–6	0.003	0.52	−0.016	−1.84	−0.004	−1.30	0.017	1.96
Number of adults	0.010	2.08	−0.043	−5.07	−0.008	−2.75	0.041	4.78
Child age	0.014	0.65	0.142	3.89	0.061	4.98	−0.217	−5.83
Child age squared	0.000	−0.21	−0.004	−2.34	−0.002	−2.79	0.006	3.33
Log of household expenditure	−0.047	−5.90	0.107	7.60	0.002	0.47	−0.062	−4.38
Father's education	−0.013	−3.15	0.037	5.19	0.003	1.38	−0.027	−3.79
Mother's education	−0.027	−5.15	0.063	7.13	0.002	0.54	−0.038	−4.16
Father not alive[a]	−0.046	−4.11	0.053	2.56	−0.017	−2.57	0.009	0.45
Mother not alive[a]	0.016	1.39	−0.052	−2.70	−0.006	−1.00	0.042	2.10
Access to water[a]	−0.077	−7.47	0.074	3.02	−0.035	−5.98	0.039	1.59
Access to electricity[a]	0.025	1.66	0.017	0.74	0.029	2.94	−0.071	−3.04

[a] dy/dx is for discrete change of dummy variable from 0 to 1.

Table A6.5.6. *Guatemala: marginal effects in urban area after bivariate probit regression*

Variable	Work only		Study only		Work and study		Idle	
	dy/dx	z	dy/dx	z	dy/dx	z	dy/dx	z
Female[a]	-0.0061	-1.36	0.0241	1.24	-0.0247	-2.10	0.0068	0.49
Child age	-0.0287	-3.48	0.1414	4.35	0.0641	2.98	-0.1768	-7.83
Child age squared	0.0018	4.42	-0.0083	-5.37	-0.0017	-1.70	0.0082	7.72
Indigenous[a]	0.0145	2.82	-0.0587	-3.00	0.0368	2.82	0.0074	0.59
Log of household income	-0.0115	-1.64	0.0533	1.76	0.0027	0.15	-0.0445	-2.07
Hh size	-0.0041	-1.84	0.0178	1.86	-0.0058	-0.97	-0.0080	-1.20
Number of children aged 0–6	0.0025	0.99	-0.0097	-0.88	0.0118	1.76	-0.0046	-0.60
Number of children aged 7–14	0.0035	1.79	-0.0157	-1.88	0.0017	0.33	0.0105	1.84
Interaction female children 0–6[a]	0.0003	0.11	-0.0034	-0.29	-0.0134	-1.80	0.0165	2.09
Father not educated[a]	0.0273	3.18	-0.1228	-4.13	-0.0041	-0.29	0.0997	4.13
Father with primary education[a]	0.0098	1.94	-0.0464	-2.16	-0.0065	-0.52	0.0431	2.72
Mother not educated[a]	0.0284	3.42	-0.1137	-3.88	0.0348	1.94	0.0505	2.39
Mother with primary education[a]	0.0094	1.59	-0.0392	-1.60	0.0194	1.28	0.0104	0.59
Collective shock[a]	-0.0019	-0.37	0.0060	0.26	0.0364	2.23	-0.0405	-2.78
Individual shock[a]	0.0062	1.17	-0.0251	-1.16	0.0269	1.95	-0.0080	-0.55
Household credit rationed[a]	0.0056	1.24	-0.0246	-1.29	0.0057	0.47	0.0133	1.02
Insurance[a]	-0.0105	-2.85	0.0473	2.92	-0.0101	-1.00	-0.0268	-2.38
Inter. credit rat.-individual shock[a]	-0.0023	-0.35	0.0091	0.32	-0.0079	-0.47	0.0011	0.05
Inter. credit rat.-collective shock[a]	0.0022	0.29	-0.0179	-0.52	-0.0174	-1.04	0.0331	1.20
Access to water[a]	-0.0036	-0.67	0.0163	0.73	-0.0014	-0.10	-0.0112	-0.73
Access to electricity[a]	-0.0236	-2.59	0.1437	4.75	0.0284	2.50	-0.1486	-5.63
Norte[a]	-0.0167	-3.45	0.0838	3.04	-0.0184	-0.93	-0.0486	-3.10
Nororiente[a]	-0.0050	-0.84	0.0140	0.47	0.0346	1.43	-0.0436	-3.12
Suroriente[a]	-0.0135	-2.71	0.0369	1.17	0.0492	1.76	-0.0725	-6.39
Central[a]	-0.0084	-1.53	-0.0147	-0.44	0.0998	3.26	-0.0767	-7.32
Surroccidente[a]	-0.0123	-2.44	0.0412	1.46	0.0397	1.66	-0.0686	-5.61
Noroccidente[a]	-0.0150	-2.93	0.0613	2.06	0.0209	0.84	-0.0672	-5.10
Peten[a]	-0.0035	-0.53	-0.0145	-0.41	0.0747	2.41	-0.0566	-4.56

[a] dy/dx is for discrete change of dummy variable from 0 to 1.

Table A6.5.7. *Guatemala: marginal effects in rural area after bivariate probit regression*

Variable	Work only dy/dx	z	Study only dy/dx	z	Work and study dy/dx	z	Idle dy/dx	z
Female[a]	-0.0496	-5.62	0.0729	3.17	-0.1339	-9.39	0.1106	6.28
Child age	-0.0787	-5.64	0.3003	9.39	0.1273	6.44	-0.3489	-13.88
Child age squared	0.0051	7.47	-0.0171	-11.37	-0.0042	-4.59	0.0162	13.44
Indigenous[a]	0.0444	6.38	-0.0964	-5.70	0.0579	5.76	-0.0060	-0.45
Log of household income	-0.0413	-2.77	0.1043	2.78	-0.0289	-1.32	-0.0341	-1.16
Hh size	-0.0183	-4.11	0.0438	3.98	-0.0168	-2.58	-0.0087	-1.01
Number of children aged 0–6	0.0128	2.96	-0.0267	-2.44	0.0189	2.99	-0.0050	-0.57
Number of children aged 7–14	0.0077	2.19	-0.0167	-1.90	0.0101	1.94	-0.0010	-0.15
Interaction female-children 0–6	-0.0027	-0.67	0.0056	0.55	-0.0041	-0.69	0.0012	0.15
Father not educated[a]	0.0699	4.21	-0.1841	-4.91	0.0182	0.83	0.0961	3.12
Father with primary education[a]	0.0429	2.89	-0.1103	-2.99	0.0247	1.15	0.0428	1.43
Mother not educated[a]	0.0542	2.94	-0.1721	-3.41	-0.0198	-0.62	0.1377	3.52
Mother with primary education[a]	0.0492	2.06	-0.1337	-2.47	0.0027	0.09	0.0818	1.77
Collective shock[a]	0.0316	3.36	-0.0651	-2.90	0.0473	3.50	-0.0139	-0.79
Individual shock[a]	0.0335	3.73	-0.0747	-3.41	0.0380	2.95	0.0032	0.18
Household credit rationed[a]	0.0205	2.69	-0.0708	-3.63	-0.0207	-1.76	0.0710	4.70
Insurance[a]	-0.0251	-3.63	0.0217	1.08	-0.0634	-6.78	0.0668	3.80
Inter. credit rat.-individual shock[a]	-0.0169	-1.61	0.0403	1.40	-0.0186	-1.16	-0.0048	-0.21
Inter. credit rat.-collective shock[a]	-0.0411	-4.70	0.1168	4.18	-0.0299	-1.93	-0.0458	-2.08
Access to water[a]	-0.0115	-1.99	0.0350	2.43	0.0027	0.32	-0.0262	-2.29
Access to electricity[a]	-0.0193	-3.06	0.0748	4.82	0.0311	3.42	-0.0865	-7.02
Norte[a]	-0.0209	-1.18	0.0703	1.36	0.0355	0.93	-0.0849	-2.54
Nororiente[a]	-0.0331	-2.18	0.1072	2.15	0.0008	0.02	-0.0748	-2.21
Suroriente[a]	-0.0383	-2.68	0.1237	2.55	0.0339	0.91	-0.1193	-4.24
Central[a]	-0.0135	-0.78	0.0499	1.01	0.0782	2.05	-0.1146	-3.88
Suroccidente[a]	-0.0531	-4.05	0.1732	4.09	0.0289	0.86	-0.1490	-5.58
Noroccidente[a]	-0.0394	-2.39	0.1209	2.49	-0.0065	-0.21	-0.0750	-2.10
Peten[a]	-0.0444	-3.43	0.1449	3.16	0.0236	0.65	-0.1241	-4.61

[a] dy/dx is for discrete change of dummy variable from 0 to 1.

Appendix 6.6 Impact of access to electricity and piped water

A6.6.1 *El Salvador*

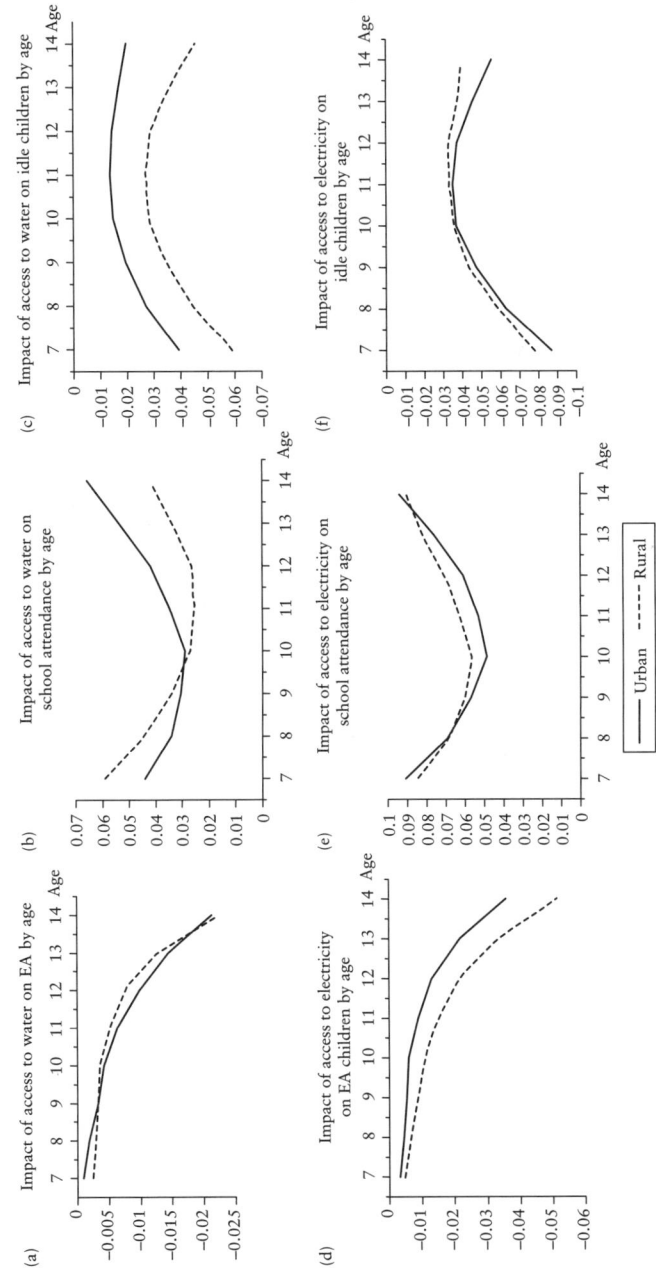

(a) Impact of access to water on EA by age

(b) Impact of access to water on school attendance by age

(c) Impact of access to water on idle children by age

(d) Impact of access to electricity on EA children by age

(e) Impact of access to electricity on school attendance by age

(f) Impact of access to electricity on idle children by age

Urban ——— Rural - - - - -

A6.6.2 *Guatemala*

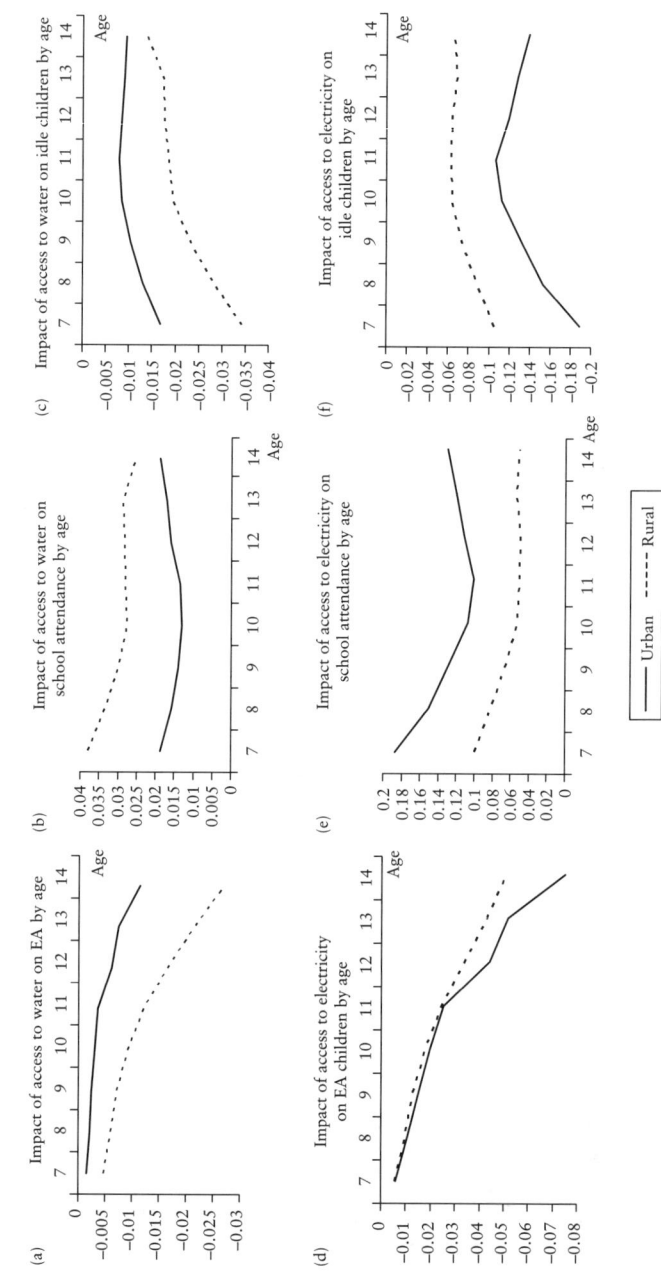

(a) Impact of access to water on EA by age

(b) Impact of access to water on school attendance by age

(c) Impact of access to water on idle children by age

(d) Impact of access to electricity on EA children by age

(e) Impact of access to electricity on school attendance by age

(f) Impact of access to electricity on idle children by age

—— Urban - - - - Rural

A6.6.3 Ghana

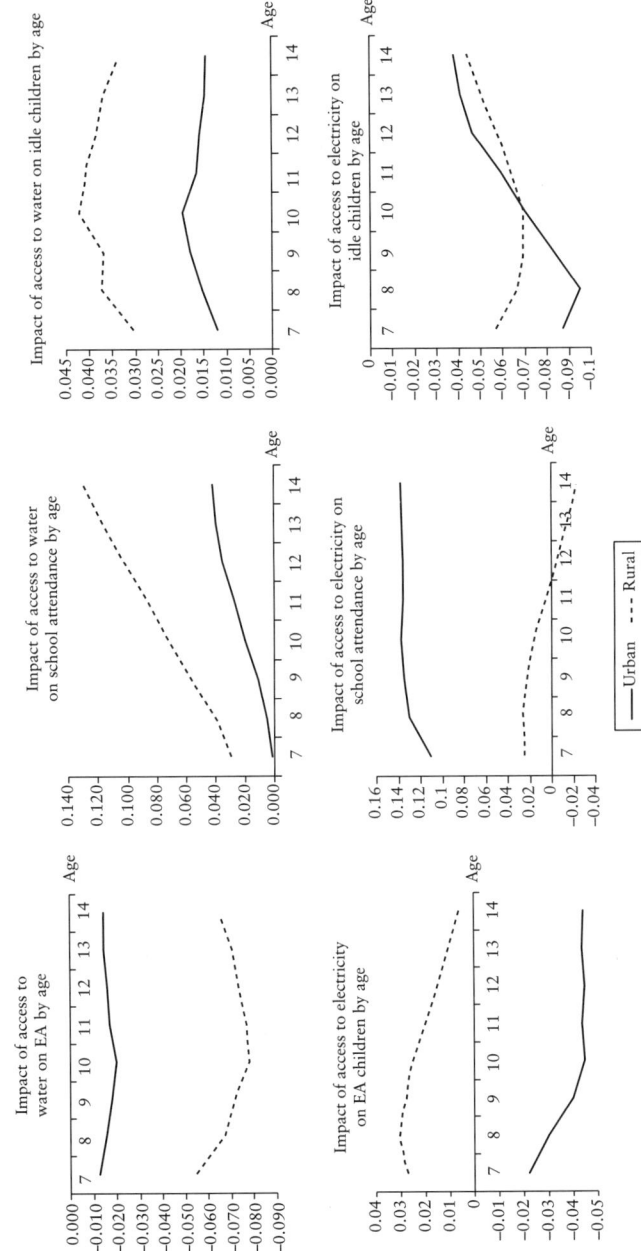

Impact of access to water on EA by age

Impact of access to water on school attendance by age

Impact of access to water on idle children by age

Impact of access to electricity on EA children by age

Impact of access to electricity on school attendance by age

Impact of access to electricity on idle children by age

—— Urban - - - Rural

A6.6.4 Yemen

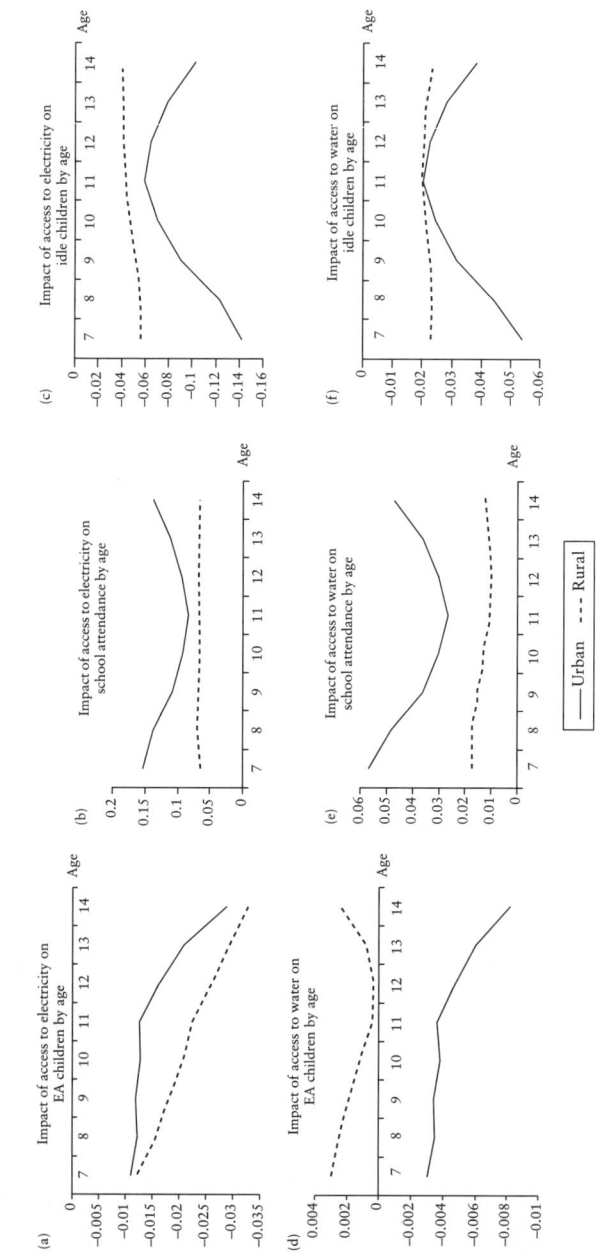

(a) Impact of access to electricity on EA children by age

(b) Impact of access to electricity on school attendance by age

(c) Impact of access to electricity on idle children by age

(d) Impact of access to water on EA children by age

(e) Impact of access to water on school attendance by age

(f) Impact of access to water on idle children by age

—— Urban - - - Rural

Appendix 6.7 Average treatment effects for 'access to water and access to electricity' for different values of the sensitivity parameters

Table A6.7.1. *Sensitivity analysis on the effect of access to water in urban area*

ATT	$\alpha = 0$ $\delta_{0w} = \delta_{1w} = 0$ $\delta_{0s} = \delta_{1s} = 0$ $\delta_{0ws} = \delta_{1ws} = 0$	$\pi = 0.1, \alpha = 0.1$ $\delta_{0w} = \delta_{1w} = -0.1$ $\delta_{0s} = \delta_{1s} = 0.1$ $\delta_{0ws} = \delta_{1ws} = 0.1$	$\pi = 0.5, \alpha = 0.5$ $\delta_{0w} = \delta_{1w} = -0.1$ $\delta_{0s} = \delta_{1s} = 0.1$ $\delta_{0ws} = \delta_{1ws} = 0.1$	$\pi = 0.1, \alpha = 0.1$ $\delta_{0w} = \delta_{1w} = -0.5$ $\delta_{0s} = \delta_{1s} = 0.5$ $\delta_{0ws} = \delta_{1ws} = 0.5$	$\pi = 0.5, \alpha = 0.5$ $\delta_{0w} = \delta_{1w} = -0.5$ $\delta_{0s} = \delta_{1s} = 0.5$ $\delta_{0ws} = \delta_{1ws} = 0.5$
Working only	−0.018	−0.018	−0.018	−0.018	−0.016
Studying only	0.107	0.107	0.106	0.103	0.097
Working and studying	−0.012	−0.012	−0.012	−0.012	−0.012
Idle children	−0.077	−0.077	−0.076	−0.073	−0.069

Source: UCW calculations based on El Salvador: *Enquesta de hogares de propósitos múltiples* (EHPM) 2001.

Table A6.7.2. *Sensitivity analysis on the effect of access to water in rural area*

ATT	$\alpha = 0$ $\delta_{0w} = \delta_{1w} = 0$ $\delta_{0s} = \delta_{1s} = 0$ $\delta_{0ws} = \delta_{1ws} = 0$	$\pi = 0.1, \alpha = 0.1$ $\delta_{0w} = \delta_{1w} = -0.1$ $\delta_{0s} = \delta_{1s} = 0.1$ $\delta_{0ws} = \delta_{1ws} = 0.1$	$\pi = 0.5, \alpha = 0.5$ $\delta_{0w} = \delta_{1w} = -0.1$ $\delta_{0s} = \delta_{1s} = 0.1$ $\delta_{0ws} = \delta_{1ws} = 0.1$	$\pi = 0.1, \alpha = 0.1$ $\delta_{0w} = \delta_{1w} = -0.5$ $\delta_{0s} = \delta_{1s} = 0.5$ $\delta_{0ws} = \delta_{1ws} = 0.5$	$\pi = 0.5, \alpha = 0.5$ $\delta_{0w} = \delta_{1w} = -0.5$ $\delta_{0s} = \delta_{1s} = 0.5$ $\delta_{0ws} = \delta_{1ws} = 0.5$
Working only	−0.013	−0.013	−0.012	−0.013	−0.010
Studying only	0.074	0.071	0.072	0.071	0.063
Working and studying	0.007	0.007	0.007	0.007	0.006
Idle children	−0.068	−0.065	−0.066	−0.065	−0.060

Source: UCW calculations based on El Salvador: *Enquesta de hogares de propósitos múltiples* (EHPM) 2001.

Table A6.7.3. *Sensitivity analysis on the effect of access to electricity in urban area*

ATT	$\alpha = 0$ $\delta_{0w} = \delta_{1w} = 0$ $\delta_{0s} = \delta_{1s} = 0$ $\delta_{0ws} = \delta_{1ws} = 0$	$\pi = 0.1, \alpha = 0.1$ $\delta_{0w} = \delta_{1w} = -0.1$ $\delta_{0s} = \delta_{1s} = 0.1$ $\delta_{0ws} = \delta_{1ws} = 0.1$	$\pi = 0.5, \alpha = 0.5$ $\delta_{0w} = \delta_{1w} = -0.1$ $\delta_{0s} = \delta_{1s} = 0.1$ $\delta_{0ws} = \delta_{1ws} = 0.1$	$\pi = 0.1, \alpha = 0.1$ $\delta_{0w} = \delta_{1w} = -0.5$ $\delta_{0s} = \delta_{1s} = 0.5$ $\delta_{0ws} = \delta_{1ws} = 0.5$	$\pi = 0.5, \alpha = 0.5$ $\delta_{0w} = \delta_{1w} = -0.5$ $\delta_{0s} = \delta_{1s} = 0.5$ $\delta_{0ws} = \delta_{1ws} = 0.5$
Working only	−0.027	−0.027	−0.027	−0.026	−0.024
Studying only	0.220	0.220	0.218	0.205	0.206
Working and studying	−0.013	−0.013	−0.013	−0.013	−0.019
Idle children	−0.180	−0.180	−0.178	−0.166	−0.164

Source: UCW calculations based on El Salvador: *Enquesta de hogares de própositos múltiples* (EHPM) 2001.

Table A6.7.4. *Sensitivity analysis on the effect of access to electricity in rural area*

ATT	$\alpha = 0$ $\delta_{0w} = \delta_{1w} = 0$ $\delta_{0s} = \delta_{1s} = 0$ $\delta_{0ws} = \delta_{1ws} = 0$	$\pi = 0.1, \alpha = 0.1$ $\delta_{0w} = \delta_{1w} = -0.1$ $\delta_{0s} = \delta_{1s} = 0.1$ $\delta_{0ws} = \delta_{1ws} = 0.1$	$\pi = 0.5, \alpha = 0.5$ $\delta_{0w} = \delta_{1w} = -0.1$ $\delta_{0s} = \delta_{1s} = 0.1$ $\delta_{0ws} = \delta_{1ws} = 0.1$	$\pi = 0.1, \alpha = 0.1$ $\delta_{0w} = \delta_{1w} = -0.5$ $\delta_{0s} = \delta_{1s} = 0.5$ $\delta_{0ws} = \delta_{1ws} = 0.5$	$\pi = 0.5, \alpha = 0.5$ $\delta_{0w} = \delta_{1w} = -0.5$ $\delta_{0s} = \delta_{1s} = 0.5$ $\delta_{0ws} = \delta_{1ws} = 0.5$
Working only	−0.029	−0.029	−0.028	−0.029	−0.025
Studying only	0.141	0.140	0.138	0.140	0.129
Working and studying	−0.003	−0.003	−0.003	−0.003	−0.004
Idle children	−0.109	−0.108	−0.107	−0.108	−0.100

Source: UCW calculations based on El Salvador: *Enquesta de hogares de própositos múltiples* (EHPM) 2001.

Table A6.7.5. *Sensitivity analysis on the effect of access to water in urban area*

ATT	$\alpha = 0$ $\delta_{0w} = \delta_{1w} = 0$ $\delta_{0s} = \delta_{1s} = 0$ $\delta_{0ws} = \delta_{1ws} = 0$	$\pi = 0.1, \alpha = 0.1$ $\delta_{0w} = \delta_{1w} = -0.1$ $\delta_{0s} = \delta_{1s} = 0.1$ $\delta_{0ws} = \delta_{1ws} = 0.1$	$\pi = 0.5, \alpha = 0.5$ $\delta_{0w} = \delta_{1w} = -0.1$ $\delta_{0s} = \delta_{1s} = 0.1$ $\delta_{0ws} = \delta_{1ws} = 0.1$	$\pi = 0.1, \alpha = 0.1$ $\delta_{0w} = \delta_{1w} = -0.5$ $\delta_{0s} = \delta_{1s} = 0.5$ $\delta_{0ws} = \delta_{1ws} = 0.5$	$\pi = 0.5, \alpha = 0.5$ $\delta_{0w} = \delta_{1w} = -0.5$ $\delta_{0s} = \delta_{1s} = 0.5$ $\delta_{0ws} = \delta_{1ws} = 0.5$
Working only	−0.166	−0.157	−0.157	−0.122	−0.133
Studying only	0.271	0.271	0.266	0.247	0.251
Working and studying	0.000	0.000	0.000	0.000	0.000
Idle children	−0.105	−0.113	−0.108	−0.125	−0.118

Source: UCW calculations based on Guatemala: *Encuesta national sobre condiciones de vida* (ENCOVI), 2000.

Table A6.7.6. *Sensitivity analysis on the effect of access to water in rural area*

ATT	$\alpha = 0$ $\delta_{0w} = \delta_{1w} = 0$ $\delta_{0s} = \delta_{1s} = 0$ $\delta_{0ws} = \delta_{1ws} = 0$	$\pi = 0.1, \alpha = 0.1$ $\delta_{0w} = \delta_{1w} = -0.1$ $\delta_{0s} = \delta_{1s} = 0.1$ $\delta_{0ws} = \delta_{1ws} = 0.1$	$\pi = 0.5, \alpha = 0.5$ $\delta_{0w} = \delta_{1w} = -0.1$ $\delta_{0s} = \delta_{1s} = 0.1$ $\delta_{0ws} = \delta_{1ws} = 0.1$	$\pi = 0.1, \alpha = 0.1$ $\delta_{0w} = \delta_{1w} = -0.5$ $\delta_{0s} = \delta_{1s} = 0.5$ $\delta_{0ws} = \delta_{1ws} = 0.5$	$\pi = 0.5, \alpha = 0.5$ $\delta_{0w} = \delta_{1w} = -0.5$ $\delta_{0s} = \delta_{1s} = 0.5$ $\delta_{0ws} = \delta_{1ws} = 0.5$
Working only	−0.080	−0.074	−0.072	−0.057	−0.067
Studying only	0.140	0.135	0.131	0.124	0.118
Working and studying	0.000	0.000	0.000	0.000	0.000
Idle children	−0.060	−0.061	−0.059	−0.067	−0.051

Source: UCW calculations based on Guatemala: *Encuesta national sobre condiciones de vida* (ENCOVI), 2000.

Table A6.7.7. *Sensitivity analysis on the effect of access to electricity in urban area*

ATT	$\alpha = 0$ $\delta_{0w} = \delta_{1w} = 0$ $\delta_{0s} = \delta_{1s} = 0$ $\delta_{0ws} = \delta_{1ws} = 0$	$\pi = 0.1, \alpha = 0.1$ $\delta_{0w} = \delta_{1w} = -0.1$ $\delta_{0s} = \delta_{1s} = 0.1$ $\delta_{0ws} = \delta_{1ws} = 0.1$	$\pi = 0.5, \alpha = 0.5$ $\delta_{0w} = \delta_{1w} = -0.1$ $\delta_{0s} = \delta_{1s} = 0.1$ $\delta_{0ws} = \delta_{1ws} = 0.1$	$\pi = 0.1, \alpha = 0.1$ $\delta_{0w} = \delta_{1w} = -0.5$ $\delta_{0s} = \delta_{1s} = 0.5$ $\delta_{0ws} = \delta_{1ws} = 0.5$	$\pi = 0.5, \alpha = 0.5$ $\delta_{0w} = \delta_{1w} = -0.5$ $\delta_{0s} = \delta_{1s} = 0.5$ $\delta_{0ws} = \delta_{1ws} = 0.5$
Working only	-0.188	-0.176	-0.185	-0.140	-0.168
Studying only	0.391	0.388	0.389	0.371	0.371
Working and studying	0.000	0.000	0.000	0.000	0.000
Idle children	-0.204	-0.212	-0.204	-0.231	-0.203

Source: UCW calculations based on Guatemala: *Encuesta national sobre condiciones de vida* (ENCOVI), 2000.

Table A6.7.8. Sensitivity analysis on the effect of access to electricity in rural area

ATT	$\alpha = 0$ $\delta_{0w} = \delta_{1w} = 0$ $\delta_{0s} = \delta_{1s} = 0$ $\delta_{0ws} = \delta_{1ws} = 0$	$\pi = 0.1, \alpha = 0.1$ $\delta_{0w} = \delta_{1w} = -0.1$ $\delta_{0s} = \delta_{1s} = 0.1$ $\delta_{0ws} = \delta_{1ws} = 0.1$	$pi = 0.5, \alpha = 0.5$ $\delta_{0w} = \delta_{1w} = -0.1$ $\delta_{0s} = \delta_{1s} = 0.1$ $\delta_{0ws} = \delta_{1ws} = 0.1$	$\pi = 0.1, \alpha = 0.1$ $\delta_{0w} = \delta_{1w} = -0.5$ $\delta_{0s} = \delta_{1s} = 0.5$ $\delta_{0ws} = \delta_{1ws} = 0.5$	$\pi = 0.5, \alpha = 0.5$ $\delta_{0w} = \delta_{1w} = -0.5$ $\delta_{0s} = \delta_{1s} = 0.5$ $\delta_{0ws} = \delta_{1ws} = 0.5$
Working only	−0.162	−0.145	−0.157	−0.118	−0.136
Studying only	0.245	0.231	0.239	0.210	0.215
Working and studying	0.000	0.000	0.000	0.000	0.000
Idle children	−0.083	−0.086	−0.082	−0.092	−0.079

Source: UCW calculations based on Guatemala: *Encuesta national sobre condiciones de vida* (ENCOVI), 2000.

7

Health Effects of Child Labour
Evidence from Guatemala and Rural Vietnam

In Chapter 2, we mentioned the possibility that work by school-age children could affect their health either while they are still children, or in adult life. If the former were true, it would follow that parents can affect the children's well-being not only through their current consumption and future human capital, c_2 and h, but also through the amount (or the type) of work that they are required to carry out at a young age. If the latter were true, parents would be affecting their children's future earnings not only through the amount of h, but also also through the probability that h is used for a long time (hence, other things being equal, that the rate at which h is remunerated, ω, is high). In the theoretical analysis, we assumed for simplicity that neither of these effects was present. If that assumption is not warranted, the amount of time worked (or type of work done) will affect the child's utility not only through c_2 and h, as in the model of Chapter 3, but also through the child's present and future health status. The net effect is thus ambiguous.

If we further allow for the possibility that c_2 affects the marginal product of child labour (the child's ability to carry out physical work) as suggested in Chapter 5, the relationship between work and utility becomes even more complicated for two reasons. First, because it is efficient, hence in the common interest of parents and children, that the additional income generated by the children's work is allocated disproportionately to the children's consumption. Secondly, because work may increase a child's bargaining power. If some children work, and some do not (because they are too young to work, or because they go to school), the amount consumed by the former will then definitely increase, because both household income and their share of this income do. But the amount consumed by children who do not work may increase or decrease, because their share of household income will decrease (Pitt et al. 1990). The policy implication is in any case that the government can affect the children's present and future health not only by spending on sanitation and health (see Chapters 3 and 5), but also either by using taxes and subsidies to modify the marginal effect of child work on family income, or by forbidding certain forms of child work.

It is thus important to establish empirically whether the direct health effect of working at a young age is indeed negative, and whether it is the amount or the type of work carried out that is detrimental to health. In the present chapter we report the results of the studies by O'Donnell and Rosati and van Doorslaer (2005) and by Rosati and Strauss (2004). International conventions define activities that children should not be allowed to carry out in terms of the consequences of such activities, rather than on the basis of the characteristics of the activity itself. For example, categories of child labour to be abolished under the provisions of International Labour Office Conventions 138 and 182 include *hazardous work*, defined as 'labour that jeopardises the physical, mental or moral well-being of a child' (ILO 2002). The ILO estimates that there are 171 million children worldwide engaged in hazardous work, of which nearly two-thirds are under the age of 15 (ILO 2002: table 1). These estimates are extrapolated from data on the prevalence of child workers in activities considered to be *potentially* damaging to child well-being.[1] There is remarkably little evidence on the *actual* health effects of child work.

To some extent, the lack of empirical evidence is not a major obstacle to policy formation. There can be little doubt that children working with dangerous materials, such as asbestos or molten glass, in unhealthy environments, such as mines or quarries, or long hours in sweatshop conditions place their health in serious jeopardy. There is little doubt also about the wretchedness of children engaging in such activities even though it is difficult to accumulate evidence on the health effects, not least because such child labour is usually illegal. However, the vast majority of child work consists of agricultural work, usually within a family context. The best available estimate is that 70 per cent of all child workers worldwide are in the agricultural sector (Ashagrie 1998: table 3).

The health consequences of such work are not obvious. On the one hand, the toll of heavy labour on young bodies, use of dangerous tools and machinery, contact with fertilizers and pesticides, sheer exhaustion, and, in the long term, forgone schooling, may all impact negatively on health. There is some evidence from the Philippines that children working on family farms experience health problems as a result of exposure to infection, heavy lifting, and lack of protective clothing (IPEC 1997). Even in the United States, work-related deaths of young workers are highest in agriculture (Bureau of Labor Statistics 2000). On the other hand, work in the open air under the supervision of parents might not be considered a particularly unhealthy environment. In addition, in very poor societies, the produce of the child's work may be crucial to the maintenance of its own sustenance and health.

Establishing the health consequences of child work empirically is not easy for a number of reasons. First, because work and health are jointly determined. This is particularly true in poor countries, and even more so among children in poor countries. Secondly, because common unobservables (e.g. preferences and

---

[1] All children aged 5–17 working in (*a*) mining or construction sectors, (*b*) occupations or processes considered hazardous by their nature, or (*c*) more than 43 hours per week are considered by the ILO to be engaged in hazardous work.

genetic health endowments) influencing both health and the decision to work may give rise to an endogeneity problem. Thirdly, because of two-way causal relationships. While work conditions and experiences can impact on health, a sick child is simply incapable of work. Physical work consumes energy required to fend off infection, but disease itself depletes the stock of energy and can leave a child incapable of work (Dasgupta 1993: 401–36). A health shock may derive from a workplace accident or be the accumulated effect of past work experience. Given any of these circumstances, the contemporaneous correlation between child work and health reveals little of the true impact of the former on the latter. Unobservable heterogeneity, simultaneity, and relationships that operate with a lag obscure any causal impact of child work on health.

The present chapter aims to establish whether there is a negative impact of work during childhood on health, controlling for observable and unobservable confounding factors. As far as we are aware, we are the first to take account of these confounding factors in a study of the health effects of child work. That is made possible by the use of a particularly rich two-wave panel data set, the 1992/3 and 1997/8 *Vietnam Living Standards Surveys*, and of the retrospective information contained in the 2000 *Guatemalan National Survey on Living Conditions* (NSLC). The panel nature of the Vietnamese data, and the availability of good instrumental variables, make it possible to correct for potential endogeneity arising from both unobservable heterogeneity and simultaneity. The Guatemala survey contains information on adult health, and retrospective information about age of entry in the labour market. Used in combination with a sub-sample of siblings selected from the main sample, such retrospective information makes it possible to identify the long-term effect of working during childhood on health in adult life.

7.1 CHILD WORK AND HEALTH

Occupational hazards jeopardize health. The risks faced by working children may be greater than those confronted by adult workers. Physiological and psychological immaturities make children more vulnerable to abuse and to given health risks. Children are more prone to injury through accidents and more sensitive to noise, heat, and toxicity (Bequele and Myers 1995, Forastieri 1997, ILO 1998, Fassa et al. 2000). The physical strain of work on growing bones and joints can lead to stunting and spinal injury (ILO 2002: 12). All these risks are higher for poorly fed children, whose physiology has already been weakened through malnourishment (ibid.). Physical work depletes a child's stock of energy. Overexertive work exhausts the energy stock below the minimum required to sustain physical growth and combat infection (Dasgupta 1993: 401–36).

Agriculture, the dominant sector of child employment, is an industry with a very poor record of safety, with 1 in 8 child workers suffering illness or injury

(Ashagrie 1998: table 6). A child working on a farm is exposed to dangerous tools and machinery, to chemicals, to water-, soil- and animal-borne infection, to heavy lifting and poor posture, as well as to heatstroke and sheer exhaustion. The difficulty of regulating child work environments that are invariably informal and small-scale, and often illegal, further raises the health risks faced by child workers (Fassa et al. 2000). Most child work is undertaken within the family unit. Perhaps surprisingly, this setting generally accounts for a disproportionately high percentage of all working children with health problems (O'Donnell, Rosati, and van Doorslaer 2002).

Health gains from child work are not inconceivable, but these benefits are indirect (coming through parental expenditure for the child's nutrition and medical care). There is evidence that a child's labour can make an important contribution to the household's living standard (Bhalotra 2003), and consequently to the health of all its members (Steckel 1995, Smith 1999). There is also a theoretical argument that a disproportionate amount of resources will be allocated to maintaining the strength and health of the most productive members (Pitt et al. 1990). This implies that a working child can be expected to receive a disproportionate share of the income he or she produces.[2]

While many of the health risks of child work threaten immediate damage to health, others are likely to develop over many years and might only become manifest in adulthood. Exposure to pesticides, chemicals, dusts, and carcinogenic agents increase the risks of developing bronchial complaints, cancers, and a wide variety of diseases (Forastieri 1997, ILO 1998, Fassa et al. 2000). Individuals working in childhood are doubly vulnerable to chronic health problems—they are exposed to risk factors for longer periods and the biological process of rapid cell growth reduces the latency period of some diseases (Fassa et al. 2000). Child work may also have a long-term impact on health through forgone education, and subsequently reduced lifetime earnings and constrained knowledge of health production mechanisms. Evidence on the trade-off between child work and schooling is mixed but, on balance, supports the crowding-out hypothesis (Rosenzweig and Everson 1977, Psacharopoulos 1997, Grootaert and Patrinos 1999, Cigno and Rosati 2002).

Existing evidence on the health consequences of child work is limited. A seventeen-year longitudinal study of rural India found that boys in paid work between the ages of 10 and 14 years grew up shorter and lighter than those who attended school (Satyanarayanan et al. 1986). But, with the exception of standardization on initial nutritional status, no control was made for confounding factors, such as household income, that could be expected to influence both work and growth experiences. In rural Ghana, a study found no growth differences between children enrolled and not enrolled in school but did find

---

[2] At the aggregate level, these arguments have less force. A large supply of child labour will reduce market wages and may leave the economy at a low-level equilibrium with low wages, low education levels, and poor health (Basu 1999).

that the latter group suffered greater morbidity of a nature apparently related to occupation-specific hazards (Fentiman et al. 2001). Again, beyond age and sex, there was no control for observable or unobservable confounding factors.

There is some evidence of a negative correlation between child work activity and health in adulthood. Kassouf, Mckee, and Mossialos (2001), using Brazilian data, find an individual is more likely to report poor health in adulthood, the lower the age of entry into the labour force. Controlling for education, the correlation is weakened but remains significant for some age and sex groups. This is suggestive of an effect of child work on adult health, in part operating through forgone education, although the limited control for covariates makes it difficult to draw firm conclusions. Giuffrida, Iunes, and Savedo (2001), also using data from Brazil, find that, controlling for age, education, wealth, housing conditions, unemployment status, and race, entry into the labour force below the age of 10 has a statistically significant and substantial negative effect on health in adulthood. Given the inclusion of so many control variables, the result is suggestive of a negative effect of child work on adult health. An alternative explanation is that unobservable characteristics, for example parental preferences vis-à-vis investment in the child's human capital, raise the probability of working in childhood and reduce health in adulthood.

7.2 VIETNAM

The Vietnam Living Standards Survey (VLSS) is a two-wave panel conducted in 1992–3 and 1997–8. The survey has detailed information on work activity for all household members aged 6 and above, as well as self-reported and anthropometric indicators of health. Work and health are primarily reported by the child itself, but can be reported by a parent on behalf of young children. Commune surveys, which can be matched to household records, provide information on health care, as well as potential instruments for child work in the form of indicators of the local economy, labour market, and school quality. In addition to these data advantages, Vietnam offers an interesting context. Child work activity is substantial and exhibited a significant decline between the two waves of the survey, which span a period of economic transition and rapid growth.

7.2.1 *Sample description*

In 1992–3, the VLSS interviewed a nationally representative (self-weighting) sample of 4,800 households. In 1997–8, 4,305 (89.6 per cent) of the original households were re- interviewed and a supplementary sample was taken to give a cross-section sample of 5,999 households. To facilitate disaggregate analysis, disproportionate sampling by region was adopted in the 1997–8 cross-section and for this reason, 96 of the original households were deliberately dropped from follow-up. No attempt was made to trace households moving out of a commune, and this probably accounts for the majority of the 400 households lost in the follow-up process.

Glewwe and Nguyen (2002) find the panel households to be broadly nationally representative. Attrition through children moving out of households does not appear to be a major problem either. Edmonds and Turk (2004) report that of 6,003 children aged 0–10 years in the first wave, 92 per cent were still in the household by the second wave. Of the missing 8 per cent, the vast majority (78 per cent) left the household when their parents moved home. There is some child attrition that is directly related to the two variables of central interest here—health and work—but the numbers are not large.

Of all the children aged 0–10 years at the first wave, 0.8 per cent had died and 0.4 per cent had moved out of the household to enter employment by the time of the second wave. Being a household survey, the VLSS does not sample street children and is unlikely to pick up all illegal forms of child work. The prevalence of child work, in general, and health-damaging work, in particular, is likely to be underestimated by the data. This is less of a problem with respect to estimation of the health effects of child work in rural areas.

We define as a 'child' a person aged 6–15 years, and include in the definition of work not only paid work outside the household, but also any unpaid work on the household farm or business, at any time in the past twelve months. The proportion of children working in Vietnam fell from roughly a third of the age group in 1992–3 to a quarter in 1997–8 (Table 7.1). This decline can be explained primarily by the impressive improvement in living standards that Vietnamese households experienced (Edmonds 2002, Edmonds and Turk 2004). Work participation is strongly correlated with age. One in ten children aged 6–11 years works (1997–8), but the ratio rises to almost one in two among children aged 12–15 years (Table 7.1).

The figures in Table 7.1 indicate little or no difference between the proportion of boys and of girls working, but this understates gender differences since household chores, a prevalently female activity, are not included in the definition of work. The exclusion is deliberate. We wish to reduce the heterogeneity of work captured by a binary indicator of participation and avoid dilution of any health effect through inclusion of work likely to be least threatening to health.[3] To completely ignore household chores, however, would be ill advised since the distinction between work in the household business or farm, and household chores, is often arbitrary. In the estimated models of health, we experimented with a separate dummy to indicate engagement in household chores for at least seven hours per week, but never found this to be significant and do not report the results.

---

[3] There is also a pragmatic reason for the omission. The data on household chores refer only to the previous seven days (not twelve months). The question is: 'During the past 7 days have you done any other work for your family at home. For example, cleaning the house, preparing, meals, washing the family's clothes, . . .'. Subsequent questions ask the number of days such work was done and for how many hours each day.

Table 7.1. *Work participation rates of children aged 6–15 years,*
Vietnam, 1992–3 and 1997–8

	Rural		Urban		Total	
	1992–3	1997–8	1992–3	1997–8	1992–3	1997–8
All	0.3747	0.2876	0.1630	0.0687	0.3395	0.2499
	0.0163	*0.0164*	*0.0310*	*0.0162*	*0.0145*	*0.0141*
Male	0.3646	0.2903	0.1599	0.0635	0.3317	0.2522
	0.0180	*0.0198*	*0.0348*	*0.0170*	*0.0161*	*0.0170*
Female	0.3852	0.2846	0.1660	0.0739	0.3476	0.2475
	0.0175	*0.0159*	*0.0309*	*0.0204*	*0.0154*	*0.0138*
Age 6–11	0.2012	0.1221	0.0575	0.0152	0.1782	0.1051
	0.0176	*0.0129*	*0.0217*	*0.0087*	*0.0153*	*0.0110*
Age 12–15	0.6742	0.5147	0.3249	0.1283	0.6126	0.4417
	0.0225	*0.0234*	*0.0523*	*0.0273*	*0.0202*	*0.0206*
Sample size	5,069	6,274	1,008	1,484	6,077	7,758

Note: Standard error appears in italic.

Child work is much more prevalent in rural areas, and the rate of decrease has been greater there than in the cities. By 1997–8, the participation rate was more than four times greater in rural than in urban areas (Table 7.1). The data offer no plausible instruments for child work in urban areas. Commune surveys were not conducted in these areas and household land holdings are obviously of limited relevance to child work decisions in towns and cities. The analysis is restricted to the rural sample, which covers the vast majority of child work undertaken in the country. In rural Vietnam, child work is predominantly (93 per cent) in household-based agriculture (Table 7.2). As already noted, this is the dominant form of child work worldwide.

Work for a household business is the second most popular form of child work. Relatively few work for pay outside the household (Table 7.2). The domination of household-based agriculture is mainly a reflection of the general structure of the Vietnamese economy, but also the outcome of legislation and cultural factors. As an early signatory to the International Convention on the Rights of the Child (1990) and ILO Convention on the Worst Forms of Child Labour (2000), Vietnam has enacted legislation that restricts the conditions under which a child, at various ages, can work (Edmonds and Turk 2004). In law, opportunities for a child to work outside the household unit are more constrained than work on behalf of the household. The latter is legal provided it is not 'harmful, dangerous or exploitative' (ibid. 15). Child work on behalf of the household has deep cultural roots, and is often considered to have positive effects on the development of the child.

A majority of working children in Vietnam also attend school, the percentage doing so increasing from 60 per cent in 1992–3 to over 70 per cent in 1997–8

Table 7.2. *Work type, hours, and job tenure of working children aged 6–15 years in rural Vietnam, 1992–3 and 1997–8*

	Proportion of working children in:				Mean hours of work per week	Mean months in current job	sample size
	Paid work	Household		School			
		Agriculture	Business				
1992–3	0.0845	0.9044	0.1420	0.6030	18.95	26.14	1894
	0.0122	*0.0122*	*0.0204*	*0.0215*	*0.724*	*0.696*	
1997–8	0.0650	0.9332	0.1100	0.7185	16.87	24.65	1487
	0.0087	*0.0120*	*0.0184*	*0.0247*	*0.897*	*0.757*	

Note: The primary objective is to determine the health consequences of this type of work. The 1998 sample consists of VLSS panel and cross-section supplementary observations. Sample weight applied for 1998; the 1993 survey is self-weighting. Standard error of estimate of population proportion appears in italics, adjusted for stratification and cluster sampling.

(Table 7.2). This is made possible by the low level of compulsory school hours (Edmonds and Turk 2004). Enrolment rates are much lower among children doing paid work outside the household. Amongst rural working children, the average number of hours worked was around seventeen hours per week in 1997–8, and the average length of employment (in the current main job) around two years. Due to an inconsistency of measurement, work hours cannot be compared across waves. In the first wave, respondents were asked to report total hours worked in agriculture. In the second wave, hours specific to each particular type of agricultural activity were reported. Aggregating the latter probably gives a more accurate, but a higher, estimate of total hours, such that the fall in average hours shown in the table understates the real decline. Given this inconsistency, we do not use the hours data from both waves, necessary to estimate the contemporaneous impact on health, but test for a long-term effect through the relationship between health at the second wave and hours worked at the first wave.

We examine three indicators of health: the weight-for-age z-score, height growth, and reported illness or injury. The z-score is a child's weight (or height) expressed in number of standard deviations from the mean weight (or height) of children of the same age and gender in a well-nourished population. The (WHO-recommended) reference population is that of the USA. Anthropometric indicators, such as z-scores and height growth, measure most directly nutritional status. As already indicated in Chapter 5, however, they are also good proxies for morbidity and survival probability (Waterlow et al. 1977, Martorell and Ho 1984, Fogel 1993, de Onis and Habicht 1996, World Health Organization 1995).

In effects, the distinction between nutritional and health status is somewhat tenuous. Malnourishment weakens defences against infection. Disease reduces the absorption of nutrients, draws down the body's stock of energy, and can lead to malnourishment (Dasgupta 1993: 405–8; Steckel 1995: 1910). Work may affect weight and growth directly through the consumption of energy, and indirectly through morbidity. Both effects are of interest. The anthropometric indicators are used here to understand the consequences of child work for both nutritional and health status. Height growth is used as a proxy for long-term health and nutritional experience. It reflects the difference between the accumulated intake of nutrients and use of energy in work and fighting disease (Steckel 1995: 1910).

The long-term consequences of child work are examined through the relationship between work at the first survey and subsequent annual average growth in height between the waves. To estimate the contemporaneous relationship between child work and health, we need an indicator of short-term health/nutritional status. BMI, used in the India study of Chapter 5, is a long-term indicator. The weight-for-height *z*-score would be an obvious choice, but it is available in the data set only up to the age of 11 years. So, we use the weight- for-age *z*-score, and control for height in the regression analysis.

The anthropometric indicators show marked improvements in the average nutritional and health status of Vietnamese children. In 1992–3, the mean height-for-age *z*-score of rural children was a little less than −2 (Table 7.3), a conventional threshold used to define stunted growth. By 1997–8, the mean *z*-score for this population had increased to −1.7. Trends in the weight-for-age *z*-score tell the same story. Descriptive statistics indicate that working children tend to be smaller, and this difference appears to have increased over time.

Table 7.3. *Health indicators of children aged 6–15 years by work status, rural Vietnam, 1992–3 and 1997–8*

	Weight-for-age *z*-score		Height-for-age *z*- score		Proportion reporting illness/injury in past 4 weeks	
	Mean	SE	Mean	SE	Mean	SE
1992–3						
All	−1.86	0.022	−2.06	0.040	0.1969	0.0117
Not working	−1.86	0.026	−1.89	0.038	0.2012	0.0112
Working	−1.85	0.026	−2.08	0.042	0.1948	0.0139
1997–8						
All	−1.67	0.021	−1.70	0.036	0.3379	0.0130
Not working	−1.65	0.023	−1.50	0.033	0.3370	0.0120
Working	−1.72	0.029	−1.86	0.044	0.3186	0.0197

Note: SE = standard error adjusted for stratification and cluster sampling.

Anthropometric indicators have the advantage of objectivity. The disadvant-
ages, for present purposes, are that the measures are more closely correlated
with health at younger ages, and might be rather insensitive to some work-
related health problems, such as injury. For these reasons, we examine the
relation of child work to morbidity, as reported by the child himself or by a
parent on behalf of a young child. There is evidence that self-reported health
is closely correlated with underlying morbidity and that, even after controlling
for clinically measured physiology, it is a good predictor of future mortality
(Kaplan and Camacho 1983, Idler and Benyamini 1997). This evidence refers
to a general self- assessment of health status. The question available in the VLSS
refers to experience of illness or injury in the previous four weeks. There are concerns about the reliability of such measures. Their subjectivity most probably
reduces the signal to noise ratio. This would not be particularly problematic
if reporting differences were random, but there is evidence, particularly from
developing countries, that it is correlated with variables, such as income, which
are potential determinants of true health (Strauss and Thomas 1998, Sadana
et al. 2000). For present purposes, this is not necessarily problematic.

In the regression analysis, we control for factors potentially correlated with
both work status and reported morbidity. It does not matter whether the control
variables are determinants of true health or reporting behaviour. If work status
is correlated with reporting behaviour through unobservables, this is reason
to treat work as endogenous, as we do. The crucial issue is whether a child's
health is reported differently *because* the child is working. Then, there is no
way to identify the work effect on true health separately from that on reporting
behaviour. When health-related benefits are available to non-workers, reporting is expected to differ with work status. It is not immediately obvious that
a child should report its health differently because he or she is working. One
possibility is that an illness becomes apparent only through interference with
work activities. Then, use of self-reported morbidity would give an overestimate of the impact of work on morbidity. On the other hand, if the prevalence
of health problems among child workers leads to their acceptance as the norm,
then use of self-reported morbidity will give an underestimate of the impact of
work on ill health. These possibilities require that the estimated relationship
between work and reported illness be interpreted cautiously, but there is no
reason to dismiss it as uninformative of the impact of child work on morbidity.

Unfortunately, the illness question was changed between survey waves. In
the first wave, individuals were asked whether they had experienced any illness
or injury in the previous four weeks and were given a few example conditions.
In the second wave, respondents were asked explicitly whether they had experienced each one of nine illnesses and/or an injury in the previous four weeks. This
form of questioning is expected to reduce noise in responses. There is evidence
that it makes individuals more likely to report illness (Kooiker 1995.) This is
evident in the data. The proportion of children reporting illness or injury apparently increased from a fifth in 1992–3 to a third in 1997–8, which is inconsistent

with improvement in child health indicated by the anthropometrics. Given this inconsistency, we do not use the self-reported morbidity data from both waves but examine the long-term relationship between child work at the first wave and illness at the second wave. Although the reference period is only four weeks, illness propensity over one month will be a decreasing function of longer-term health status. To the extent that child work has a sustained negative impact on health status, this should be reflected in a positive relationship between past work and current illness propensity.

Both child work status and health status are strongly correlated with living standards. Child work participation falls as household consumption per capita rises, such that participation amongst the poorest quintile of children was more than twice that of the richest quintile in 1997–8. Child height and weight both rise with household consumption. Inequality is less apparent in the distribution of reported morbidity, an indication of the discrepancies in reporting behaviour discussed above.

7.2.2 *Contemporaneous versus longer-term work–health relationships*

As usual, the main statistical issue is endogeneity, which may arise from both unobservable heterogeneity and simultaneity. In a short-term context, unobservable heterogeneity refers to the joint dependence of both measured (transient) health and work activity on unobservable (permanent) health endowments and preferences. Assuming that health is positively associated with labour market productivity, *ceteris paribus*, the inherently healthiest individuals are most likely to be available for employment and to be appointed. This *healthy worker selection effect* would tend to induce a positive statistical relationship between child health and work status. Other sources of unobservable heterogeneity may bias the relationship in the opposite direction. The more altruistic parents are vis-à-vis their child, the more they will invest in the health of the child, and strive to keep the child from working. Such a *preference effect* would create a negative statistical relationship between child health and work status. Endogeneity can also arise through reverse causality—current work activity depends directly on the individual's transient health and nutritional status. A temporary bout of illness can leave the individual incapable of work. This will tend to induce a positive correlation between health/nutrition and work status. A number of estimation strategies, described in Appendix 7.1, are employed to deal with these endogeneity problems. Instruments are described and justified in section 7.4.3.

The longer-term health consequences of child work are examined through the relationship between childhood work at the time of the first survey and two indicators of subsequent health experience (reported illness four to five years later, and average annual growth in height between waves). Restricting attention to the longer-term health consequences of work eliminates the reverse causality problem. Health shocks cannot impact on past work. Lagged work status may still be endogenous, due to unobservable factors that impinge on work and health status in all periods. The impact of child work at the first wave on the probability of illness at the second is estimated through the bivariate probit system described in Appendix 7.1.

7.2.3 *Definition of variables*

At the individual level, the regressors are basic demographics (*age, female,* and *ethnic minority*). Over the age range considered, growth spurts and the onset of puberty will result in highly non-linear relationships of weight and height-to-age, which can be expected to differ by gender. For each model, we search for the most suitably flexible functional form for the age effect. In gender-pooled estimates, we interact a gender dummy with polynomials in age. In addition, all models have been estimated separately by gender. With respect to the health–work relationship, the results are generally consistent across genders. We concentrate on the pooled estimates and present disaggregated results only when important gender differences emerge. At the household level, we control for household composition (# *infants,* # *kids,* # *adults, dad in household*), mother's age and education (*mum's age, mum has diploma*) and housing/hygiene conditions (*drinking water OK, sanitation OK, house walls*).

Living standards are proxied by the logarithm of the value of household consumption per capita (*hhold consumption*). Controlling for living standards deals with an important confounding factor but also takes out any positive indirect effect from child work to health through the household income. We are testing for a negative effect of child work on health, not estimating the total effect through all possible pathways. This needs to be kept in mind in drawing policy conclusions from the results. For each model, exogeneity of household consumption is tested and relaxed where necessary and feasible. Household consumption is an important determinant of child nutritional intake and medical care. As a further proxy for nutrition, we include the (log) quantity of household rice consumption per capita (*rice consumption*). Nutrition should increase with rice consumption but not linearly. Where it is a staple food, as in Vietnam, rice is essential to the sustenance of malnourished children. But a rice-dominated diet is not a nutritious one. To better capture nutritional intake, we experimented with the disaggregation of household consumption into food and non-food expenditures but it made no difference to the results.

Commune-level survey data allow control for the availability of medical facilities and personnel (*doctor/pharmacy in commune, distance to hospital, most births at home*) and services provided by the local health centre, including child growth and nutrition-specific interventions, such as mothers' health/nutrition education programmes and the provision of oral rehydration salts (*child health exam, child growth chart, mum health education, oral rehydration, nutrition education*). Medical interventions, such as oral rehydration salts, affect the nature of the relationship between nutrition and health. Controlling for such services increases the health information content of residual variation in the anthropometrics. Our initial specification included a much longer list of medicines and health services, including the availability of iron supplements and vitamin A. Many were not significant. The weight-for-age z-score equation is estimated in differences. Not all of the commune health services variables are available in both waves and so a restricted set are used to estimate this equation.

School attendance is deliberately left out of the empirical specification to avoid yet another potentially endogenous regressor. Consequently, the estimated effect of child work on health includes any indirect effect operating through schooling. We expect the contemporaneous effect of schooling on health during childhood to be small. In the longer term, an indirect schooling effect is more plausible, but the five-year period we examine, spanning into early adulthood for only part of the sample, is unlikely to be sufficient to pick up much of the impact that education has on health.

The instruments include three types of variables—household land holdings, indicators of the commune economy/labour market, and indicators of school quality. Household agricultural land is a plausible determinant of both child work and household living standards and, controlling for all else, there seems no reason for child health to be influenced by land possessions. There is widespread evidence of child work activity increasing with the size of household land holdings (Rosenzweig and Everson 1977, Cigno and Rosati 2002, Bhalotra and Heady 2003). This may operate through a positive effect on the productivity of child workers in the presence of labour and land market imperfections (Bhalotra and Heady 2003).

In Chapter 5, we have shown that, with full income controlled for, the propensity for a child to work in India increases with the size of the land holding. Using the VLSS, Edmonds and Pavcnik (2001) find that the propensity for a child to work in Vietnam increases slightly if the household has any land but, conditional on this, is decreasing with the size of the land holding. As full income is not controlled, the latter result may be explained by a wealth effect, strengthened by credit market imperfections, outweighing the productivity effect (Bhalotra and Heady 2003). Glewwe et al. (2002), also using the VLSS, argue that land holdings are a valid instrument for household consumption as a determinant of child health, proxied by height-for-age z-scores. Land markets are underdeveloped in Vietnam and simply do not exist in many rural areas. To a large extent, agricultural land is controlled by the government and allocated to households. There is thus little opportunity for a household to adjust its land holdings in response to the sickness of a child (Glewwe et al. 2002: 16). When estimating in differences, we use total household agricultural land holdings (*land*), which are measured consistently across waves. For estimation of lagged relationships, where we need instruments at wave 1 only, we use land that has been allocated to the household or which it has for long-term use (*any allocated land, allocated land size*). This should be an even more exogenous source of variation in household wealth and farm productivity.

The remaining instruments are defined at the commune level. Edmonds and Pavcnik (2003) find the commune relative price of rice (*rice price*) to be a substantial determinant of child work activity in Vietnam. According to their estimates, the rise in the price of rice, as a result of market liberalization, was a major factor contributing to the fall in child work activity between 1992–3 and 1997–8. Since much of this effect operated through household earnings opportunities, the rice price should be a determinant of household living standards, as well as child work. Controlling for all regressors, including total household expenditure and the quantity of rice consumed, the rice price is assumed to have no independent influence on child health. Living standards and child work will be influenced by the condition of the economy and labour market at the commune level, which we proxy by indicators of work-related migration to and from the commune (*immigration, emigration, migrant ratio*).

The quality of schooling on offer is a potentially important determinant of child work. As a proxy for school quality, we use the year in which the commune primary school was built (*school year*) and, for the estimation of longer-term relationships, the pupil–teacher ratio in the nearest secondary school (*pupil–teacher*), which is available for wave 1 only. For each model, the relevance of the instruments is checked through tests of significance in first-stage regressions. For linear estimators, overidentification restrictions are tested formally (Wooldridge 2002: 122–4). For the bivariate probit, overidentification is checked, somewhat informally, by tests of exclusion of each instrument from the illness equation conditional on the assumption that the remaining instruments are valid. Sensitivity of the estimates to dropping variables from the instrument set is also checked, and reported on.

For each dependent variable, we test down from a very general specification, sequentially removing variables of low significance, to arrive at the most appropriate empirical model. In the main tables (7.4–7.6), we present, for each dependent variable, the work coefficients for a variety of estimators and specifications. In the baseline specification, work activity is represented through a dummy for any work in the past year. We experiment with effects from paid work outside the household (*paid work*), household chores for at least seven hours in the past week (*hhold chores*), number of months in the current job (*job tenure*), and, for the longer-term relationships, total hours of work in the past year (*work hours*). These effects are reported when significant.

7.2.4 *Results*

We now present, separately for the short and the long term, the Vietnam estimates of the health effects of child work.

7.2.4.1 *Contemporaneous work–health relationship*

Estimates of the contemporaneous relationship between child work status and weight-for-age *z*-score (*waz*) are presented in Table 7.4. The sample consists of children within the 6–17 years age range in both waves. *z*-scores are only computable up to the age of 17. We control for height (third degree polynomial) and interpret coefficients as reflecting relationships with thinness, or wasting. Pooled OLS gives a significantly positive relationship between child work participation and current *waz*. The possibility that this reflects selection of the stronger kids into work is supported by the FD-OLS results, which show no relationship between child work status and *waz*.[4]

The coefficient of (log) household consumption changes from positive and significant under pooled OLS, to negative and marginally significant under FD-OLS. The direction of change suggests that fixed unobservables raise both household expenditure and child weight. The negative FD-OLS estimate is surprising and might reflect simultaneity bias. To deal with this, along with any remaining endogeneity of child work, we proceed to FD-2SLS. The instrument set consists of *land, rice price, immigration, emigration*, and *school year*. Their relevance to the determination of child work and household consumption is confirmed by significant rejection of exclusion restrictions on the respective reduced form regressions (see Table 7.4, column 3). In the case of child work, IV significance is only at the 7 per cent level, and the R^2 is low, which could indicate a weak instruments problem. Overidentification is not rejected at the 5 per cent level, but is on the margin at the 10 per cent significance level (Table 7.4, column 3).

We also test the exclusion of each instrument from the structural equation while relying on the remaining instruments for identification. In each case, the exclusion condition cannot be rejected. The Hausman (1978) F-test rejects joint exogeneity of child work status and household per capita consumption. On an individual basis, examining the *t*-statistics on the respective reduced-form residuals, only the exogeneity of household consumption is rejected (Wooldridge 2002: 118–22). As with FD-OLS, the FD-2SLS estimate of the child work effect is insignificantly different from zero (Table 7.4, column 3). The FD-OLS estimate of a negative relationship between household consumption and child weight becomes positive and significant when estimated by FD-2SLS. The direction of change is as expected in the case that the medical needs of a low-weight, sick child force a household to increase expenditure financed by dissaving and/or raising labour supply. Estimation by FD-2SLS greatly increases the magnitude of the estimate of the household consumption effect, which corresponds to an elasticity of 0.39 at the sample mean.

---

[4] Splitting the sample by gender does not alter this conclusion. The work coefficient is negative for boys and positive for girls, but in neither case does it remotely approach significance.

Table 7.4. *Weight-for-age z-score against current child work activity (sample: 6–17 years in both waves)*

	Pooled OLS	First difference OLS		First difference 2SLS			
				Work and household consumption instrumented		Household consumption only instrumented	
				Full IV set[a]	Full IV set less rice price	Full IV set	Full IV set less school year
Child in work	0.0359** (0.0147)	−0.0001 (0.0144)		0.0863 (0.3318)	−0.0302 (0.2778)	0.0147 (0.0218)	0.0077 (0.0215)
Child in paid work							0.0876** (0.0390)
(log) Household consumption	0.0649*** (0.0232)	−0.0428* (0.0246)		0.6643** (0.3294)	0.2780 (0.4067)	0.6424** (0.3132)	0.6714** (0.3237)
Sample size	5572	2786		2542	2593	2582	2582
R^2	0.6419	0.5526		0.4068	0.5210	0.4203	0.4099
F-test of joint significance	160.93 ($p = .000$)	69.12 ($p = .000$)		42.07 ($p = .000$)	52.92 ($p = .000$)	44.24 ($p = .000$)	43.36 ($p = .000$)
Hausman test of exogeneity[b]			Work	$t = -0.26$ ($p = .795$)	$t = 0.02$ ($p = .998$)		
			Hhold consumption	$t = -2.52$ ($p = .013$)	$t = -0.59$ ($p = .556$)	$t = -2.72$ ($p = .008$)	$t = -2.79$ ($p = .006$)
			Work and hhold consumption	$F(2, 105) = 3.77$ ($p = .026$)	$F(2, 107) = 0.31$ ($p = .737$)		
Reduced forms: R^2 F-test of IV significance			Work	$R^2 = 0.0736$ $F(5, 105) = 2.09$ ($p = .072$)	$R^2 = 0.0733$ $F(4, 107) = 3.03$ ($p = .206$)		
			Hhold consumption	$R^2 = 0.2845$ $F(5, 105) = 2.35$ ($p = .046$)	$R^2 = 0.2784$ $F(4, 107) = 1.95$ ($p = .107$)	$R^2 = 0.2831$ $F(4, 107) = 2.80$ ($p = .029$)	$R^2 = 0.2837$ $F(4, 107) = 2.77$ ($p = .031$)
Overidentification[c]				$X^2(3) = 6.16$ ($p = .104$)	$X^2(2) = 1.02$ ($p = .602$)	$X^2(3) = 5.90$ ($p = .116$)	$X^2(3) = 5.57$ ($p = .135$)

Note: Cluster adjusted robust standard errors in parentheses. *, **, and *** denote significance at 10%, 5%, and 1% respectively; p = denotes p- value.

[a] land, rice price, emigration, immigration, school year.

[b] t-test of individual significance and F test of joint significance of reduced form residuals in augmented structural equation (Hausman 1978; Wooldridge 2002: 118–22).

[c] Overidentification test robust t. heteroskedasticity (Wooldridge 2002: 122–4).

The FD-2SLS estimates are robust to dropping variables from the instrument set, with the exception that exclusion of *rice price* reduces the magnitude of the coefficients on the endogenous variables and leaves the household consumption effect insignificantly different from zero (Table 7.4, column 4). The work effect remains insignificant. Without the rice price in the instrument set, exogeneity is not rejected for household consumption as well as child work. The remaining instruments perform better with respect to the overidentification test but are weaker. Given that exogeneity of child work is not rejected in any case, we estimate treating only household consumption as endogenous and returning *rice price* to the IV set but dropping *school year* since this is not a plausible determinant of household living standards (Table 7.4, column 5). The household consumption effect is robust to the assumption that work status is exogenous. Without instrumentation, the work effect is estimated more precisely, but it remains insignificantly different from zero.

There is no evidence to support a contemporaneous negative impact of child work on weight for age. The same conclusion emerges using two alternative health indicators—body mass index and reported illness.[5] The lack of a work participation effect may mask differential effects by type and tenure of work. We test this by including, in turn and in addition to work participation, *Household chores*, *paid work*, and *job tenure*. Given the change in measurement of hours in agricultural work between waves, it is not possible to test for a contemporaneous health effect from hours of work. *Household chores* and *job tenure* are never significant. Irrespective of the estimator, the coefficient on *paid work* is positive and significant. In first differences, exogeneity of *paid work*, as well as any work participation, is not rejected.

In the final column of Table 7.4, we give FD-2SLS estimates with household consumption only instrumented and *paid work* included. While non-paid work within the household environment has no significant impact on child weight, children working for pay are significantly heavier. Given that selection effects have been eliminated through differencing and there is no indication of remaining endogeneity in the work variables, the analysis supports a causal relationship. Working for pay makes the child heavier and, by extension, healthier. This is not the effect one might expect and it should certainly be interpreted with caution.

Failure to detect simultaneity in the relationship between child work and weight is a little surprising. If *paid work* is instrumented, the effect remains positive but is no longer significant. Significance is lost also if the sample is split by gender, but the estimated coefficient is roughly the same for boys and girls.

---

[5] Body mass index is weight divided by the square of height. In estimating the contemporaneous impact on illness, we try to deal with the change in the illness question through flexible time effects. Correcting for both unobservable heterogeneity and simultaneity through instrumentation, the illness propensity is *lower* for working children (10% significance) but the estimate is not robust to the instrument set.

On the other hand, it is not implausible that working for pay may benefit the child nutritionally. As explained at the outset of this chapter, work may in fact increase a child's claim on household resources. At least in the short term, it is thus possible that the nutritional and health benefits of a child engaging in paid work are positive. Of course, in the longer term there may be legitimate concerns about the health consequences of sustained exposure to workplace risks. We now turn to estimates of such longer-term effects.

7.2.4.2   *Longer-term work–health relationship*

Estimates of the relationship between illness propensity in 1997–8 and child work activity up to five years earlier are presented in Table 7.5. The sample consists of wave 2 observations of children that were aged 6–15 years at wave 1. The gender-pooled univariate probit estimates (column 1) indicate a positive but insignificant relationship between current illness and past child work. The relationship increases substantially in magnitude and significance in moving to the bivariate probit model (Table 7.5, column 2). This is consistent with a *healthy worker selection effect*. The univariate model does not allow for the fact that the inherently more healthy individuals are more likely to have worked in the past. The negative correlation between the work and illness equation error terms is also consistent with selection into work on the basis of unobserved health endowments. This correlation is significant only at the 11 per cent level, but the magnitude of the correlation and the difference between the estimates support the bivariate probit model.

The bivariate probit is identified through the exclusion of *any allocated land*, *allocated land size*, *rice price*, *emigration*, *migrant ratio*, *pupil–teacher ratio*, and *school year* from the illness equation. We confirm the significance of the instruments in the work equation (results not reported) and check the validity of the identification restrictions by testing the exclusion of each of the instruments from the illness equation under the assumption that the remaining instruments are valid. The exclusion restriction is not rejected in any case. The estimates are fairly robust to variations on the identification strategy. Dropping household land holdings from the model, and so relying principally on commune-level factors for identification, increases the work coefficient from 0.5140 to 0.6370 and raises its significance. The correlation of the errors also increases in magnitude and becomes significant at the 5 per cent level. Omitting the commune-level factors has the opposite effect, reducing the magnitude and significance of both the work coefficient and the error correlation. Dropping the school quality variables reduces the work coefficient to 0.4739, with significance preserved at 1 per cent. Dropping the commune rice price and migration indicators gives a work coefficient of 0.4896, not significant at 10 per cent.

Besides the significant work effect, illness propensity is greater for ethnic minorities and less if the child's mother has a school diploma. Safe drinking

Table 7.5. *Illness/injury in 1997–1998 against child work activity in 1992–1993 (sample: 6–15 years in 1992–3)*

	Males and females (N = 3370)			Males (N = 1803)			Females (N = 1567)		
	Univariate probit	Bivariate probit	Bivariate probit	Univariate probit	Bivariate probit	Univariate probit	Univariate probit	Bivariate probit	Bivariate probit
Child work in 1992–3	0.0987 (0.0715)	0.5140** (0.2582)	0.3472 (0.3086)	0.0422 (0.0948)	0.2926 (0.3459)	−0.2952* (0.1665)	0.1632* (0.0866)	0.7351** (0.3238)	0.9112*** (0.3434)
Job tenure in 1992–3 (months)			0.0140 (0.0088)			0.0255** (0.0112)			−0.0058 (0.0042)
Job tenure squared (/100)			−0.0241* (0.0129)			−0.0348** (0.0158)			
Correlation of errors (rho)		−0.2639 (0.1579)	−0.2536 (0.1647)		−0.1592 (0.2083)			−0.3677 (0.1989)	−0.4009 (0.1979)
Wald test of rho = 0		2.54 ($p = 0.1113$)	2.17 ($p = 0.1409$)		0.5647 ($p = 0.4524$)			2.81 ($p = 0.0935$)	3.24 ($p = 0.0717$)
Log-likelihood	−1950.5	−3366.0	−3363.7	−1039.2	−1792.13	−1036.6	−894.4	−1538.9	−1538.0
LR test of pooling across gender	40.46 ($p = 0.0000$)	75.77 ($p = 0.3273$)							

Note: Cluster adjusted robust standard errors in parentheses. *, **, and *** denote significance at 10%, 5%, and 1% respectively. p = denotes p-value.

water and satisfactory sanitation also significantly reduce the probability of illness. Illness is greater in communes where more than half of women give birth at home and less where there is a pharmacy in the commune, a child growth chart in the health centre, where there was a mothers' health education programme within a year of the first survey, and where the commune has received food relief within the past year. These estimates make sense and suggest that the reported illness measure is reflecting variation in underlying health and its determinants.

Other regressors capture reporting behaviour. Illness is more likely to be reported when the question is answered by the subject (*self report* = 1) rather than by a parent on behalf of a young child. The propensity to report illness is greater where the commune health centre conducts a child health exam. Most likely, such examinations make families aware of child health problems, which are subsequently reported. The one counter-intuitive result is the positive and significant effect of both current and past household consumption. This may reflect reporting behaviour and/or endogeneity. In developing countries, strong pro-rich inequalities in objective indicators of health, such as infant mortality rates, are often not apparent in more subjective measures, such as reported morbidity. The better off may be more aware of their health problems and have higher expectations of health. These differences will be reflected in reported illness, for any given level of true health. As argued in section 7.3, such reporting behaviour need not bias our estimates of the child work effect on illness. The control variables are intended to pick up variation in both true health and reporting behaviour. There is a problem only if any remaining variation in reporting behaviour is determined by work status itself.

If the positive household consumption coefficient reflects endogeneity, there is a problem, since this could contaminate the work effect. We test exogeneity by the two-step method of Rivers and Vuong (1988), which is a test of the significance of reduced-form (OLS) residuals in a probit containing all the regressors of the structural model. We test the exogeneity of past work participation, as well as that of current and past household consumption. The instruments are as defined for the bivariate probit. Exogeneity of all three variables is not rejected ($\chi^2(3) = 4.94, p = 0.1765$). On an individual basis, the z-ratios on the reduced form residuals indicate marginal rejection of exogeneity of lagged consumption ($z = 1.68, p = 0.094$) but not of current consumption ($z = -0.52$).

Maximum likelihood estimation allowing for the potential endogeneity of both current and past household consumption, in addition to that of work status, is likely to prove difficult.[6] Given it is the work effect that is of central

---

[6] A two-stage conditional maximum likelihood procedure (Rivers and Vuong 1988) would not be consistent due to the binary nature of one of the potentially endogenous varibles (work).

interest, we simply check whether the estimate of this parameter appears to be contaminated by any endogeneity of consumption. Since we are treating work as endogenous, we can drop household consumption from the model and avoid omitted variables bias in the coefficient of interest. The bivariate probit work coefficient is robust to dropping either or both household consumption variables, varying between 0.5129 and 0.5332, and remaining significant at 5 per cent.

A further alternative is to replace the value of total household consumption in the model with the value of food consumption alone. Since the latter does not include expenditures on health care and medicines, it should be less endogenous to sickness. Food expenditures are the least discretionary component of the household budget and should be less sensitive to unobservable household preferences that are correlated with both child work and health investment decisions. The Rivers and Vuong test gives no indication of any endogeneity of current food expenditure, and exogeneity of lagged food expenditure is not rejected even at the 15 per cent significance level (z-ratio $= 1.38, p = 0.166$). Replacing total household consumption with food consumption raises the work coefficient in the bivariate probit from 0.5140 to 0.5711, with significance preserved at the 5 per cent level. These sensitivity checks suggest that the positive and significant effect of past child work on illness propensity is not an artefact of endogeneity bias deriving from household consumption.

Representation of child work activity through a simple participation dummy obscures any variation in the work effect with the intensity, nature, and tenure of work. Conditional on participation, hours of work at wave 1 have no significant effect on illness propensity at wave 2. In contrast to the result for weight for age, there is no significant difference between the illness effects for children working within the household and those working outside the household for pay. Illness propensity does rise non-linearly with the length of time an individual worked as a child. We estimate a bivariate probit for illness and past work status with a quadratic in past *job tenure*, in addition to work participation, included in the illness equation (Table 7.5, column 3). The assumed exogeneity of past *job tenure* is tested and not rejected. With *job tenure* included, the participation effect falls in magnitude and loses individual significance, but participation and tenure are jointly significant ($\chi^2(3) = 7.81, p = 0.0502$). Illness propensity is increasing with time in work up to a period of twenty-nine months, which corresponds to the 67th percentile of distribution for those in work.

The relation of illness propensity to past work activity differs by gender. For males, there is evidence of a job tenure effect, while for females it is participation itself that is most important. Failure to reject error independence at any reasonable level of significance in the bivariate probit for males suggests a univariate probit is adequate (Table 7.5, columns 4 and 5). This is confirmed by a Rivers and Vuong test that does not reject exogeneity of work participation and job tenure in a univariate probit. The participation effect is negative and significant at 10 per cent, while illness propensity rises significantly with job tenure until a turning point at thirty-six months, equivalent to the 75th percentile of the distribution for males in work (column 6). For females, there is a positive and significant impact of past work participation on illness propensity irrespective of the model and specification adopted. The magnitude and significance of the effect rise in moving from the univariate to bivariate probit and the latter is supported by rejection (10 per cent) of zero error correlation. The tenure effect is negative but not significant.

The explanation of these gender differences in the work–illness relationship most likely lies in the nature of work undertaken and the differential burden of other activities. Our definition of work does not include household chores. Amongst the children working at wave 1, one-third of girls were also performing household chores for at least seven hours per week, while only 13 per cent of boys were doing so. Given the greater energy that girls are exerting in the performance of household chores, the marginal burden of entering work is probably greater than that experienced by boys. Working girls are more likely to be withdrawn from school than working boys, suggesting that the intensity and nature of work undertaken by girls is more onerous.[7] For boys, work participation itself does not appear to endanger health but the risk of illness increases, up to a point, the longer they are exposed to workplace health hazards.

There is no evidence of any significant relationship between child work and subsequent growth in height (Table 7.6). The OLS estimate is slightly positive, but not significantly different from zero (column 1). Joint exogeneity of work and initial height is rejected (at the 5 per cent level). On an individual basis, only the exogeneity of initial height is rejected (column 2). Instrumenting both work and initial height, the work effect remains insignificantly different from zero (column 2). The instruments are the same as those used for past work in the determination of illness. These are significant determinants of work but are not jointly significant in the reduced form for initial height. It is difficult to find a plausible instrument for initial height in an equation for subsequent growth in height.[8] One solution is to drop initial height from the model, and allow for omitted variable bias by instrumenting work. This is implemented using only the school quality variables as instruments.

The other variables, such as the indicators of economic conditions and wealth, may have explanatory power for height and so become relevant regressors in the growth equation once initial height is dropped. This is confirmed by rejection of overidentification with the full instrument set. Following this strategy, the work coefficient switches sign, rises in magnitude, but remains insignificant (Table 7.6, column 3). The exogeneity of work is not rejected.

---

[7] Amongst non-working children there is no difference in school participation rates by gender. For working children, the school participation rate is 70% for boys but only 65% for girls.

[8] One possibility would be to use mother's age and education, on the grounds that these may influence growth in early, but not later, childhood. Tests did not support this hypothesis.

Table 7.6. *Average annual growth in height 1992/3–1997/8 against child work status in 1992–3 (sample: 6–15 years in 1992/3)*

	OLS	2SLS—Work and height instrumented	2SLS—Height dropped and work instrumented
Child worked in 1992/3	0.0293 (.0478)	0.0110 (0.4682)	−0.9941 (0.6998)
Height in 1992/3	−0.0764*** (.0048)	−0.193*** (0.0698)	
Sample size	3,164	2,870	2,870
R^2	0.6158	0.4048	0.4866
F-test of joint significance	127.01 ($p = 0.0000$)	110.19 ($p = 0.0000$)	96.95 ($p = 0.0000$)
Hausman test of exogeneity	Work	$t = 0.00$ ($p = 0.998$)	$t = 1.31$ ($p = 0.194$)
	Height	$t = 3.07$ ($p = 0.003$)	
	Work and height	$F(2.94) = 4.71$ ($p = 0.0113$)	
Reduced form: R^2 F-test of IV significance	Work	$R^2 = 0.3709$ $F(7.94) = 7.82$ ($p = 0.0000$)	$R^2 = 0.3709$ $F(2.94) = 5.48$ ($p = 0.0056$)
	Height	$R^2 = 0.7929$ $F(7.94) = 1.41$ ($p = 0.2125$)	
Overidentification		$\chi^2(5) = 6.54$ ($p = 0.2571$)	$\chi^2(1) = 4.39$ ($p = 0.0361$)

Note: Cluster adjusted robust standard errors in parentheses. *, **, and *** denote significance at 10%, 5%, and 1% respectively. $p =$ denotes p-value.

Estimating by OLS with initial height omitted gives a negative work effect significant at 10 per cent but, despite the result of the exogeneity test, one suspects this reflects OV bias—initially taller children are more likely to work and have less potential to grow. Exogeneity of initial household consumption is not rejected. But, even if this variable is instrumented, along with initial work and height, there is no change in the result that the effect of work is not significant.[9] This holds for both males and females.

The lack of a work participation effect does not mask any significant effects of work hours, work outside the household environment, or job tenure (results not presented). While childhood work appears to raise vulnerability to subsequent illness, the health impact is not sufficiently strong to impede the growth of the child. This is consistent with evidence from rural Ghana showing differences in morbidity, but not in growth, between children enrolled and children not enrolled in school (Fentiman et al. 2001).

---

[9] The change in household consumption is left out of the model to avoid any possible simultaneity. This does not appear to introduce any OV bias. The correlation between initial child work status and subsequent change in household consumption, conditional on all other regressors, is not significantly different from zero. Including the change in household consumption in the model has little or no impact on the work coefficient.

## 7.3	GUATEMALA

We have seen that child work can have immediate and delayed helth effects. We now try to assess whether the delayed effects extend as far as adult life. The retrospective information on the age at which adults begun to work contained in the Guatemala survey permits the formulation of a relatively simple empirical test. The test consists in assessing whether having worked as a child has an impact on current health status. However, the interpretation of a possible correlation as a causal relationship poses several problems.

### 7.3.1	*Econometric issues in the estimation of the effect of childhood work on adult health*

According to Behrman and Wolfe (1989), the reduced-form determinants of an adult's health generally fall into four categories: observed indicators of earlier childhood and environment, unobserved household-specific indicators, observed individual-specific indicators (e.g. gender, age), unobserved individual-specific effect and the price structure. The main concern to be addressed is that the impossibility of controlling for a set of potentially relevant variables in the estimates may generate spurious results. We can identify two sets of unobservables that are relevant to our problem at both the individual and household level.

As mentioned earlier in this chapter, one possible source of bias is the so-called 'healthy worker effect'. All else equal, and assuming that health is positively related with labour productivity, healthier individuals are more likely to be selected for work. Hence, a negative effect of work on health could be confounded by the fact that unobservable individual characteristics are not taken into account. This effect may account for the measured positive (or weakly negative) relationship in simple correlation analysis between working children and health status. Since it obviously depends on the genetically given characteristics of the individual, we call this the unobservable 'individual effect'.

A second source of bias depends on the fact that our data do not contain information on the household characteristics of the adult during his childhood: correlation between these unobserved characteristics and adult health outcomes might lead to biased estimates. Consider, for example, the relationship between the income of the household where the individual under observation was born, the work performed during childhood, and the current (adult) health status of the individual. Poor households, invest less in health and education and are more likely to send their children to work. A negative correlation between child work and adult health might be spurious as it might reflect (also) the low level of the unobserved investment in health during childhood.

Ideally, we would like to ensure that our conclusion about the relationship between child labour and health is not distorted by unobservables. One possible way to achieve this is to find a valid instrument that is uncorrelated with the unobservable term but highly correlated with the endogenous explanatory variable. However, as explained in Bound, Jaeger, and Baker (1995), and Staiger and Stock (1997), the validity of the instruments depends highly on the correlation between the instruments and the endogenous explanatory variable. The weaker the correlation, the closer the IV estimator is to the standard OLS result. Another stream of the literature—see for example Imbens and Angrist (1994)—uses experimental or quasi-experimental data to handle the endogeneity problem. The variable of interest is considered under these circumstances as a treatment. Assuming that treatment is assigned completely at random, hence uncorrelated with the unobserved characteristics of the individual, the estimation results are unbiased. Under these conditions, the random assignment can be considered as a valid instrument.

In our case, the use of any of these approaches appears to be precluded. The data set does not offer information on variables that can be used as good instruments for either unobservable individual characteristics, or unobserved past household characteristics. Also, it is difficult to assume that selection for child labour can be considered as a randomly assigned treatment. For these reasons, we decided to follow a different route, similar to the methodology chosen by Ashenfelter and Krueger (1994) to measure the return to schooling. To overcome the problems linked to unobservables, those authors used a sample of twins. We use a self-constructed sample of siblings from the Guatemalan NLSC to analyse the long-run impact of child labour on health. To control for unobservable household-specific characteristics, we transform the data in a panel structure, and estimate the model by conditional fixed effects. In this way, the household effects are taken care of by the fixed effects, and the estimated coefficient can be considered as unbiased by the unobserved past household characteristics.

Since our data set is not restricted to monozygotic, genetically identical, twins as in the case of Ashenfelter and Krueger, we still have the problem that the coefficient of interest to us might be contaminated by individual-specific characteristics. Were that the case, the estimator would be biased according to the formula

$$E(b_2) = \beta_2 + \beta_3 \gamma_2, \tag{1}$$

where $E(b_2)$ is the estimated coefficient of the effect of child labour on adult health, β_2 is the unbiased impact, β_3 is the effect of the unobservable variable on health, and γ_2 is the correlation between the unobservable individual-specific characteristic and child labour. The question is the sign of γ_2. As there is no rationale for assuming that less healthy, hence weaker, children are sent to work—and there certainly is no evidence, even anecdotal, pointing in that direction—we cannot assume that γ_2 is negative. There is more support, both theoretical and empirical, for assuming that the correlation between the unobservable genetic health endowment and child labour is positive (i.e. that healthier children are more likely to be selected to work).[10] Hence, it seems reasonable to assume that, if biased, our estimator will underestimate the true impact of child labour on health.

7.3.2 *Sample description*

The Guatemalan National Survey on Living Conditions (NSLC) of the year 2000 provides information on household composition, education, migration, economic activities, and health indicators. The two main variables of interest are the health status, and the age of entry into the labour market. As the true health status is not observable, we use a self-reported health indicator taking value 1 if the person reports having had bad health in the last month, 0 otherwise. This might cause a measurement error in the dependent variable. If the measurement error is systematically related to one or more of the explanatory variables, the estimator will be biased. However, epidemiological studies show that self-reported health indicators seem to be good predictors of bad health status and mortality. Over a nine-year period, individuals reporting a health problem have a death rate three times greater than that of individuals reporting good health (Kaplan and Camacho 1983).

Child labour is defined as a dummy taking value 1 if the person entered the labour market before the age of 15, value 0 otherwise. Around 67 per cent of the individuals in the sub-sample reported having worked during childhood; 25 per cent declared they had health problems (see Table 7.7).The average age of the individuals in the sub-sample was about 24. The average age of labour market entry was 13. The majority (52 per cent) were rural residents, and only 22 per cent were born in an urban area. Forty-two per cent were women. Fourteen per cent had some education. Almost 80 per cent reported being employed in the week preceding the interview. Forty-three per cent reported having suffered from an individual shock, and 31 per cent from a collective shock, during the six months prior to the interview.

7.3.3 *The logit model*

In this subsection, we present the estimates obtained by a standard logit regression. The dependent variable is the self-reported health index. The independent variable is the dummy indicating whether the individual was a child labourer.[11]

---

[10] This is the well-known healthier work effect, which, however, has not found overwhelming empirical support.

[11] We also run regressions replacing the dummy for child labour with the actual age of labour market entry in both the standard logit and conditional logit set-up. These results confirm the negative impact of early labour market entry on health (although with varying levels of significance). However, since using the age of labour market entry as a proxy for child labour assumes that the effect is linear and independent of being an adult or not, we consider these results not as sound as the ones presented in this section. Nevertheless, for completeness we show the results in the Appendix.

Table 7.7. *Summary statistics*

Variable	Obs.	Mean	Std. dev.	Min.	Max.
Age	3,409	23.96	9.09	16	85
Gender	3,409	0.42	0.50	0	1
Labour market entry	3,407	12.94	4.04	6	45
Child labour	3,409	0.66	0.47	0	1
Self-reported health index	3,409	0.25	0.43	0	1
Collective shock	3,409	0.31	0.46	0	1
Individual shock	3,409	0.43	0.49	0	1
Education	3,409	0.14	0.35	0	1
Employed last week	3,409	0.79	0.40	0	1
Worked last week	3,409	0.70	0.45	0	1
Born urban	3,324	0.22	0.41	0	1
Rural resident	3,409	0.52	0.50	0	1
Income	3,399	6.44	1.08	2.52	9.11

Source: Guatemalan NSLC.

The control variables include the education of the parents as an indicator of the childhood environment of the current adult,[12] a dummy for an urban birthplace to control for the price structure of health services in earlier childhood, and one for each Guatemalan state to control for geographical differences. The other controls are individual-specific characteristics like age, gender, education, and current household characteristics like income, individual and collective shocks,[13] a dummy for rural residency, and a dummy for indoor plumbing. Education is a dummy taking value 0 if the individual has nothing less than completed primary education, 1 otherwise.[14] The inclusion of income and education allows us to distinguish the direct effects of child labour from the indirect ones it might have through higher earnings, or reduced educational achievement.

Table 7.8 shows the results. The coefficient of the child labour dummy has the expected positive sign in all model specifications, but the coefficient is never highly significant (the *p*-values are all around 0.10). As neither education nor household income is significant, the main effect of child labour on health appears to be direct, rather than indirect. Age, gender, and individual and collective shocks are highly significant. As was to be expected, age is positively

[12] As we have very few observations in some groups we aggregated the variable in three categories. No education, preparatory school, and adult's education are grouped together and indicate the lowest level of education. Primary school constitutes the second category. Secondary, higher, and postgraduate education are combined to indicate the highest level of education. The reference category in the estimates is the lowest level of education.

[13] For the precise definition of these variables see Chapter 8.

[14] We also experimented with various different cut-off points, but this had no significant effect on the results.

Table 7.8. *Logit estimates*

	(1)	(2)	(3)	(4)
Child labour	.161	.159	.151	.148
	(.096)*	(.097)*	(.097)	(.097)
Born urban	.069	.073	.079	.079
	(.119)	(.119)	(.12)	(.119)
Father primary school	.11	.096	.111	.11
	(.1)	(.101)	(.108)	(.108)
Father higher education	.428	.404	.414	.409
	(.174)**	(.176)**	(.176)**	(.176)**
Mother primary school	−.118	−.118	−.104	−.106
	(.104)	(.104)	(.105)	(.105)
Mother higher education	.113	.102	.109	.108
	(.188)	(.192)	(.192)	(.192)
Age	.017	.017	.017	.017
	(.004)***	(.004)***	(.005)***	(.005)***
Rural resident	−.181	−.157	−.161	−.161
	(.102)*	(.181)	(.181)	(.181)
Gender	.251	.254	.244	.237
	(.084)***	(.084)***	(.085)***	(.087)***
Water	.013	.035	.05	.051
	(.107)	(.108)	(.109)	(.109)
Individual shock	.378	.282	.281	.281
	(.085)***	(.09)***	(.09)***	(.09)***
Collective shock	—	.331	.333	.334
		(.094)***	(.094)***	(.094)***
Income	—	.101	.108	.109
		(.175)	(.176)	(.176)
Education	—	—	.144	.143
			(.129)	(.129)
Worked last week	—	—	—	−.037
				(.093)
Controls	—	—	—	—
Obs.	3248	3246	3246	3246
Log likelihood	−1765.253	−1757.343	−1756.727	−1756.644
χ^2 statistic	95.817	108.27	109.501	109.666

Note: Standard errors in brackets. The results of several further controls are not depicted.

associated with bad health. Women are more likely to experience bad health. Individual and collective shocks also increase the probability of bad health. The finding that having a father with higher education has a detrimental effect on health is puzzling. The mother's education has no significant effect.

7.3.4   *The Conditional-Fixed-Effects Logit model*

The results obtained by the logit model suffer from the defect that we do not control for unobserved heterogeneity. There are several ways in which one can address the problem in a cross-section analysis. If there is a suitable proxy for the unobserved effect, one can estimate an equation by the logit model described before. If there are suitable instruments for the explanatory variables, one can apply instrumental variable methods. As none of these strategies appears to be feasible in the present case, however, we resorted to using a sub-sample of adult siblings. If siblings have a common household-specific background, we can hope to capture the effect of this unobservable characteristic through the information contained in the sub-sample.

The sub-sample was selected in two stages. First, we selected all persons aged 16 or more. Secondly, we selected all households that included siblings.[15] In some cases, we found more than one set of siblings in the same household. Since each household member was required to declare his or her relationship to the household head, we dealt with the problem of multiple sets by considering the offspring of the household head, and that of each sibling of the household head, as a different 'household'. Table 7.9 shows the frequency distribution of the number of siblings in each set. The sub-sample is clearly not representative of Guatemalan society. As we shall control for the unobservable common household background of each set of siblings, and other relevant factors, however, the estimates should not be affected by the selection criteria.

Table 7.9. *Household composition*

No. of siblings	No. of households	Observations in the sample
2	935	1,870
3	339	1,017
4	96	384
5	21	105
6	2	12
7	3	21
All	1,396	3,409

Source: Guatemalan NSLC.

[15] The latter was only possible in the case where the siblings lived in the same household at the time of the interview. This might pose a section problem, but as our estimates are based on within-household variation rather than on between-household variation we do not think this might be a serious problem.

After identifying the sets of siblings, we transformed the data in a panel by defining Y_{ij} (the dependent variable), X_{ij} (the independent variables) as observable characteristics of person j in household i (i.e. sibling j in the set i). Assuming that the unobserved household-specific effect is constant within siblings, we are able to control for this effect by using the Conditional-Fixed-Effects Logit Estimator described in more details in Appendix 7.1.3.[16]

While not contaminated by the household-specific effect, the estimator will still be influenced by the individual-specific effect. Since correlation between the unobservable individual-specific effect and child labour is assumed to be non-negative, we can however interpret our estimator as a lower bound of the true impact. The results of the Conditional- Fixed-Effect estimation are reported in Table 7.10.

The estimate of the β vector gives us the effect of each element of x_t on the log-odds ratio. Unfortunately, we cannot estimate partial effects on the response probabilities unless we plug in a value α_i, and we cannot estimate average partial effects because that would require specifying the distribution of α_i.

All 'households' (sets of siblings) that have the same value of the dichotomous dependent variable health status are automatically eliminated from the sample. Any variable that takes the same value for all siblings belonging to the same 'household' is also dropped. The omitted variables represent common household-specific characteristics. Of the remaining variables, gender and age remain highly significant. As in the last subsection, the effect of child labour on health appears to operate directly, rather than indirectly through education.

Notice that, once the household unobservables are taken into account, the effect of child labour on health becomes highly significant and of a relevant magnitude. Since the coefficient of child labour is equivalent to the log-odds ratios, our results predict an over 40 per cent increase in the probability of having health problems as an adult if the person worked as a child. This is a substantial effect. Since our result is a lower bound, the 'true causal effect' could be even larger. Another interesting point is that, in contrast with received wisdom, our results indicate that the unobserved household-specific effect generates a downward bias in the coefficient. The point estimates reported in Table 7.8 (the logit estimates) are in fact lower and less significant than those estimated by the Conditional-Fixed-Effects Logit.

---

[16] Unconditional-Fixed-Effects and Random-Effects estimation methods are not applicable in our framework. Random-Effect estimation requires the additional assumption that the unobserved error terms, α_i (for household-specific effect) and d_j (for individual-specific effect) are uncorrelated with the explanatory variables. Since it is hard to assume that unobserved household- and individual-specific effects are uncorrelated with child labour, we will employ the Fixed-Effect estimation techniques. Although the name suggests it, fixed effect does not necessary mean that the unobserved effect is non-random. In our application, it rather means that we allow for arbitrary correlation between the unobserved effect and the observed variables (see Wooldridge 2002). As shown by Andersen (1970) and Chamberlain (1980), however, the Unconditional-Fixed-Effects Estimator is not able to control for the household-specific effect under general circumstances, because of the incidental parameter problem described by Neyman and Scott (1948).

Table 7.10. *Conditional-Fixed-Effects Logit*

	(1)	(2)	(3)	(4)
Child labour	.369	.369	.363	.348
	(.188)**	(.188)**	(.184**)	(.185*)
Born urban	.04	.04	.04	.06
	(.29)	(.291)	(.291)	(.291)
Father primary school	1.596	1.596	1.603	1.699
	(1.116)	(1.116)	(1.115)	(1.12)
Mother primary school	.33	.33	.326	.275
	(.847)	(.847)	(.847)	(.845)
Mother higher education	.863	.865	.857	.73
	(1.659)	(1.659)	(1.659)	(1.655)
Age	.025	.025	.025	.027
	(.014)*	(.014)*	(.0.14)*	(.014)*
Rural resident	—	—	—	—
Gender	.394	.394	.387	.358
	(.135)***	(.135)***	(.137)***	(.139)***
Water	—	—	—	—
Individual shock	—	—	—	—
Collective shock	—	—	—	—
Income	—	—	—	—
Education	—	—	.081	.078
			(.271)	(.271)
Worked last week	—	—	—	−.192
				(.161)
Controls	—	—	—	—
Obs.	1080	1078	1078	1078
Log likelihood	−381.684	−380.953	−380.908	−380.192
χ^2 statistic	16.923	16.999	17.089	18.521

Note: Standard errors in brackets. The results of several further controls are not depicted.

7.4 CONCLUDING REMARKS

Does work during childhood have a negative impact on health? We tried to answer this question by looking for possible short- and long-term effects during childhood, and for even longer-term effects in adult life. We also tried to distinguish the effects of different types of work.

The evidence from rural Vietnam suggests that work has no negative short-term effect on childhood health. It also shows that children doing paid work are significantly heavier than their contemporaries who are either working for the household, or not working. Assuming that health is an increasing function of weight for this age group, the dominant form of child work—unpaid agricultural work for the household—appears to have no short-term impact on health. Paid work may even be beneficial to nutrition and health. The most likely pathway for this effect is through the direction of household nutritional resources to the child earner. Health does appear to determine the selection of children for work. Controlling for a large range of covariates, the simple cross-section relationship between child work status and weight for age is significantly positive. Differencing out fixed individual and local factors, the relation weakens and becomes insignificant, suggesting that the initial positive relationship is attributable to selection of the inherently stronger and healthier children into work. The absence of a contemporaneous negative impact of child agricultural work on health is robust to a variety of estimators, identification strategies, specifications, and health indicators.

In the longer term, child work appears to have negative health repercussions. Individuals working during childhood are significantly more likely to report illness up to five years later. This is true after controlling for an extensive range of individual, household, and community-level covariates and for common unobservable determinants of past work and current illness. The result is robust to different empirical specifications and identification strategies, and is consistent with evidence from Brazil showing that self-reported health in adulthood is lower, the younger the age at entry to the workforce (Giuffrida, Iunes, and Savedo 2001, Kassouf, Mckee, and Mossialos 2001). We add to this evidence, and strengthen it by correcting for any correlation through unobservables. The nature of the effect differs by gender. For females, work participation appears to provoke illness in the long term. For males, there is no work participation effect, but illness propensity increases with the period of time spent in childhood work. While childhood work raises the risk of future illness, the health impact is not sufficiently large to impede the growth of the child.

The analysis of the Guatemalan data reveals that adult health is influenced by the age of entry into the labour market. Using a sample of Guatemalan siblings, and thus controlling for unobserved household characteristics, we have shown that having worked as a child increases by about 40 per cent the probability of reporting a bad health status. There are two general pathways through which this effect may operate. First, it may be that a child suffers a workplace accident with long-term consequences for health. Secondly, it may be that there is a latency period in the development of work-related health problems (e.g. of conditions that are the cumulative effects of sustained exposure to chemicals, poor posture, or heavy lifting). The evidence that male illness propensity is increasing with past job tenure is consistent with the latent development of health problems. This justifies public concern for chilòdren working over extended periods (ILO 2002).

Some caveats are in order. The data at our disposal have led us to focus on the most common form of child labour, agricultural work. That was made explicit in the case of Vietnam, but was implicit also in that of Guatemala, because the data show that the vast majority of children in that country work in agriculture today (and this was even more true twenty years ago). Although work in agriculture is the most commonly practised form of child labour, it is however fair to say that it is unlikely to be more damaging than some of the work undertaken by children in large urban centres.

It must be kept in mind, furthermore, that we have also uncovered evidence of a positive effect of paid work. As we control for total household consumption, this effect appears to operate through a reallocation of household resources in favour of working children. That is indeed the theoretical prediction of Pitt et al. (1990). If the reallocation in favour of working children is at the expense of others, however, this may still be bad for other children in the family. There is empirical support for this hypothesis. Using data on calorie intakes from rural Indonesia, Ralston (1997) found the intra-household calorie allocation to be positively related to children's labour contributions, and morbidity to be negatively related to calorie intake. On the other hand, child work raises household resources. If household income increases more than the share of non-working children decreases, the net effect on non-working children could be positive. The available evidence suggests that it is not. A study of rural Guatemala, Immink and Payongayong (1999), does in fact find that, while participation of school-age children in farm production does not appear to reduce their own growth and development, its effect on the growth of younger siblings is negative.

The international community wants better evidence on the health consequences of different types of child work in order to identify hazardous work, make effective its prohibition, and offer rehabilitation to children withdrawn from such activities (ILO 2002: 12). Our finding of significantly negative health effects of child work strengthens the case for policies that reduce children's work engagement. Our finding that this is true also of the bulk of child economic activity, agricultural work, does not make the task politically any easier.

Appendix 7.1   ECONOMETRIC METHODOLOGY

A7.1.1   *Estimation of contemporaneous effects*

The estimation of the contemporaneous relationship between health and child labour is based on the following model,

$$h_{ijt} = \alpha l_{ijt} + X_{ijt}\beta + Z_{jt}\delta + \tau_t + \lambda_j + \mu_i + \varepsilon_{ijt} \tag{A1}$$

where is h_{ijt} health/nutrition status, proxied by weight-for-age z-score, of child i belonging to community j at time t. l_{ijt} is a binary indicator of work status, X_{ijt} and Z_{jt} are vectors of health/nutrition determinants defined at the individual/household and commune levels respectively. As we control for height, the other regressors inform of relationships with thinness. The individual-specific effects (μ_i) represent unobservable heterogeneity in health endowments and preferences. The community effects (λ_j) capture unmeasured health determinants that vary across location but not time, such as climate, infrastructure, and public hygiene. The time effect (τ_t) captures, for example, the impact, not fully reflected in the measured variables, of the rapid economic transition that Vietnam has experienced over the period. We also allow time dummy inter-actions with time-constant regressors (region and ethnicity). The idiosyncratic errors are represented by ε_{ijt}.

Endogeneity of work status can arise through its dependence on μ_i (unob-servable hetergeneity) and/or its correlation with ε_{ijt}. To eliminate the first, we estimate by ordinary least squares in first differences (FD-OLS). This procedure removes also the community effects. Standard errors are made robust to hetero-skedasticity, and adjusted for clustering at the commune level.[17] Having purged the individual effects, we use instrumental variables to test and, where appro-priate, allow for simultaneity bias. Estimation is by two-stage least squares on first differences (FD-2SLS). In addition to child work status, the proxy for living standards—household consumption—is a potential source of simultan-eity bias. A sick child may lose weight, stop work, and cause the household expenditure to rise through medical care expenses. Out-of-pocket payments account for more than 80 per cent of health care finance in Vietnam, and absorb a large share of total household expenditure for a substantial fraction of the population (Wagstaff and van Doorslaer 2003). Household living stand-ards may also be responsive to child health through the labour supply of other household members. Measurement error in household consumption is also a potential problem.

A7.1.2 *A model for long-term effects of child labour on health*

The impact of child work at the first wave on the probability of illness at the second is estimated through a bivariate probit system with latent indices of illness and work propensity specified as

$$h_{ij2}^* = \alpha l_{ij1} + X_{ij2}\beta_2 + X_{ij1}\beta_1 + Z_{j2}\delta_2 + Z_{j1}\delta_1 + \upsilon_{ij2} \qquad (A2)$$

$$l_{ij1}^* = X_{ij1}^*\psi + Z_{j1}^*\zeta + \upsilon_{ij1} \qquad (A3)$$

$$(\upsilon_{ij1}, \upsilon_{ij2}) \sim N(0, \Omega) \qquad (A4)$$

where 1, 2 index first and second wave values, (X, X^*) are defined at the individual/household level and (Z, Z^*) at the community level. Observed bin-ary indicators are given by the indicator functions $h_{ij2} = 1(h_{ij2}^* > 0)$ and $l_{ij1} = 1(l_{ij1}^* > 0)$. Testing the significance of the error correlation coefficient provides a test of exogeneity. Identification requires at least one argument of (X_{ij1}^*, Z_{j1}^*) to be excuded from (X_{ij1}, Z_{j1}) It is assumed that household land

[17] Adjustment for clustering is necessary in the case that the commune effects do not enter in the additive form specified in (A1).

holdings, community labour market conditions, and school quality influence child work at time 1 but, conditional on all else, do not influence health at time 2.

The growth regression, with the dependent variable defined as the average annual change in height between waves (Δh_{ij}), is specified as follows,

$$\Delta h_{ij} = \alpha l_{ij1} + \theta h_{ij1} + X_{ij1}\beta_1 + \Delta X_{ij}\beta_2 + Z_{j1}\delta + \Delta Zj\delta + \varepsilon_{ij} \qquad (A5)$$

where h_{ij1} is initial height, index 1 indicates first wave values, and Δ indicates across-wave differences. Starting from a specification including initial values and changes in all variables, restrictions supported by the data are imposed. Some commune-level health/nutrition determinants are only available for wave two and these are included as proxies for conditions prevailing over the previous period. The error term includes any unobservable permanent factors that govern potential growth at every point in time. Endogeneity is a problem in the instance that such factors are correlated with unobservable determinants of initial work status and/or height. Such correlation cannot be ruled out, although it is probably much smaller than that between unobservable determinants of work status and the *level* of height. To allow for this, we complete a recursive model with equations for initial work status and height as follows,

$$l_{ij1}^* = \gamma h_{ij1} + X_{ij1}^*\psi + Z_{j1}^*\zeta + v_{ij1}, \quad l_{ij1} = 1\left(l_{ij1}^* \geq 0\right) \qquad (A6)$$

$$h_{ij1} = X_{ij1}^{**}\xi + Z_{j1}^{**}\varsigma + v_{ij1}. \qquad (A7)$$

The child's height influences work decisions. But height, as seems reasonable, is assumed to be unresponsive to *current* work status. Estimation is by 2SLS. Finding a variable that determines initial height but not subsequent growth, and so acts as an instrument for the former, is difficult. Consequently, we also estimate a restricted model from which initial height is omitted.

A7.1.3 *Conditional-Fixed-Effects Logit Estimator*

One way to estimate the model describe in the text would be to include dummy variables for the different households, and then maximize the unconditional likelihood function. Chamberlain (1980) and Andersen (1970) offer an estimator of the structural parameters that is consistent even in the presence of incidental parameters.[18] The so-called Conditional-Fixed-Effects Logit

---

[18] The unconditional maximum-likelihood estimator of the incidental parameters (household-specific effects) is consistent as $T \to \infty$ (which is the number of siblings per set in our case) for fixed N (sets of siblings) but inconsistent as $N \to \infty$ for fixed T. The inconsistency arises because the number of incidental parameters increases without bound, while the information about each incidental parameter remains fixed. Since the MLEs for α_i and β are not independent of each other for the discrete choice model, the MLE estimator remains inconsistent.

Estimator is obtained by conditioning the likelihood function on minimal sufficient statistics for the incidental parameters, and then maximizing the conditional likelihood function. In the logit case, such a statistic can be $\sum y_{i,j}$ (the sum of the dependent variables in one unit). The conditional probability for y_i given $\sum y_{i,j}$ is

$$\Pr\left(y_i \Big| \sum_{j=1}^{M} y_{i,j}\right) = \frac{\exp\left[\beta' \sum_{j=1}^{M} x_{i,j} y_{i,j}\right]}{\sum_{d \in B_i} \exp\left[\beta' \sum_{j=1}^{M} x_{i,j} d_{i,j}\right]}$$

$$\text{where } B_i = \left\{(d_{i1}, \ldots, d_{iM},) | d_{ij} = 0 \text{ or } 1, \text{ and } \sum_{j=1}^{M} d_{i,j} = \sum_{i=1}^{M} y_{i,j}\right\}. \quad (A8)$$

Equation (A8) is in a conditional logit form, with the alternative sets B_i varying across observations i. Since the probability does not depend on the incidental parameter α_i, the conditional-maximum-likelihood estimator β can be obtained by maximizing the corresponding likelihood function.[19]

[19] An obvious drawback of this approach is that it cannot produce estimates for the incidental parameters. Furthermore, explanatory variables that do not vary with time cancel out in the likelihood function.

8

Credit Markets and Child Labour
The Effect of Shocks, Credit Rationing, and Insurance

If there were perfect capital and insurance markets, human capital accumulation would depend only on the relative benefits and costs of education, and its path over time would not be influenced by idiosyncratic shocks. But we know that capital markets are far from perfect, especially in developing countries, and that this is even truer of insurance markets, formal or informal. We saw in Chapter 2 that, in the absence of perfect asset and credit markets, investment in human capital may be either inefficiently low or inefficiently high, and that an erratic shock can put a family in a state of extreme poverty. In the present chapter, we try to assess the extent to which capital market imperfections, and lack of insurance, *actually* affect the supply of child labour.

From a theoretical point of view, changes in child labour supply and investment in human capital are two of the possible responses to the occurrence of adverse events. This has important policy implications. If the role of child labour as a buffer against uninsured shocks is substantial, policies aimed at reducing household risk exposure may have a substantial bearing on children's labour supply. The strategic relevance of policies aimed at promoting the development of capital markets, and at improving risk-coping and risk-reduction mechanisms, is stressed in Holzmann and Jorgensen (2002), and World Bank (2001).

We saw in Chapter 5 that income has a relatively small impact on the supply of child work. Sustained income growth, or large transfer programmes, would thus be required to substantially reduce child work by that route. Moreover, Deb and Rosati (2002) find that households with very similar observable characteristics may have very different propensities to invest in children's education. These findings are coherent with a potential role of credit rationing and lack of insurance mechanisms, but the direct evidence of the effects of these market imperfections is limited essentially to the seminal contribution of Jacoby and Skoufias (1997). Beyond that, Dehejia and Gatti (2002) find that credit market development has an impact on child labour. Another recent paper, Edmonds (2002), performs an indirect test of the relevance of credit constraints for child work by evaluating the effects of an expected change in household income.

The Guatemalan Living Standards Measurement Survey ENCOVI 2000 contains information on shocks, access to credit, and availability of insurance mechanisms. The amount of detail on themes related to vulnerability makes this survey quite unique. In what follows, we draw heavily on the analysis of this data set by Guarcello, Mealli, and Rosati (2003) to show how access to credit, and the presence of insurance programmes, affect domestic responses to several kinds of shocks. Details of the questions used to construct these variables are reported in Appendix 8.2.

8.1 THE GUATEMALAN DATA SET

ENCOVI 2000 covers 7,276 (3,852 rural and 3,424 urban) households following a probabilistic survey design. The survey is representative at the national and regional level, as well as at the level of urban and rural areas. There are separate modules on (1) risks and shocks, (2) conflict, crime, and violence, (3) social capital, and (4) migration.

8.1.1 *Access to credit, insurance, and shocks*

As most of our attention will be devoted to the effects of shocks, and access to credit and insurance, we start by providing precise definitions, and presenting summary statistics, of these variables.

Credit rationing. The survey contains questions relating to access to credit. In particular, households are asked whether they have applied for credit and, in case of application, whether they were denied credit. We define as 'credit rationed' households that did not apply for credit for one of the following reasons:

(*a*) institutions offering credit are not available,
(*b*) does not know how to ask for credit,
(*c*) does not have the required characteristics,
(*d*) does not have collateral,
(*e*) interest rates too high,
(*f*) insufficient income,
(*g*) institutions do not give credit to this kind of household.

Households that applied for, but were denied, credit will also be classified as credit rationed.

Table 8.1 shows descriptive statistics of credit-rationed households, broken down by poverty level.[1] About 50 per cent of the households in Guatemala are credit rationed according to our definition. The incidence rises with poverty,

---

[1] The 'extreme' poverty line is defined as the yearly cost of the *canasta basica*, the food basket that provides the minimum daily caloric requirement, estimated in Q. 1912. The 'non-extreme' poverty line (being just poor) is defined as the extreme poverty line plus an allowance for non-food items, estimated in Q. 4319.

Table 8.1. *Distribution of credit-rationed households by poverty level*

	Extremely poor	Poor	Not poor	Total
Reasons for not applying for credit Institutions offering credit not available	5.13	1.98	1.86	2.39
Does not know how to ask for credit	5.92	4.78	3.05	4.2
Does not have the required characteristics	8.28	11.34	11.02	10.76
Does not have the collateral	12.23	12.5	8.43	10.7
Afraid of losing collateral	5.13	5.53	4.58	5.06
Interest rates too high	5.33	6.56	12.42	8.92
Insufficient income	34.12	36.82	37.85	36.87
Institutions do not give credit to households in that condition	22.09	18.24	13.01	16.54
Other reasons	1.78	2.25	7.77	4.57
Total	100	100	100	100
Credit refused following application	14.43	14.47	10.71	12.28
Credit-rationed households	67.84	58.65	39.78	49.41

Source: *Encuesta de condiciones de vida* (ENCOVI) 2000. Instituto Nacional de Estadísticas (INE) Guatemala.

ranging from about 40 per cent for households above the poverty line to almost 70 per cent for extremely poor households. In absolute terms, lack of income, lack of collateral, and household conditions are the most common reasons for not applying for credit. Credit rationing through the interest rate mainly applies to non-poor households. The rate of rejection of credit applications is similar for poor and non-poor households.

Shocks. ENCOVI 2000 contains a set of questions pertaining to the occurrence of shocks (see Appendix 8.2 for details). Shocks are divided into two broad categories: collective and individual (idiosyncratic). Collective shocks include events like earthquakes, floods, fires, etc. Individual shocks include loss of employment, death, etc.[2] Households can report more than one shock from each category. A household is classified as hit by a shock if it reported at least one shock. The analysis used two dummies, one for each of the broad categories of shocks (collective and individual). Other classifications were also tried, but did not change the main results.

About 50 per cent of the households surveyed reported experiencing one or more shocks in the year 2000, as shown in Table 8.2. Of these, 12 per cent

[2] For a detailed description and analysis see Tesliue and Lindert (2002).

Table 8.2. *Percentage of households affected by collective or individual shocks*

		Yes (%)	No (%)		Shock	No. of households	%
Collective shock	Yes (%)	18	12		Individual	2,769	38.06
	No (%)	20	50		Collective	2,142	29.44
				Total 100	Total households surveyed	7,276	

Source: *Encuesta de condiciones de vida* (ENCOVI) 2000. Instituto Nacional de Estadísticas (INE) Guatemala.

reported experiencing natural or economic shocks affecting the community, 20 per cent shocks directly affecting the family, and 20 per cent affecting both. Of the 7,276 households surveyed, 38 per cent were affected by individual (idiosyncratic) shocks and about 30 per cent by collective shocks (see Appendix 8.4 for additional details). The most frequently reported collective shock is a general increase in prices, as shown in Table 8.3. This could reflect a misperception of the economic environment, or just a generic complaint about the cost of living. In any case, excluding this form of shock from the definition of the dummy variables does not change the results obtained.

Risk reduction and risk-coping mechanisms. The questionnaire permits us to identify whether an individual has medical insurance (public or private). A dummy variable (*Insurance*) was created, taking the value of 1 if at least one member of the household has medical insurance. Information was insufficient to identify whether households belonged to an informal social support network.

'Expected' expenditure. Expected expenditure is computed by regressing household expenditure on a set of variables (age and sex of the household head, parents' education, parents' occupation and sector of employment, urban/rural area, regional dummies, household structure).

Child and household characteristics. A set of control variables is used to take into consideration individual and household characteristics. These include: the age of the child (*age, age^2*); a gender dummy (*Female*); a dummy taking value 1 if the child belongs to an indigenous household (*Indigenous*); the number of household members (*Hhsize*); the number of children aged 0–5 in the household (*numkidsy*) and the number of school-age children (*numkidso*); a dummy taking value 1 if the child is a girl and there are children aged 0–5 in the household (*femkidsy*); a series of dummies for the the mother's (*M_*) and for the father's (*F_*) education.

8.1.2 *Child work*

Child work is very common in Guatemala. Some 506,000 children aged 7–14 years, one-fifth of total children in this age group, are engaged in work.

Table 8.3. *Percentage of households affected by different types of shock*

Individual shock	%	Collective shock	%
Loss of employment of any member	13.67	Earthquake	0.87
Lowered income of any member	17.42	Drought	6.32
Bankruptcy of a family business	2.55	Flood	2.33
Illness or serious accident of a working member of the household	15.64	Storms	3.28
Death of a working member of the household	2.19	Hurricane	1.66
Death of another member of the household	3.03	Plagues	16.69
Abandonment by the household head	1.67	Landslides	1.41
Fire in the house/business/property	0.27	Forest fires	1.1
Criminal act	4.79	Business closing	0.81
Land dispute	1.56	Massive lay-offs	0.85
Family dispute	1.82	General increase in price	63.01
Loss of cash or in-kind assistance	1.82	Public protests	0.87
Fall in prices of products in the household business	7.54	Other covariate shocks	0.82
Loss of harvest	24.95		
Other idiosyncratic shocks	1.08		
Total	100	Total	100

Source: *Encuesta de condiciones de vida* (ENCOVI) 2000. Instituto Nacional de Estadísticas (INE) Guatemala.

Most are employed on the family farm or in petty business, and live in rural areas. Guatemala ranks third highest, after Bolivia and Ecuador, in child work prevalence among the fourteen Latin American and Caribbean (LAC) countries for which data are available. In terms of per capita GDP, on the other hand, the country ranks fifth lowest. Guatemala's relative level of child work is therefore high compared to its relative level of income.

The decision to consider the age range 7–14 in order to define child work is based on several considerations. School in Guatemala starts at 7, and no significant amount of child labour is found below the age of 7. The basic education cycle (*ciclo basico*) requires, in most cases, nine years of study. It should also be noted that current legislation allows children to work legally from the age of 14. Results do not change if child work is taken to refer to the 7–13 age range.

Table 8.4. *Children aged 7–14, by sex, type of activity, and residence*

Sex	Activity	Urban		Rural		Total	
		%	No.	%	No.	%	No.
Male	Work only	4.3	19,285	12.3	104,161	9.5	123,446
	Study only	73.9	334,299	53.9	455,964	60.9	790,263
	Work and study	10.1	45,587	19.7	166,924	16.4	212,511
	Total work[a]	14.4	64,872	32.0	271,085	25.9	335,957
	Total study[b]	78.2	379,886	73.6	622,888	67.3	1,002,774
	Neither	11.8	53,308	14.1	119,329	13.3	172,637
Female	Work only	4.1	17,820	6.8	54,249	5.9	72,509
	Study only	74.6	323,451	58.4	464,030	64.1	787,764
	Work and study	7.6	32,764	8.3	66,386	8.1	99,546
	Total work[a]	11.7	50,584	15.1	120,635	14.0	172,055
	Total study[b]	82.2	356,215	66.7	530,416	72.2	887,310
	Neither	13.8	59,770	26.5	210,491	22	270,371
Total	Work only	4.2	37,105	9.7	158,410	7.7	195,515
	Study only	74.2	657,750	56.1	919,994	62.4	1,577,744
	Work and study	8.8	78,351	14.2	233,310	12.3	311,661
	Total work[a]	13.0	115,456	23.9	391,720	20.0	507,176
	Total study[b]	83.0	736,101	70.3	1,153,304	74.7	1,889,405
	Neither	12.8	113,078	20.1	329,820	17.5	442,898

[a] 'Total work' refers to children that work only *and* children that work and study.
[b] 'Total study' refers to children that study only *and* children that work and study.

Source: *Encuesta de condiciones de vida* (ENCOVI) 2000. Instituto Nacional de Estadísticas (INE) Guatemala.

Table 8.4 gives more detailed information on children's activities in Guatemala. It shows that a significant proportion of children, 17 per cent, are reportedly neither working nor attending school. This group includes children, mainly girls, performing full-time household chores, undeclared workers, and children who cannot attend school (either because there is no school near home, or because getting to the nearest school is too expensive), but do not have the opportunity to perform any productive activity. These 'idle' children are nearly as numerous as working children, and constitute as great a policy concern. This group is the most sensitive to changes in policy and in exogenous variables. The table shows important gender differences in child activity status. Boys are more likely to work, but girls are more likely to be neither working nor attending school. It also shows that indigenous children have a lower school attendance rate, and a higher work participation rate than the rest.

8.2 ECONOMETRIC METHODOLOGY

The theoretical analysis of Chapter 2 leads us to expect that parental decisions regarding whether a child will study only, work only, work and study, or do neither are guided by an unobservable utility index,

$$I = f(Z, X, C, S),$$

where Z is a vector of household characteristics (including household expected or 'permanent' income net of children's contribution), X a vector of proxies for the marginal rates of return to child work and education, C a vector of variables relating to credit rationing, and access to public or private insurance mechanisms, and S a vector of realized shocks.

The main econometric problem is endogeneity. Being credit rationed, belonging to an insurance scheme, or being part of a social security system, may all be endogenous to a certain extent. Not even the occurrence of certain idiosyncratic shocks is entirely exogenous. Whether strong winds will take the roof off a house may partly depend on how well the house is built. The decision to spend more or less money on making the house safe is not independent of decisions regarding the labour supply and school attendance of the children who will live in it. Given the relevance of the endogeneity issue, we discuss the approach followed at some length in the Appendix to the volume.

The approach followed by Guarcello, Mealli, and Rosati (2003) is based on propensity score matching methods, and regression analysis. Given that adjusting for unobservables tends to be quite subjective, and very sensitive to distributional and functional assumptions, and usually relies on the existence of a valid instrument, the analysis rests on the so-called unconfoundedness assumption. The latter is similar to the so-called selection-on-observables assumption: exposure to treatment is random within cells defined by the observed variables X. We now discuss how the propensity score is to be specified, and used for analysing the effects of shocks, insurance, and credit rationing on child labour and school attendance.

Shocks, insurance, and credit rationing are defined at the household level. A child is said to be 'treated' if his or her household is affected by the shock. This impliess that, even though we want to analyse the effects of the treatment variables on children, these variables are assigned at the household level. The clustered structure of the units of analysis (children) has some methodological implications. First of all, since the assignment is at the household level, assignment can be assumed ignorable (or even unconfounded) only if we condition on the household and its characteristics. The propensity score is thus defined at the household level, and represents the probability that a single household with vector of characteristics x is credit rationed (or subject to a shock, or insured). In order to be consistent with the hypothesized assignment mechanism, x should include also summary characteristics (e.g. number and age) of the children in each household. Once the propensity scores are estimated using households as units of analysis, the estimated propensity score for treated and untreated households can then be used to check the degree of overlap between the two groups in terms of the distribution of their characteristics.

The propensity score can also be used to estimate the ATT using a matching strategy. Even if the outcome involves the children within the household, the outcome Y in this case must be defined at the household level. Summary measures of child labour or school attendance, such as the proportion of school-age children going to school, to work, etc. are appropriate.

Matching is done by a nearest neighbour matching procedure that, for each of the N^T treated (e.g. rationed) households, looks for the nearest neighbour matching sets in the group of control households, defined as

$$C(i) = \min_j \|p_i - p_j\|,$$

which usually contains a single control unit (household). Denoting the number of controls matched with treated observation i by N_i^C, the matching estimator of ATT is

$$A\hat{T}T = \frac{1}{N^T} \sum_{i \in T} \left[Y_i^1 - \sum_{j \in C(i)} \frac{1}{N_i^T} Y_j^0 \right].$$

An estimate of the variance of this estimator can be derived either analytically, or using bootstrap methods (for details, see Becker and Ichino 2001).

A further complication is that we are interested in at least three potentially endogenous variables, namely credit rationing, insurance, and the occurrence of shocks. The order of these treatments cannot be determined from the questionnaire. In principle, one could define a treatment variable as the combination of the three, but that would render the propensity score based analysis, as well as the interpretation of the results, more complicated. Propensity scores and ATT estimates are thus obtained separately for each variable.[3]

The consequences that a violation of the unconfoundedness hypothesis could have on any causal conclusion are tested by performing the sensitivity analysis proposed by Rosenbaum and Rubin (1983a), extended here to a multinomial outcome. This method allows one to assess the sensitivity of the causal effects to assumptions about an unobserved binary covariate that is associated with both the treatments and the outcome. Details of the methodology are reported in the Appendix to the volume and the results are reported in Appendix 8.1.

---

[3] Preliminary tests showing conditional independence of the occurrence of the three variables considered confirm the validity of this procedure.

8.3 THE EFFECTS OF SHOCKS AND ACCESS TO CREDIT AND INSURANCE

Household decisions concerning the four possible activities in which a child can engage (work only, work and study, study only, or do neither) are modelled as a multinomial logit.[4] The detailed results are reported in Appendix 8.6. Appendix 8.4 shows that the distributions of the propensity scores for treated and untreated groups of households overlap to a large extent. It also shows similar covariates' distributions for the treatment and control groups. As reported in Appendix 8.1, the results are robust with respect to the sensitivity analysis carried out to assess the consequences of a violation of the unconfoundedness assumption. This gives us confidence in the causal interpretation of the results.

Table 8.5 reports the marginal effects calculated (at the mean) from the estimated coefficients of the multinomial logit model. All the coefficients for individual and household-level characteristics are significant, and have the expected sign. Holding expenditure and other characteristics constant, girls are less likely than boys to become part of the labour force. They are more likely to attend school, and even more likely to be 'idle'. This indicates that girls are more likely than boys to be involved full time in household chores. Indigenous children are more likely to be working than other children (the probability of work increases by 8 percentage points). Parents' education (above primary education, the omitted category) has a negative effect on child labour, and a positive one on school attendance. A child with an uneducated father is about 5 percentage points more likely to work full time, and 13 percentage points more likely to be idle, than a child with an educated father. It appears that, in Guatemala, there are no large differences between the impact of the mother's and the father's education. Household expenditure reduces child labour, and increases full-time school attendance. At the mean, a 10 per cent increase in income reduces the probability that a child works only, or works and studies, by about 7 percentage points.

The proxies for access to credit and insurance, and shocks, are significant, and have strong effects on household decisions regarding the children's activities. These results are consistent with those found in the propensity score based analysis. Credit rationing strongly reduces school attendance. The probability that a child belonging to a credit-rationed household attends school is about

---

[4] The multinomial logit model is even more flexible than the usual bivariate probit model, which takes account of the simultaneity of the decisions only through the correlation of the error terms. In fact, the covariates in the multinomial logit model may explicitly have a different effect on the probability of taking one of the four decisions. Also note that the usual weakness of the conditional logit model, namely the Independence of Irrelevant Alternatives (IIA) property, does not apply when, as in the present case, most or all of the covariates are individual (as opposed to choice-specific) characteristics, and each of these characteristics has choice-specific coefficients (i.e. such that each of them enters the underlying stochastic utility with a different coefficient). In such a case the cross-elasticities are not constant, and including another alternative to the choice set does not leave the odds of the other alternatives unchanged.

Table 8.5. *Multinomial logit model marginal effects*

Variable	Work only		Study only		Work and study		No activities	
	dy/dx	*z*	*dy/dx*	*z*	*dy/dx*	*z*	*dy/dx*	*z*
Female	−0.022	−4.02	0.036	2.13	−0.078	−7.26	0.064	4.94
Age	−0.023	−2.48	0.178	7.09	0.094	5.51	−0.249	−13.5
Age2	0.002	4.4	−0.010	−8.6	−0.003	−3.77	0.011	12.76
Indigenous[a]	0.013	3.02	−0.096	−7.19	0.065	7.07	0.018	1.8
Hh expenditure	−0.032	−5.01	0.152	7.95	−0.035	−2.95	−0.084	−5.41
Hhsize	−0.013	−5.89	0.052	7.99	−0.016	−3.74	−0.023	−4.61
Numkidsy	0.009	3.59	−0.013	−1.63	0.012	2.49	−0.007	−1.12
Numkidso	0.003	1.46	−0.018	−2.75	0.008	1.87	0.007	1.42
Femkidsy	−0.004	−1.8	0.003	0.36	−0.009	−1.64	0.010	1.64
M_none[a]	0.050	3.22	−0.155	−5.61	−0.014	−0.84	0.118	4.99
M_primary[a]	0.047	2.36	−0.092	−3.14	−0.006	−0.38	0.051	2
F_none[a]	0.048	3.72	−0.177	−7.13	−0.004	−0.27	0.132	5.7
F_primary[a]	0.023	2.47	−0.099	−4.53	0.002	0.19	0.073	3.8
Collective[a]	0.006	0.96	−0.055	−3.08	0.055	4.62	−0.005	−0.37
Individual[a]	0.015	2.51	−0.051	−3.00	0.039	3.65	−0.002	−0.17
Credit[a]	0.006	1.3	−0.066	−4.49	−0.002	−0.22	0.062	5.55
Insurance[a]	−0.014	−3.38	0.037	2.66	0.039	−4.94	0.016	1.37
Credit_Individual[a]	−0.006	−0.97	0.023	1.06	0.017	−1.34	0.000	0.01
Credit_Collectivet[a]	−0.010	−1.54	0.081	3.91	0.037	−3.18	−0.034	−2.11
Regional dummies:								
Norte[a]	−0.008	−0.94	0.067	2.43	0.005	−0.22	−0.054	−3.06
Nororiente[a]	−0.009	−1.08	0.051	1.84	0.003	0.16	−0.045	−2.54
Suroriente[a]	−0.017	−2.44	0.088	3.32	0.021	0.94	−0.092	−6.73
Central[a]	0.008	0.72	0.035	1.25	0.050	2.1	−0.092	−6.66
Surroccidente[a]	−0.021	−3.21	0.113	4.62	0.017	0.81	−0.108	−8.1
Noroccidente[a]	−0.016	−2.08	0.106	4.15	−0.015	−0.78	−0.075	−4.47
Peten[a]	−0.003	−0.32	0.080	3.06	0.003	0.12	−0.080	−5.64

[a] For dummy variables, *dy/dx* is the effect of a discrete change from 0 to 1.

7 percentage points lower compared with a unrationed household. Children from credit-rationed households are more likely to be not only out of school, but also out of the labour force. This finding seems to indicate that credit rationing influences especially investment in the human capital of children. Since credit-rationed parents would send their children to school if they could borrow, this finding seems to indicate that, at the margin, returns to education are higher than returns to work. In the presence of fixed costs of access to work, low returns to child labour would in fact induce credit-rationed parents to keep their children idle.

Households affected by shocks reduce their children's full-time school attendance, and increase child labour. Following a collective shock, child participation increases by 5.5 percentage points. Most of the additional participation comes from formerly full-time students, who start to work without dropping out of school. The overall effect of individual shocks is similar to that of collective shocks. Child labour participation in households hit by an individual shock is about 5 percentage points higher than average. Individual shocks, however, affect mainly children attending school, and increase the probability of work full time (by 1.5 percentage points). Idle children are barely affected. About two-thirds of the children that enter the labour force continue to attend school.

These findings seem to show that inability to obtain credit affects household investment in human capital, rather than child labour participation. Shocks, by contrast, affect child labour participation, most likely because of the need to compensate for an unexpected loss of resources. This confirms the importance of credit rationing for investment in human capital, but seems to indicate that improving access to credit is not very useful for removing children from the labour force. Children who do not attend school nor work are at risk of becoming workers (or worse, see Chapter 2), and may be actually worse off than working children, as they might receive a smaller allocation of resources,[5] and do not even benefit from any increase in human capital from on-the-job training that working children might receive.

Information on the availability of formal or informal insurance mechanisms and 'safety nets' is limited to the indicator of whether any household member is covered by health insurance. But the effect of this variable is far from negligible. Children belonging to households where at least one member (usually the household head) is covered by health insurance are about 5 percentage points less likely to work only, or work and study. Such a large effect should not come as a surprise, if one considers that about 15 per cent of the idiosyncratic shocks are linked to health conditions, and that other kinds of shocks can be at least in part influenced by health conditions. Since the estimates are obtained controlling for the income and education of the parents, we can be reasonably confident that insurance cover does not act as a proxy for either of those variables.

8.4 DISCUSSION

Policies aimed at reducing the vulnerability of families with children, and promoting risk-reducing behaviour, deserve attention. The World Bank has recently developed a social risk management strategy but, so far, this has focused mainly on vulnerability by poverty, as defined by consumption.

The empirical findings reported in the present chapter indicate that credit rationing is an important determinant of the household decision to invest in the human capital of children, but less relevant where child work is concerned. The children kept away from school tend to remain idle, rather than work. As idle children may find themselves in circumstances that are much worse than those associated with work in the usual sense (see Chapter 2), credit rationing thus puts children at considerable risk. Shocks substantially alter household decisions. In particular, a negative shock substantially increases the probability that a child will work. Coupled with evidence from other research that child

---

[5] This is confirmed by the tabulations available for many countries at www.ucw-project.org.

labour shows a high degree of persistence, this finding highlights the importance of protection from shocks for reducing children's labour supply, and increasing human capital investment. Risk-reduction schemes, proxied by the availability of medical insurance, also have a beneficial and substantial effect on child work.

In order to get a rough impression of the size of the effects of the possible policies, consider that in order to achieve an increase in school attendance equal to that due to the elimination of credit rationing, household income would have to increase by as much as 30 per cent. To match the effects of eliminating the consequences of a negative individual shock on child work, household income would have to increase by about 40 per cent. The effects on the other variables have a similar order of magnitude. Policies aimed at improving access to credit and providing safety nets, especially for poorer households, thus appear to be among the most powerful instruments for promoting school attendance and reducing child work. As the amount of income needed to match the effects of a reduction in either shocks or credit rationing is very large, this suggests that policies aimed at reducing risk may be not only effective, but also cost efficient.

Appendix 8.1   Sensitivity analysis

The estimates of the ATT for credit rationing, and different combinations of values for π , α, and δ_{ti}, are reported in Table A8.1.1. The elements of X are the same as those used in the estimation of the multinomial logit model, and by the propensity score method. The results are clearly not very sensitive to a range of plausible assumptions about U. Notice that an α or δ_{ti} of 0.5 almost doubles the odds of receiving the treatment, or the odds of a certain value of the outcome. These values are larger than most of the coefficients of the estimated multinomial logit. Setting the values of the association parameter to bigger numbers may change the results. Given the large number of observed covariates already included in the model, however, the existence of a residual unobserved covariate so highly correlated with T and Y appears implausible. The sensitivity analysis of the ATT estimates of the effects of individual and collective shocks, and of the availability of insurance, gave similar results.

Table A8.1.1. *Average effects of treatment with 'credit rationing', for different values of the sensitivity parameters*

ATT	$\alpha = 0$ $\delta_{0w} = \delta_{1w} = 0$ $\delta_{0s} = \delta_{1s} = 0$ $\delta_{0ws} = \delta_{1ws} = 0$	$\pi = 0.1, \alpha = 0.1$ $\delta_{0w} = \delta_{1w} = -0.1$ $\delta_{0s} = \delta_{1s} = 0.1$ $\delta_{0ws} = \delta_{1ws} = 0.1$	$\pi = 0.5, \alpha = 0.5$ $\delta_{0w} = \delta_{1w} = -0.1$ $\delta_{0s} = \delta_{1s} = 0.1$ $\delta_{0ws} = \delta_{1ws} = 0.1$	$\pi = 0.1, \alpha = 0.1$ $\delta_{0w} = \delta_{1w} = -0.5$ $\delta_{0s} = \delta_{1s} = 0.5$ $\delta_{0ws} = \delta_{1ws} = 0.5$	$\pi = 0.5, \alpha = 0.5$ $\delta_{0w} = \delta_{1w} = -0.5$ $\delta_{0s} = \delta_{1s} = 0.5$ $\delta_{0ws} = \delta_{1ws} = 0.5$
Working only	0.011	0.011	0.012	0.011	0.018
Studying only	−0.049	−0.050	−0.052	−0.053	−0.060
Working and studying	−0.028	−0.023	−0.028	−0.028	−0.031
Idle children	0.066	0.062	0.067	0.070	0.073

Appendix 8.2   Questions used to define some of the variables used in the estimation

Questions used to define credit-rationed households

What is the principal reason that no one applied for a loan?

In the community no one offer loans 1
Do not know how to apply for a loan 2
They ask for too many requirements 3
Don't have the goods to give guarantees.................. 4
Fear of losing the guarantees............................ 5
Interest rate is too high 6
Prefer to work with own resources 7
Do not have opportunity to invest........................ 8
There was no need....................................... 9
Insufficient income.....................................10
They don't give loans to people like us 11
Other what?..12

Did they approve any loan that was applied for?
Yes... 1
No.. 2

Questions used to define the collective and individual shocks

Collective shocks	Individual shocks
In the last 12 months, has the household been affected by any of the following general types of problems?	In the last 12 months, has the household been affected by any of the following problems?
Earthquake..................... 1	Loss of employment of any member 1
Drought........................ 2	Lowered income of any member........ 2
Flood 3	Bankruptcy of a family business........ 3
Storms 4	Illness or serious accident of a working
Hurricane...................... 5	member of the household............. 4
Plagues........................ 6	Death of a working member of the
Landslides...................... 7	household 5
Forest fires 8	Abandonment by the household head... 6
Business closing 9	Fire in the house/business/property 7
Massive lay-offs 10	Criminal act 8
General increase................11	Land dispute......................... 9
Public protests..................12	Family dispute.......................10
Other 13	Loss of cash or in-kind assistance.......11
	Fall in prices of products in the household business................12
	Loss of harvest.......................13
	Other 14

Questions used to define the 'health insurance' and 'social security' variables

Health insurance	Social security
Is [NAME] affiliated or covered by:	Do you pay a quota to social security (IGSS) for the work that you do as (.....)?
Private health or illness insurance...1	
IGSS............................2	Yes................................1
IGSS and private...................3	No.................................2
Other, what.......................4	
None 5	

Appendix 8.3 Detailed descriptive statistics on shocks

Table A8.3.1. *Collective shocks that resulted in loss of income, loss of inheritance, or neither of these*

	Loss of income normally received		Loss of inheritance		Loss of income and inheritance		None		Total	
	%	No.	%	No.	%	No.	%	No.	%	No.
Earthquake	20.1	4,166	32.0	6,625	7.4	1,524	40.6	8,407	100	20,722
Drought	41.2	62,231	8.6	12,933	6.5	9,749	43.8	66,118	100	151,031
Flood	29.5	16,405	14.8	8,240	7.7	4,293	48.0	26,673	100	55,611
Storms	33.4	26,186	14.4	11,248	3.3	2,554	48.9	38,310	100	78,298
Hurricane	37.1	14,663	17.3	6,835	9.8	3,886	35.8	14,179	100	39,563
Plagues	48.9	195,039	7.4	29,469	5.8	23,077	38.0	151,401	100	398,986
Landslides	33.1	11,125	12.6	4,237	15.3	5,137	39.0	13,115	100	33,614
Forest fires	13.0	3,396	12.8	3,346	7.5	1,960	66.8	17,473	100	26,175
Business closing	54.7	10,545	2.1	409	6.8	1,301	36.4	7,021	100	19,276
Massive lay-offs	72.9	14,861	0.0	0	7.3	1,485	19.8	4,046	100	20,392
General increase in price	90.5	1,363,135	2.6	38,430	2.4	36,066	4.6	68,490	100	1,506,121
Public protests	35.5	7,401	0.6	132	1.4	289	62.5	13,011	100	20,833
Other	39.3	7,706	13.7	2,694	11.1	2,177	35.9	7,029	100	19,606
Total	72.7	1,736,859	5.2	124,598	3.9	93,498	18.2	435,273	100	2,390,228

Note: The totals exceed the number of households because of multiple answers.

Table A8.3.2. *Idiosyncratic shocks that resulted in loss of income, loss of inheritance, or neither of these*

	Loss of income normally received		Loss of inheritance		Loss of income and inheritance		None		Total	
	%	No.	%	No.	%	No.	%	No.	%	No.
Loss of employment of any member	93.3	166,753	2.18	3,900	1.9	3,394	2.62	4,680	100	178,727
Lowered income of any member	93.53	213,037	2.18	4,963	2	4,545	2.3	5,230	100	227,775
Bankruptcy of a family business	83.36	27,794	5.11	1,705	9.39	3,130	2.14	713	100	33,342
Illness or serious accident of a working member of the household	85.88	175,671	2.75	5,620	5.41	11,060	5.96	12,197	100	204,548
Death of a working member of the household	87.75	25,103	0.3	86	8.5	2,431	3.45	986	100	28,606
Death of another member of the household	55.02	21,814	2.95	1,171	1.71	679	40.32	15,987	100	39,651
Abandonment by the household head	63.93	14,000	0.79	172	8.55	1,872	26.74	5,855	100	21,899
Fire in the house/business/property	17.04	604	65.6	2,325	17.35	615	0	0	100	3,544
Criminal act	69.93	43,795	10.84	6,786	8.6	5,386	10.64	6,661	100	62,628
Land dispute	29.56	6,047	3.83	783	5.12	1,048	61.5	12,582	100	20,460
Family dispute	31.65	7,513	2.96	702	3.05	725	62.34	14,798	100	23,738
Loss of cash or in-kind assistance	81.62	19,412	0.66	156	8.62	2,051	9.1	2,165	100	23,784
Fall in prices of products in the household business	79.16	78,046	0.65	645	16.44	16,208	3.74	3,691	100	98,590
Loss of harvest	76.67	250,179	8.82	28,788	11.39	37,182	3.12	10,168	100	326,317
Other	83.54	11,835	1.52	216	0.88	125	14.05	1,991	100	14,167
Total	81.18	1,061,603	4.44	58,018	6.92	90,451	7.47	97,704	100	1,307,776

Note: The totals exceed the total number of household because of multiple answers.

Appendix 8.4   Comparison of the distributions of propensity scores for treated and control groups

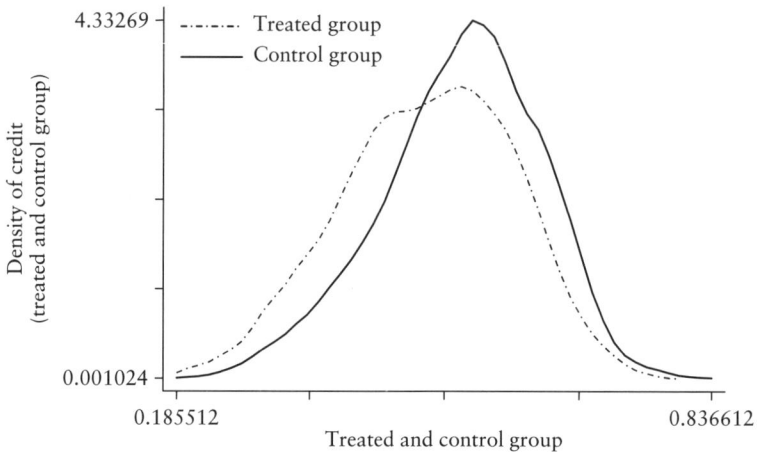

Figure A8.4.1. *Propensity score comparison for 'Credit Rationing'*

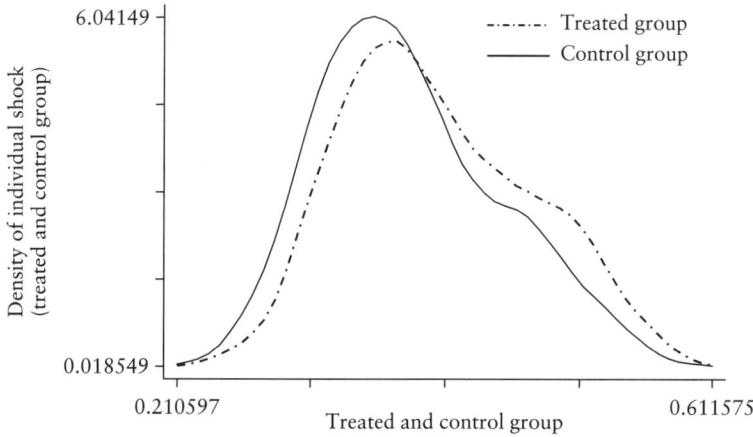

Figure A8.4.2. *Propensity score comparison for 'Individual Shocks'*

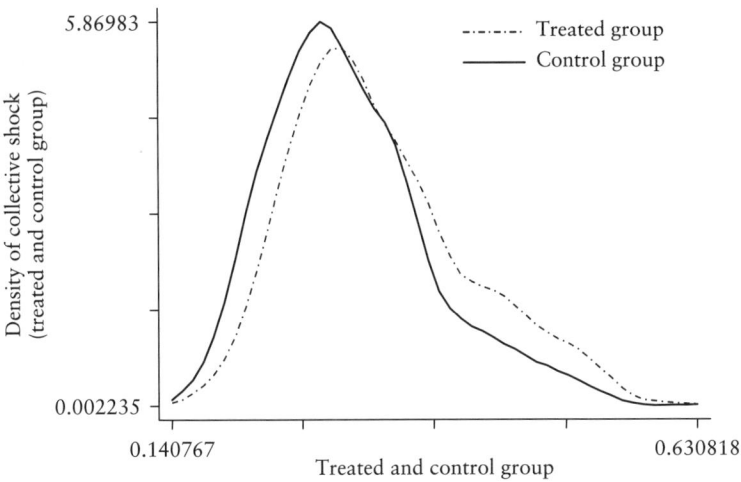

Figure A8.4.3. *Propensity score comparison for 'Collective Shock'*

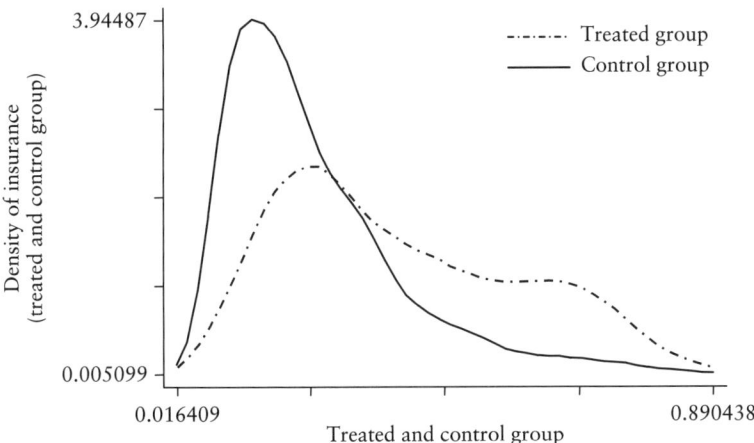

Figure A8.4.4. *Propensity scores comparison for 'Insurance'*

Appendix 8.5　Definition of variables

Child activities

Working	1 if individual currently works, 0 otherwise
Attending school	1 if individual currently attends school, 0 otherwise
Work only	1 if individual currently works and does not attend school
Study only	1 if individual currently attends school and does not work
Work and study	1 if individual currently works and attends school
Neither	1 if individual currently neither works nor attends school

Other variables

Female	1 if female, 0 otherwise
Household expenditures	logarithm of per capita household expenditure

Father's education

F_None	1 if he has no completed education, 0 otherwise
F_Primary	1 if he has completed primary education, 0 otherwise

Mother's education

M_None	1 if she has no completed education, 0 otherwise
M_Primary	1 if she has completed primary education, 0 otherwise
	(Secondary or higher education is the comparison group)
Indigenous	1 if the child is indigenous, 0 otherwise

Shocks

Collective	1 if a household reported experiencing at least a collective shock, 0 otherwise
Individual	1 if a household reported experiencing at least one idiosyncratic shock, 0 otherwise

Social risk indicator

Insurance	1 if at least one member of the household has medical insurance, 0 otherwise

Credit rationing indicator

Credit	1 if the household is credit rationed, 0 otherwise

Appendix 8.6 Results of multinomial logit estimates

(Reference Group: children neither working nor studying)

Variable	Work only		Study only		Work and study	
	Coeff.	Z	Coeff.	Z	Coeff.	Z
Female	−1.03	−6.11	−0.39	−3.65	−1.20	−8.27
Age	1.06	3.85	1.94	13.04	2.60	11.62
Age squared	−0.02	−1.96	−0.09	−12.77	−0.11	−10.22
Indigenous[a]	0.22	1.68	−0.26	−3.17	0.47	4.18
Hh expenditure	−0.31	−1.5	0.78	6.29	0.23	1.34
Hh size	−0.19	−2.82	0.23	5.61	0.01	0.13
Numkidsy	0.29	3.6	0.03	0.59	0.17	2.44
Numkidso	0.03	0.5	−0.07	−1.8	0.03	0.5
Femkidsy	−0.19	−2.4	−0.07	−1.28	−0.16	−2.19
M_none[a]	0.51	1.13	−1.03	−5.36	−0.94	−3.76
M_primary[a]	0.74	1.65	−0.46	−2.45	−0.39	−1.59
F_none[a]	0.30	1.01	−1.07	−6.78	−0.84	−4.09
F_primary[a]	0.13	0.45	−0.63	−4.14	−0.47	−2.37
Collective[a]	0.18	1.01	−0.04	−0.37	0.52	3.55
Individual[a]	0.40	2.25	−0.06	−0.5	0.38	2.65
Credit[a]	−0.26	−1.74	−0.52	−5.63	−0.45	−3.42
Insurance[a]	−0.52	−3.36	−0.05	−0.6	−0.52	−4.12
Credit_Individual[a]	−0.18	−0.78	0.03	0.21	−0.18	−0.93
Credit_Collectivet[a]	−0.03	−0.13	0.36	2.39	−0.16	−0.78
Regional Dummies						
Norte[a]	0.18	0.54	0.52	2.76	0.38	1.4
Nororiente[a]	0.07	0.2	0.42	2.29	0.39	1.4
Suroriente[a]	0.26	0.76	0.96	5.11	1.04	3.85
Central[a]	1.00	3.36	0.85	4.96	1.23	4.95
Surroccidente[a]	0.25	0.8	1.13	6.43	1.13	4.5
Noroccidente[a]	0.10	0.3	0.75	4.09	0.46	1.73
Peten[a]	0.63	1.96	0.82	4.43	0.74	2.72
_cons	−7.19	−2.94	−13.35	−9.53	−16.10	−8.12

9

Further Evidence on Fertility, Education, and Child Labour

The theoretical analysis of Chapters 2 and 3 highlighted the links between fertility, education, and child labour. Chapter 5 brought some evidence on the effects of certain policies. Here, we investigate whether the educational and child labour effects of realized fertility uncovered by the study reported in Chapter 5 can be given a causal interpretation, and then go on to review the available evidence on the fertility effects of a number of policies (including public pensions) and variables (including wage and interest rates). In both parts of the chapter, we pay special attention to the question whether fertility is indeed endogenous as assumed in the theoretical analysis of Chapters 2 and 3, and apparently confirmed by the empirical analysis of Chapter 5.

9.1 THE EFFECTS OF POLICY AND REALIZED FERTILITY ON EDUCATION AND CHILD LABOUR DECISIONS

In Chapters 2 and 3, we hypothesized that couples take decisions by backward induction. They first choose what to do with any given number of school-age children. Then, they decide how well to feed and care for the health of any given number of pre-school children they might have, taking into account the effect that this will have on the future number and well-being of school-age children. Finally, they choose the level of birth control, taking into account the effect that this will have on the future number of pre-school children. The analysis of rural Indian data reported in Chapter 5 finds, among other things, that the number and age distribution of children, and a number of policy and other exogenous variables, affect educational and child labour decisions in the way predicted by the theory. These particular effects are the focus of a follow-up study, Deb and Rosati (2004), of the same data set. This more narrowly focused study goes in greater depth into the econometric problems (endogeneity, lack of robust instruments, unobserved heterogeneity) that, as we saw in Chapters 6 to 8, plague any attempt at estimating causal relationships in a non-experimental setting.

9.1.1 *Econometric issues*

Given the backward-induction structure of the household decision model, and given that children are not born all at the same time, the effect of realized fertility on labour supply decisions cannot be properly determined without taking into account the endogeneity of the number of children present in the household. The issue has been recognized and modelled in a variety of different ways in the empirical literature on adult labour supply, and the results generally show strong evidence of the endogeneity of fertility.[1] In the empirical literature on child labour, by contrast, the issue has not been addressed. Deb and Rosati (2002), Jensen and Nielsen (1997), Maitra and Ray (2002), Ravallion and Wodon (2000), and Ray (2000) include controls for the number and ages of children in models of child labour and schooling, but these variables are treated as if they are exogenous. Under the same assumption, we found in Chapter 5 that children are more likely to work, and less likely to attend school, if they have many brothers and sisters of the same age or younger. The evidence reported in the rest of the existing labour literature is mixed. In any case, however, it is difficult to give these findings a causal interpretation.

It is reasonable to expect that important sources of heterogeneity, common to fertility and child activity equations, are not reported by the data. In addition to unobserved preferences, the data typically offer poor proxies for income, wealth, and returns and costs of education and child labour. Therefore, econometric models of children's activity that treat the number of children as exogenous may provide biased estimates of the effect of this number. While endogeneity is to be expected, the direction and magnitude of such effects is not clear. In the literature on adult labour supply, Angrist (2001) finds that the effect of children on female labour supply when endogeneity is accounted for is just over half as large as the effect when fertility is treated exogenously. Lundberg and Rose (2002), on the other hand, find evidence that the effect of children on male labour supply is substantially larger when endogeneity is taken into account.

Deb and Rosati (2004) depart from the practice of estimating a structural model by a linear instrumental-variables approach. Instead, they develop a structural econometric model of fertility and children's activities that respects important features of the data. The first is that survey data typically show a substantial fraction of children neither attending school nor participating in work activities (in general, and especially outside the home). We saw that to be true, for example, of the data sets used in earlier chapters. Deb and Rosati (2004) show that reportedly idle children are different from children reported working or attending school. This highlights the importance of modelling child activities as a multinomial process. Since the linearization of children's activities

---

[1] See, for example, Angrist (2001), Angrist and Evans (1998), Francesconi (2002), Gong and van Soest (2002), Hotz and Miller (1988), Lundberg and Rose (2002), and Moffit (1984).

requires that the multinomial variable be reduced to a binary variable, this has substantive and statistical consequences. The second feature is that fertility can take only a small number of integer values; hence it is a count process. Linearizing it leads to substantially inefficient estimates with poor finite sample properties. Consequently, the number of children in the household is better modelled as a Poisson process, and children's activities as a multinomial logit process.

Latent factors are incorporated into the equations for the number of children, and for children's activities, to allow for unobserved influences on fertility to affect children's activities. The latent factor structure has three advantages over alternative ways of generating correlated errors. First, it can be used to combine sets of any marginal distributions into an appropriate joint distribution. Secondly, correlated errors have a natural interpretation as proxies for unobserved covariates since they enter the equations in the same way as observed covariates. The factor loadings can therefore be interpreted in much the same way as coefficients on observed covariates. Thirdly, the approach provides a parsimonious representation of error correlations in models with large numbers of equations. Deb and Rosati (2004) apply maximum simulated likelihood (MSL) techniques to estimate the parameters of the models. As no closed-form solutions exist, simulation is used to evaluate integral expressions in the likelihood function of the model.[2]

This approach bears similarities to those adopted in a number of other microeconometric papers. In a fertility context, Olsen and Farkas (1989) examine the effect of childbirth on the hazard of dropping out of school, while Carrasco (2001) examines the effect of childbirth on labour force participation of women in a panel data context. In other contexts, Bingley and Walker (2001) examine the effect of duration of husbands' unemployment on wives' discrete labour supply choices, Jensen (1990) examines the effect of contraceptive use on duration between births, and Pitt and Rosensweig (1990) study the effect of endogenous health status of infant children on their mothers' main daily activity.

The econometric models used in these studies share a number of statistical features. One is that both treatment and outcome processes are non-normal and non-linear: multinomial, count, discrete, or censored. Another is that the treatment is endogenous. Yet another is that the investigator often has good a priori reasons for choosing a particular (and incontrovertible) marginal model for both treatments and outcomes. But, the transition from given marginal distributions to a joint model for treatment and outcome continues to be a

---

[2] MSL using pseudo-random draws can be computationally very expensive if the number of observations and parameters is large, and a large number of draws is required to reduce the simulation error to acceptable levels. For computational efficiency, Deb and Rosati (2004) thus adapt an acceleration technique that uses quasi-random draws based on Halton sequences (Bhat 2001, Train 2003).

methodological challenge, because multivariate distributions are typically non-normal. In some cases (e.g. in count and duration models), the marginal models have no (or very restrictive) tractable multivariate counterparts. In others, treatment and outcome belong to different statistical families (e.g. treatment is multinomial, and the outcome is a hazard rate), as a consequence of which analytically tractable multivariate distributions often do not exist.

Reliable estimates of the effects of realized fertility on child labour are very important for policy purposes. Consider, for example, the introduction of a subsidy for school attendance. This will reduce the cost of attending school, but also the cost of raising children. While the direct objective is to increase school attendance, the policy might thus have the (possibly undesirable) effect of also increasing fertility. If there is a significant effect of fertility on child labour and schooling, this policy would have an effect on schooling not only directly, but also indirectly through fertility. Correct information on the effects of realized fertility on child labour is needed also to assess the importance of cross-sectoral policies. For example, policies aimed at modifying fertility behaviour, such as those that improve the children's survival probabilities (see Chapter 3), will have unintended consequences for the supply of child labour and school attendance.

9.1.2   *Data, variables, and econometric analysis*

The theory suggests that the econometric model should have a recursive structure, with the number of children entering the equation for the children's activities.[3] Decisions regarding the latter may be assumed to made when the children are of school age. Deb and Rosati (2004) model only the activities of the youngest child in each family. In families where all the children are 7 years of age or older, the youngest of these children can be taken to be the 'marginal' child. In the case of families where some (but not all) of the children are less than 7 years old, it is assumed that the survival of the youngest children is uncertain. Where decisions concerning children's activities are concerned, the 'marginal' child is then taken to be the youngest child aged at least 7. Assuming that the youngest child in the relevant age group is also the least entrenched in a possibly undesirable activity (working or being idle), he or she may be taken to be also the target of social policy.[4]

As only 0.71 per cent of children are reported working and attending school, it is assumed that a child can only do one of the following: attend school,

---

[3] A recursive structure is required for logical coherency also in models with discrete and count outcomes; see Maddala (1986), and Blundell and Smith (1994).

[4] This choice is not without statistical consequences. One may wish to model the activities of each of the children in the relevant age group, thus absolving the analyst of making a choice of which child to consider. Since the activities of all children within the family share the same unobserved heterogeneity, however, the model is considerably more complicated to programme and estimate than the one described.

work, or do nothing (children working and attending school at the same time are classified as working). These activities are modelled as a multinomial logit process conditional on the number of children. The econometric model is set out in detail in the Appendix to this chapter. In what follows, we describe the data and define the variables used in the estimation.

The data set is a sub-sample of households drawn from the 1994 Human Development of India survey already used in Chapter 5. The sub-sample includes only households with at least one child between the ages of 7 and 15. The sub-sample consists of 12,830 observations. Summary statistics for the variables used in the analysis are presented in Table 9.1.

Table 9.1. *Summary statistics*

Variable	Definition	Mean	Std. dev.
School	=1 if child is in school	0.703	0.457
Work	=1 if child is working	0.086	0.280
Idle	=1 if child is neither in school nor working	0.211	0.408
Number of children	number of children	3.374	1.336
Child is female	=1 if female	0.449	0.497
Child's age	age in years/10	0.977	0.252
Mother's education	education of mother	1.374	0.816
Father's education	education of father	1.993	1.321
Primary school in village	=1 if primary school is in the village	0.457	0.498
Secondary school in village	=1 if secondary school is in the village	0.441	0.497
Cost of education	village mean of education cost in Rs./1,000	0.660	0.577
Household is poor	=1 if household income is in lowest quintile	0.559	0.497
Household owns land	=1 if household owns land	0.669	0.471
Household owns livestock	=1 if household owns livestock	0.693	0.461
Number of appliances	number of appliances in household	0.912	1.168
Household is Hindu	=1 if Hindu	0.836	0.370
Household is Muslim	=1 if Muslim	0.106	0.307
Household is Christian	=1 if Christian	0.024	0.153
Household is in low social class	=1 if scheduled caste or tribe	0.370	0.483
First child is male	=1 if first child was male	0.669	0.470
Mother's age	age of mother in years/10	3.663	0.881
Father's age	age of father in years/10	4.136	1.130
Mortality rate in village	village mean of child mortality rate	0.082	0.029

Notes: Income quintiles are defined over urban and rural populations, although the sample consists of only rural households.
Education costs include expenditures on exams, fees, books, stationery, and uniforms.

The variables are largely those of Chapter 5. The explanatory variables common to the fertility and the children's activities equations include two proxies for full household income: a dummy for the household being poor (belonging to the lowest income quintile),[5] and the number of appliances in the household. Two other dummies, showing whether the household owns land and whether the household owns livestock, may also be thought of as proxies for full household income, but they are also proxies for returns to work. The costs of education are proxied by three variables: two dummies indicating the presence of primary and secondary schools in the village, and the village-level average monetary cost of school attendance. The other household-level variables are the education levels of the parents, and dummies for religion and caste. A full set of state dummies is used to control for geographical heterogeneity. Two child-specific explanatory variables, age and gender of the child, are included in the multinomial logit equations for the child's activities, but excluded from the fertility equation.

A dummy variable for the gender of the first-born child, the ages of the parents, and the village-level mortality rate are used as instruments in the exclusion-restriction sense. It is assumed, in other words, that these variables directly affect the number of children in the family, but do not directly affect the chosen activity of the youngest (eligible) child. The gender of the eldest child controls specifically for the well-known preference for male children in India. The ages of the parents control for the possibility that the observed number of children may not reflect completed fertility, or that there may be cohort effects in fertility. The village-level mortality rate is used as a proxy for the effects of expected child mortality on fertility decisions (see Chapter 5). This choice of instruments is obviously open to discussion, but informal checks suggest that the instruments are valid in a statistical sense.[6] To check the robustness of the results to the choice of instruments, the models were also estimated with subsets of these instruments. The results of these checks are described below, after the discussion of the main results.

9.1.3 *Results*

The reduced-form estimates presented in Chapter 5 did not reject the predictions of the theoretical analysis, but did not address the problem of unobserved heterogeneity. The more sophisticated econometric analysis of Deb and Rosati (2004) broadly confirms those results, and is thus stronger evidence of the validity of the theoretical model.

---

[5] See Chapter 5 for a discussion of the arguments against using actual household income as a proxy for full household income.

[6] There are no formal tests for validity of overidentification restrictions in the context of non-linear models such as the present one.

Table 9.2. *Truncated Poisson model for number of children*

	Parameter
First child is male	−0.060[a]
	(0.013)
Mother's age	0.085[a]
	(0.008)
Father's age	0.048[a]
	(0.007)
Village mortality rate	−0.627[b]
	(0.371)
Mother's education	−0.069[a]
	(0.009)
Father's education	0.010[a]
	(0.005)
Primary school present	−0.031
	(0.020)
Secondary school present	−0.018
	(0.020)
Cost of education	0.017
	(0.011)
Household is poor	−0.099[a]
	(0.012)
Household owns land	0.002
	(0.013)
Household owns livestock	0.047[a]
	(0.013)
Number of appliances	−0.000
	(0.005)
Household head is Hindu	−0.094[a]
	(0.036)
Household head is Muslim	0.140[a]
	(0.040)
Household head is Christian	−0.265[a]
	(0.055)
Household head is low caste	0.041[a]
	(0.012)

[a] The estimate is statistically significant at the 5% level.

[b] The estimate is statistically significant at the 10% level.

Notes: The model is estimated jointly with multinomial logit equations for a child's activities.

Asymptotic standard errors are in parentheses.

Table 9.2 reports the estimated parameters of the truncated-Poisson fertility model. The ages of the parents have positive effects on the number of children, supporting the view that fertility may be incomplete for younger parents, or that there may be cohort effects. Households where the eldest child is male are found to have fewer children (parents need not look any further for a son). This supports the claim of a gender bias in India. Households with more-educated mothers are found to have fewer children. By contrast, households with better-educated fathers have more children. Religion and caste have large and statistically significant effects on fertility.

The dummies for land and livestock ownership are not statistically significant, possibly because they are proxies for both full household income and the marginal return to child work. The cost of education proxies are not significant either, possibly because they are crude aggregate proxies that do not capture differences in the actual costs of education within households. The negative coefficient on the village survival rate indicates that an exogenous reduction in mortality reduces the number of births, but may increase the number of surviving children.

Parameter estimates and marginal effects of the multinomial logit model for a child's activities are reported in Table 9.3. In order to evaluate the statistical and substantive impact of the endogeneity of fertility, these estimates should be compared with those obtained treating fertility as exogenous, reported in Table 9.4. The coefficient of the number of children in the equation for *idle* is statistically significant and of roughly the same magnitude in the two cases, but the coefficient on *work*, negative and statistically insignificant in the exogenous case, is positive and statistically significant when endogeneity is taken into account.

The effects of realized fertility are thus different according to whether its endogeneity is taken into account or not. Although the effect on the probability of being idle is the same in either case, the probability of attending school in the case where endogeneity is allowed for is twice as large as in the case where fertility is assumed exogenous. The finding that the effect of fertility on the probability of work changes sign and becomes statistically significant when endogeneity of fertility is taken into account indicates that the number of children, and the allocation of these children's time, are closely linked.

The factor loading parameter, λ, is not statistically significant in the *idle* equation, but it is negative and highly significant in the *work* equation. A negative value of λ is indicative of a negative correlation between the unobserved components of the choice of work (relative to schooling) and the unobserved components of fertility choice. This is consistent with the a priori belief that the most likely sources of common unobserved heterogeneity between fertility and choice of the child's activities are household-level costs of education, returns to education, and unobserved components of full income. It is also consistent with the finding in Lundberg and Rose (2002) of a negative correlation between the errors of the fertility and female labour supply equations.

The marginal effects show that the youngest child is about 2 percentage points less likely to attend school, 1 percentage point more likely to work, and 1 percentage point more likely to be idle in households with more children. The presence of a primary school raises the probability of attending school by about

Table 9.3. *Multinomial logit model for a child's activities*

	Parameters		Marginal effects		
	Work	Idle	School	Work	Idle
Number of children	0.208[a]	0.110[a]	−0.019[a]	0.008[a]	0.011[a]
	(0.083)	(0.033)	(0.004)	(0.004)	(0.004)
Child is female	1.263[a]	0.719[a]	−0.126[a]	0.054[a]	0.072[a]
	(0.103)	(0.051)	(0.008)	(0.005)	(0.006)
Child's age	−0.920	−9.720[a]	1.041[a]	0.016	−1.056[a]
	(1.552)	(1.019)	(0.137)	(0.065)	(0.118)
Child's age squared	2.519[a]	4.161[a]	−0.526[a]	0.086[a]	0.440[a]
	(0.730)	(0.490)	(0.064)	(0.031)	(0.057)
Mother's education	−0.759[a]	−0.687[a]	0.100[a]	−0.029[a]	−0.071[a]
	(0.119)	(0.080)	(0.009)	(0.005)	(0.008)
Father's education	−0.419[a]	−0.461[a]	0.064[a]	−0.016[a]	−0.048[a]
	(0.053)	(0.029)	(0.004)	(0.002)	(0.003)
Primary school present	−0.087	−0.353[a]	0.039[a]	−0.002	−0.038[a]
	(0.159)	(0.089)	(0.012)	(0.007)	(0.010)
Secondary school present	−0.295[b]	−0.527[a]	0.065[a]	−0.010	−0.055[a]
	(0.161)	(0.092)	(0.012)	(0.007)	(0.010)
Cost of education	0.185[a]	0.201[a]	−0.028[a]	0.007[b]	0.021[a]
	(0.082)	(0.053)	(0.007)	(0.004)	(0.006)
Household is poor	0.005	0.105[b]	−0.011	−0.000	0.011[b]
	(0.095)	(0.060)	(0.008)	(0.004)	(0.006)
Household owns land	−0.159	−0.170[a]	0.024[a]	−0.006	−0.018[a]
	(0.100)	(0.060)	(0.008)	(0.004)	(0.007)
Household owns livestock	0.025	−0.135[a]	0.013[b]	0.002	−0.015[a]
	(0.100)	(0.060)	(0.008)	(0.004)	(0.006)
Number of appliances	−0.414[a]	−0.406[a]	0.058[a]	−0.016[a]	−0.042[a]
	(0.054)	(0.035)	(0.005)	(0.003)	(0.004)
Household head is Hindu	−0.518[b]	0.171	0.006	−0.027[b]	0.021
	(0.276)	(0.208)	(0.025)	(0.015)	(0.020)
Household head is Muslim	−0.027	0.900[a]	−0.119[a]	−0.008	0.127[a]
	(0.314)	(0.221)	(0.038)	(0.012)	(0.038)
Household head is Christian	−1.373[a]	0.069	0.025	−0.037[a]	0.013
	(0.529)	(0.366)	(0.043)	(0.009)	(0.042)
Household head is low caste	0.274[a]	0.338[a]	−0.047[a]	0.010[a]	0.036[a]
	(0.087)	(0.055)	(0.007)	(0.004)	(0.007)
λ	−1.256[a]	−0.096			
	(0.407)	(0.164)			

[a] The estimate is statistically significant at the 5% level.

[b] The estimate is statistically significant at the 10% level.

Notes: The model is estimated jointly with a truncated Poisson equation for fertility. Asymptotic standard errors are in parentheses.

Table 9.4. *Multinomial logit model for a child's activities assuming exogeneity of fertility*

	Parameters		Marginal effects		
	Work	Idle	School	Work	Idle
Number of children	−0.026	0.093[a]	−0.009[a]	−0.003[b]	0.012[a]
	(0.031)	(0.020)	(0.003)	(0.002)	(0.002)
Child is female	1.162[a]	0.720[a]	−0.134[a]	0.062[a]	0.072[a]
	(0.075)	(0.051)	(0.007)	(0.005)	(0.006)
Child's age	−0.675	−9.721[a]	1.106[a]	0.116	−1.221[a]
	(1.382)	(1.013)	(0.141)	(0.092)	(0.120)
Child's age squared	2.207[a]	4.171[a]	−0.565[a]	0.072[b]	0.493[a]
	(0.623)	(0.487)	(0.065)	(0.038)	(0.061)
Mother's education	−0.720[a]	−0.692[a]	0.110[a]	−0.034[a]	−0.076[a]
	(0.102)	(0.080)	(0.011)	(0.006)	(0.010)
Father's education	−0.383[a]	−0.461[a]	0.069[a]	−0.017[a]	−0.052[a]
	(0.043)	(0.029)	(0.004)	(0.003)	(0.004)
Primary school present	−0.103	−0.348[a]	0.043[a]	−0.001	−0.042[a]
	(0.142)	(0.089)	(0.013)	(0.009)	(0.011)
Secondary school present	−0.295[a]	−0.523[a]	0.072[a]	−0.010	−0.061[a]
	(0.144)	(0.092)	(0.013)	(0.009)	(0.011)
Cost of education	0.171[a]	0.201[a]	−0.030[a]	0.008	0.023[a]
	(0.072)	(0.053)	(0.007)	(0.005)	(0.006)
Household is poor	−0.054	0.099[b]	−0.008	−0.005	0.013[b]
	(0.083)	(0.059)	(0.008)	(0.005)	(0.007)
Household owns land	−0.155[b]	−0.172[a]	0.026[a]	−0.007	−0.019[a]
	(0.090)	(0.060)	(0.008)	(0.006)	(0.008)
Household owns livestock	0.048	−0.129[a]	0.012	0.005	−0.017[a]
	(0.089)	(0.059)	(0.009)	(0.006)	(0.007)
Number of appliances	−0.382[a]	−0.406[a]	0.063[a]	−0.018[a]	−0.045[a]
	(0.045)	(0.035)	(0.005)	(0.003)	(0.004)
Household head is Hindu	−0.410[b]	0.121	0.006	−0.028[b]	0.022
	(0.248)	(0.205)	(0.027)	(0.016)	(0.026)
Household head is Muslim	0.196	0.854[a]	−0.104[a]	−0.001	0.105[a]
	(0.276)	(0.218)	(0.029)	(0.017)	(0.027)
Household head is Christian	−1.273[a]	−0.011	0.061	−0.081[a]	0.019
	(0.479)	(0.364)	(0.050)	(0.029)	(0.047)
Household head is low caste	0.280[a]	0.337[a]	−0.050[a]	0.012[a]	0.038[a]
	(0.078)	(0.054)	(0.008)	(0.005)	(0.008)

[a] The estimate is statistically significant at the 5% level.

[b] The estimate is statistically significant at the 10% level.

Note: Asymptotic standard errors are in parentheses.

4 percentage points, reduces the probability of being idle by 4 percentage points, and has no effect on child labour. Land ownership increases school attendance by 2.4 percentage points and decreases the probability of being idle by less than 2 percentage points.

The effect of fertility on the likelihood of school attendance is twice as large when the endogeneity of fertility is taken into account than when it is not. If fertility is assumed exogenous, a child belonging to a large household is less likely to work than a child belonging to a small household, but this effect is on the margin of significance. By contrast, if endogeneity of fertility is taken into account, a child is significantly more likely to work in a large than in a small household, and the size of the effect is more than double that found in the exogenous case. The effect of fertility on the likelihood that the child is idle appears robust to whether fertility is assumed exogenous or not. Consequently, accounting for endogeneity does make a substantial qualitative and quantitative difference.

Accounting for the endogeneity of fertility has little impact on the effects of other exogenous covariates on a child's activities. The effects have the signs predicted by the theory, and are of plausible magnitudes. Girls are more likely than boys to work, and to be idle. This may simply be a consequence of the fact that the work of girls is more likely to be regarded and reported as work. Children of better-educated parents, and especially of better-educated mothers, are more likely to attend school. The presence of a primary or secondary school in the village increases school attendance and reduces the probability that a child works or is idle. The same is true of the village-level cost of education. Ownership of both land and livestock increases the probability of attending school, but leaves the probability of working almost unchanged. Families owning land or livestock are less likely to have idle children. The number of appliances appears, on the other hand, also to reduce the probability that a child works.[7]

9.2   FERTILITY EFFECTS OF PENSIONS, WAGES, AND INTEREST RATES

The theoretical analysis contained in the first part of Chapter 3 predicts that a rise in the fixed cost of a pre-school child, or in the marginal cost of the goods consumed by children in that age range, reduces fertility. By contrast, full household income raises aggregate fertility. Since the gender analysis contained in the second part of Chapter 3 leads us to expect that, in most households, the father's wage rate affects essentially full household income, while the mother's wage rate affects also the costs in question, we can expect that an increase in male wage rates would have a positive effect on aggregate fertility, while an

---

[7] Changes in the set of instruments does not alter substantially the results of the estimates. For details, see Deb and Rosati (2004).

increase in female wage rates would have an ambiguous one. The theory also predicts ambiguous fertility effects of an increase in either the interest rate, or public pension coverage (the latter more likely negative).

Direct evidence of the effects of pension policy, child benefits, male and female wage rates, and the rate of interest on fertility behaviour can be found in aggregate national data. However, pension policy has three dimensions: the number of persons covered, the level of coverage, and the extent to which it is actuarially fair. The first is the ratio of the number of persons receiving public pension benefits to the number of persons of retirement age (the 'extensive' measure of coverage). The second is the amount of pension benefits received on average by persons covered by a public pension scheme. The ratio between total pension payments and number of persons of retirement age (the so-called 'intensive' measure of coverage) reflects both these dimensions of pension policy. The third dimension is measured by the difference between the discounted value of pension benefits received, and the capitalized value of pension contributions paid, by a generation at the date of retirement. Child benefits may include cash transfers, tax allowances, and benefits in kind. Wage rates are intended net of income tax (where it exists). The relevant interest rate is obviously the long-term one.

Using cross-country data, Hohm (1975) and several others find a negative correlation between fertility and some measure of pension coverage. Entwisle and Winegarden (1984) do the same specifically for developing countries. Two more recent cross-country studies, Ehrlich and Zhong (1998) and Zhang and Zhang (2004), treat fertility as jointly determined with per-capita income growth and household saving (in the case of Zhang and Zhang, also private educational expenditure). These later studies contradict each other over a number of signs, but concord with each other and with the earlier studies in finding that pension coverage has a negative effect on fertility. As none of these cross-country studies controls for actuarial fairness and child benefits, however, the estimates may be biased.

One of the problems with cross-country studies is that information on child benefits and actuarial fairness is available only for a limited number of countries. A better alternative is time-series studies for countries that do provide this information. The drawback is that none of these countries can be classified as underdeveloped. We now report on a family of such time-series studies that use co-integration techniques to get at the long-term relationships between the relevant variables. In all these studies, fertility is measured by the total fertility rate. Pension coverage is measured either as the ratio of the number of persons receiving pension payments to the number of persons over the age of 65 (the 'extensive' measure), or as the ratio between total pension payments and number of persons aged 65 or over (the 'intensive' measure). The degree of actuarial fairness is proxied by the pension fund deficit, the yearly difference between pension benefits and pension contributions. In steady state, this difference coincides with that between the discounted value of pension benefits received, and the capitalized value of pension contributions paid, by each generation at the date of retirement. Over a sufficiently long run of years, it may thus be expected that the pension deficit (surplus) in the annual account of the pension administration will tend to behave like the surplus (deficit) in the lifetime account of the representative individual. The interest rate is proxied by the yield on long-dated government bonds. All monetary variables are obviously in real terms.

Cigno and Rosati (1992) use Italian time series to estimate reduced-form equations for saving and fertility. The paper shows that the pension deficit has no significant fertility, but pension coverage has a powerfully negative one. Controlling for the expansion of capital markets, which also compete with family transfer systems for the provision of old-age security, the paper does indeed find that as much as three-quarters of the total fertility reduction which occurred between 1930 and 1984 can be attributed to the increase in the proportion of the population covered by mandatory pension arrangements. This confirms the role of these markets as an alternative to intra-family arrangements. Foster and Rosenzweig (2000) find the same in a developing country.

Cigno and Rosati (1996, 1997) find the same sign pattern as Cigno and Rosati (1992) in the post-war time series of West Germany, Italy, Japan, the UK, and the USA. In all these studies, the male wage rate (or household income) is found to affect fertility positively, and the female wage rate to affect it negatively. The effect of the interest rate is positive in some countries, and negative in others. Where data are available, the fertility effect of the child benefit rate (equivalent to that of a reduction in the fixed cost of a child) is estimated to be positive. These findings relate to developed economies, but are consistent with earlier findings on developing economies, and with the predictions of the theory developed in Chapters 2 and 3. However, in all these time-series studies, the saving and fertility equations are estimated separately, and causation is simply *assumed* to run from policy to individual behaviour.

Cigno, Casolaro, and Rosati (2003) redo the analysis for West Germany only, using VAR methods that allow for all possible interactions, and directions of causation, among the variables concerned.[8] A preliminary analysis of the data revealed a discontinuity of the child benefit series in the year 1986, and a sharp fall in fertility between the end of the 1960s and the first half of the 1970s. To account for the possibility of structural breaks, the authors use a dummy for the year 1986, and another for the 1968–75 period. Confirming the presence of these breaks, the 1986 dummy turns out to be a significant determinant of fertility,[9] and the1968–75 step dummy to be a highly significant

---

[8] The data are better than in Cigno and Rosati (1996), because they are the longest time series (1960–95) that will ever be available for West Germany (after 1995, no separate statistics have been collected for the two parts of reunited Germany), and also because the measures of pension coverage and pension deficit are based on a more stringent definition of pension benefits.

[9] Its inclusion in the regression is also crucial for obtaining a normal distribution of the residuals in the system.

determinant of both saving and fertility. The econometric analysis establishes that the relationship between policy and fertility is causal, and that causality runs from policy to fertility. The new estimates confirm the negative effect of pension coverage on fertility. The fertility effect of the pension deficit, statistically insignificant according to the earlier estimate, is now positive. Fertility is again affected positively by the male wage rate, and negatively by the female one. The interest rate has a positive effect on fertility.

The policy change picked up by the 1986 dummy consists of the introduction of a new kind of fertility-related benefits, and of a sharp increase in existing ones. The 1968–75 dummy is a crude but effective way of accounting for shifts in the supply schedule of contraceptives.[10] The sharp fall in fertility between those dates does in fact coincide with the rapid diffusion of the contraceptive pill. This diffusion is likely to reflect shifts in both the demand for, and supply of, contraception. Since the demand for contraception is derived from the demand for children, the demand for the pill is a function of the same variables that figure in the demand for children. Shifts in the demand schedule for contraception may thus be thought to be adequately taken care of by the regressors used to explain fertility. The same cannot be said, however, about shifts in the supply schedule. Interestingly, the introduction of the 1968–75 dummy leads to a higher estimate of the effect of the child benefit rate on fertility. Put another way, ignoring the negative effect of the pill would have resulted in an underestimate of the positive effect of the fertility subsidy.

These findings complement those reported in Chapter 5, and in section 6.1 above. Education and health policies affect fertility, child benefits and subsidized family planning do too, but so does pension policy. Since pension coverage has a strongly negative effect on aggregate fertility, and given that realized household fertility has a positive effect on the probability that a child works, it then follows that extending pension coverage would reduce child labour.

Appendix 9.1   Econometric model

Assume that the random utility of the youngest child in household $i = 1, 2, ..., N$ engaged in activity $j = 0, 1, 2$ is

$$y_{ij}^* = \beta_{0j} + x_i\beta_{1j} + c_i\gamma_j + u_{ij}\lambda_j + \varepsilon_{ij}. \tag{1}$$

The elements of vector x_i are the observed individual and exogenous household-specific covariates; c_i denotes the number of children. The elements of vector

---

[10] Data limitations made it impossible to split the sample, and perform a test on the constancy of the parameter. The authors checked, however, for a possible correlation between the step dummy and the variables of interest by interacting it with pension coverage, pension deficit, the child benefit rate, and male and female wage rates. The effect turned out to be always very weak, and not to affect the value of the coefficient. These interaction terms were thus excluded from the final estimates.

u_{ij} describe household-specific and alternative-specific unobserved heterogeneity (e.g. parental preferences regarding the children's activities, unobserved components of income and wealth, costs of and returns to education, etc.). The errors ε_{ij} follow i.i.d. extreme-value distributions. Alternative j is chosen over alternative j' if $y_{ij}^* > y_{ij'}^*$. Let y_i be an indicator variable denoting an actual choice. Then, conditional on u_{ij},

$$\Pr(y_i = j | u_{ij}) = \frac{\exp(\beta_{0j} + x_i\beta_{1j} + c_i\gamma_j + u_{ij}\lambda_j)}{\sum_{j'=0}^{2} \exp(\beta_{0j'} + x_i\beta_{1j'} + c_i\gamma_{j'} + u_{ij}\lambda_{j'})}, \quad j = 0, 1, 2. \qquad (2)$$

The number of children in a family is assumed to follow a Poisson process with mean

$$E(c_i) = z_i\alpha + \sum_{j=1}^{2} u_{ij}\delta_j, \qquad (3)$$

where z_i is a vector of observed household-specific covariates that determine the number of children.[11] Notice that u_{ij} also enters (3). If unobserved heterogeneity is dominated by unobserved components of relative education prices, income and wealth, the theory leads us to expect that λ_j and δ_j will have opposite signs.

As only households with at least one child in the 7–15 age group are included, the stochastic fertility process is truncated at one. Therefore, conditional on u_{ij},

$$\Pr(c_i = c | c_i \geq 1, u_{ij}) = \frac{\exp(-\exp(z_i\alpha + \sum_j u_{ij}\delta_j))(z_i\alpha + \sum_j u_{ij}\delta_j)^c}{c![1 - \exp(-\exp(z_i\alpha + \sum_j u_{ij}\delta_j))]}. \qquad (4)$$

Conditional on u_{ij}, the joint probability of observing a certain number of children in a family and the activities of these children is given by the product of the marginal probability of observing the number of children and the conditional probability of the type of activity,

$$\Pr(y_i = j, c_i = c | c_i > 0 | u_{ij'}) = \Pr(y_i = j | u_{ij'}) \times \Pr(c_i = c | c_i > 0 | u_{ij'}),$$
$$j' = 0, 1, 2. \qquad (5)$$

If u_{ij} were known, the error terms of the two processes could be treated as independent. But they are not. It is assumed instead that each u_{ij} is drawn from a standard normal distribution with joint density denoted by $\mathbf{f}(\mathbf{u})$. Then u_{ij} can be integrated out of (5) to form a likelihood function that will yield consistent parameter estimates. Specifically, the contribution of the ith household to the

---

[11] Identification will be discussed after the data description.

log likelihood is given by

$$l_j = \ln \int_{-\infty}^{\infty} \left[\frac{\exp(\beta_{0j} + x_i\beta_{1j} + c_i\gamma_j + \sum_j u_{ij}\lambda_j)}{\sum_{j'=0}^{2} \exp(\beta_{0j'} + x_i\beta_{1j'} + c_i\gamma_{j'} + \sum_j u_{ij}\lambda_{j'})} \right.$$

$$\left. \times \frac{\exp(-\exp(z_i\alpha + \sum_j u_{ij}\delta_j))(z_i\alpha + \sum_j u_{ij}\delta_j)^c}{c![1 - \exp(-\exp(z_i\alpha + \sum_j u_{ij}\delta_j))]} \right] \mathbf{f}(\mathbf{u})d\mathbf{u}. \qquad (6)$$

The main problem with the estimation of the parameters of (6) is that the integral does not have a closed-form solution. However, this difficulty can be addressed using maximum simulated likelihood (MSL) (Gouriéroux and Monfort 1996).

Standard errors are calculated using the robust, sandwich formula for the covariance matrix of parameters, because it also correctly incorporates simulation noise (McFadden and Train 1997), while other formulae do not. Marginal effects of covariates on the outcomes are also calculated by simulation. The marginal effects are calculated as discrete changes for dummy variables, as derivatives for continuous ones. These marginal effects are calculated at the means of all other covariates. Note that each of these calculations requires averaging over simulated draws of the latent factors. Standard errors of the marginal effects are calculated using a Monte Carlo technique using 500 replications.[12]

A number of normalization restrictions are necessary before estimation algorithms can be implemented. The first one is the standard normalization for the multinomial logit model, $\beta_{00} = \beta_{10} = \gamma_0 = \lambda_0 = 0$. Without loss of generality, it can then be assumed that $u_{i0} = 0$. School attendance is normalized so that the u_{ij}, $j = 1, 2$ are unobserved determinants of child labour and idleness relative to school attendance. Since the variances of the unobserved factors cannot be identified, a normalization is required on either either λ_j or δ_j. Without loss of generality, it is assumed that $\delta_j = 1$.

Once these normalization restrictions are imposed, the model can be identified via non-linearity, even if the same variables determine fertility and child activity. However, identification by this route is not desirable. The chosen alternative is to include in z_i a set of variables that are excluded from x_i (in other words, to use a set of instruments that are assumed to affect fertility, but do not directly affect the choice of the child's activity, conditional on the covariates in the child's activities equations). Details of these variables, and their justification, are given in the main text.

---

[12] For details, refer to the original paper.

Conclusion

We started this book by noting that (i) international conventions have set the international community the objective of eliminating the 'unconditional worst' forms of child labour (in plain English, child exploitation), and (ii) there may be arguments for reducing child labour in any form. That raised two questions. In which circumstances should child labour be allowed to continue? What can be done to stop children working in the circumstances where we think that they should not work? The answer to both questions lies in the positive analysis of the sequence of events that culminates in parents making their children work and, in extreme cases, delivering them into the hands of cruel exploiters. The individual optimization assumption underlying standard economic thinking implies that public intervention is justified only if there is a coordination failure (efficiency considerations), or on grounds of social justice (equity considerations).

This general principle applies also in the case of child labour, but with two provisos. The first is that young children are not free agents. Decisions concerning their consumption, education, and work activities are taken by their parents. This implies that efficiency must reign within the family, as well as in the market place. It also implies that there may be a conflict of interest between parents and young children (and between grown-up children and elderly parents). Altruism does not make the conflict go away. The second proviso is that consumption at any stage of the life-cycle cannot fall below the subsistence level. This constraint (or, rather, set of constraints) is generally assumed away in standard economic analyses, but cannot be ignored in an analysis of child labour. As we saw in Chapter 2, when this constraint is binding, optimization gives way to the algebra of survival. The usual marginal conditions no longer apply.

The analysis of parental decisions contained in Chapters 2 and 3 leads us to conclude that child labour may be inefficiently high, or inefficiently low. The former had already been established in Baland and Robinson (2000). The latter appears to be novel. Leaving aside the possibility that labour may be bad *per se*, we find that child labour may be inefficiently high if parents cannot borrow and do not have sufficient assets to sell, inefficiently low if parents are not allowed to buy assets with a higher yield than the marginal return to education. We also find that the same applies if parents are not rich or altruistic enough to want to spend for their young children, or make transfers to their grown-up children, in excess of the minimum prescribed by self-enforcing family rules (but the existence of these rules actually *relaxes* the non-negative-bequest constraint generated by the legal principle that a child is not obliged to accept a negative estate).

Bommier and Dubois (2005), also cited in Chapter 2, argue that, if young children dislike work, child labour may be inefficient even in the absence of market imperfections or corner solutions. The same must be true if work early in life has adverse health effects. In Chapter 7, we reported evidence that working at a young age is likely to have an adverse effect on health both immediately, and in adult life. The finding that this is true also of agricultural work reinforces the case for curtailing child labour even outside the 'unconditional worst' cases. The fact that agricultural work is not only the predominant form of child work, but takes also place very often on the family's own farm, makes prohibition very difficult to enforce.

In Chapters 5 and 9, we reported evidence supportive of the predictions made by the theoretical analysis. In particular, we report evidence that child labour increases with poverty, with the cost of access to education, with the opportunity cost of a child's time, and with the number of children. A reduction in the opportunity cost of a child's time would thus reduce the probability that the child works. This implication is confirmed by evidence reported in Chapter 6 that access to basic utilities (piped water or electricity connection) reduces child labour. In this case, the reduction in the opportunity cost comes through a reduction in the time spent fetching water and fuel.

Evidence mentioned in Chapters 2 and 5 that the household-level income elasticity of child labour is high only at very low levels of income implies that income redistribution would help reduce child labour especially if it were directed primarily at taking families out of extreme poverty (defined as families effectively bound by the subsistence constraints). Redistributing land, by contrast, could have the opposite effect (if the substitution effect of the opportunity cost of child labour dominates the income effect) because the marginal product of child labour increases with the amount of land farmed.

Chapters 5 and 9 bring also evidence that school availability has only a small effect on the probability that a child works, but a strong one on the probability that a child attends school. This suggests that reducing the cost of access to education would boost enrolment, but have very little impact on child labour. The additional students would come out of the ranks of children who would otherwise do nothing. While not reducing actual child labour much, capillary school provision would thus reduce the number of children at risk of becoming workers or, worse still, of being sold or bonded (see Chapter 3). Evidence also reported in those two chapters, that fertility and child labour are lower in a low infant mortality environment, implies that policies aimed at reducing infant mortality (either directly, or indirectly by inducing parents to spend more for the survival of each child born to them) also reduce child labour. Indeed, we find evidence of a positive cross-sectional correlation between fertility and child labour.

In Chapter 4, we examined the theoretical proposition that (i) the absolute and relative levels of remuneration of workers with different levels of education are internationally determined like the interest rate, and (ii) skill premia (the ratios of skilled to less skilled wage rates) would be higher in countries with a comparatively better-educated labour force. Cross-country evidence reported in the same chapter appears to vindicate the assumption made throughout this book that one can go a long way in the explanation of child labour by looking at parental responses to government policies and internationally determined wage rates. In particular, the evidence says that, depending on the educational composition of the existing labour force, exposure to international trade may help reduce child labour. It also tells us that public expenditure on health and sanitation reduces child labour. The latter is consistent with the household-level evidence reported in Chapters 5 and 9, that mortality-reducing public expenditure discourages fertility and reduces child labour. It is also consistent with already mentioned evidence that piped (hence, presumably, safe) water reduces child labour.

The theoretical analysis of Chapters 2 and 3 attributes great importance to credit accessibility. The analysis of the consequences of extreme poverty, in particular slavery and labour bondage, attribute an important role also to uninsured risk. Chapter 8 brings evidence that credit rationing reduces educational investment, and that child labour is used as a buffer against adverse shocks. Chapter 3 argues also that the special role of women in the generation and upbringing of children may adversely affect the allocation of family resources between boys and girls. In particular, it may reduce the probability that a baby girl survives to school age, and that she will go to school if she does. All the empirical studies reviewed in this book confirm that being female makes a child's condition definitely worse. By contrast, evidence of the advantage of having an educated mother is not clear-cut.

Taking all these theoretical and empirical findings into account leads us to expect that, in the great majority of cases, child labour is inefficiently high rather than inefficiently low. Since child labour is predominantly (but far from exclusively) a characteristic of poor households—in particular a characteristic of households living close to subsistence level—efficiency and equity considerations point towards a reduction of child labour beyond unconditional worst cases. It should be clear from all we have said, however, that there is no single remedy for child labour.

Poverty alleviation policies certainly help reduce child labour. Land redistribution, desirable though it may be on other grounds, probably does not. Easy school access—meaning not only that fees and educational materials are subsidized, but also that children do not need to travel a long way, or leave home, in order to attend school—certainly helps too. It will help even more if the policy is aimed especially at girls, for in that case it will mitigate the gender bias, and if it is financed by taxes levied disproportionately on the rich, for in that case there will also be a redistributive effect. Removing obstacles to international trade helps if education and other policies have created the premisses for trade to have a positive effect on the relevant skill premium. A ban on the trade of goods with a child labour content will have the desired effect if universally agreed and applied, and if former exporters of these goods are compensated (see the discussion at the end of Chapter 4).

Mortality-reducing policies (from mass immunization to safe piped water) reduce fertility and, largely but not exclusively through that, child labour. This spill-over effect does not appear to have been pointed out by anyone other than the present authors. Evidence cited in Chapter 3, that the introduction or extension to wider strata of society of an actuarially fair pension system would have a strongly negative effect on fertility, suggests that this policy also would help. Policies aimed at giving wider strata of society access to asset and credit markets would have pretty much the same effect.

The same can be said of public intervention in favour of households affected by either collective or idiosyncratic shocks. In developed countries, the former are covered by the government because they are uninsurable, the latter are usually covered by private insurance. In developing countries, neither type of risk is generally covered, and children tend to be used as a buffer against uninsured shocks. By providing cover against these shocks (or, at least, against the collective ones, where there is not moral hazard problem) the government would reduce the probability that children are sent to work, bonded or suppressed.

All the policies we have mentioned are conducive to growth and, more broadly, to economic and social development. Although child labour is a feature of underdevelopment, it is thus not necessary to wait for a country to be fully developed before child labour disappears. It is possible to alleviate the child labour problem ahead of the others.

General Appendix
Econometric Issues in the Estimation
of Policy Effects

Empirical applications in economics often struggle with the question of how to accommodate (often binary) endogenous regressor(s) in a model aimed at capturing the relationship between the endogenous regressor(s) and an outcome variable. Problems of causal inference motivated by policy concerns involve 'what if' statements, and thus counterfactual outcomes. In this Appendix, we discuss the approaches followed in the present book.

A.1 THE TREATMENT CONTROL APPROACH

In some cases, it is possible to put the policy question in the treatment control form typical of the experimental framework. The fact that the treatment is endogenous reflects the idea that the outcomes are jointly determined with the treatment status or that there are variables related to both treatment status and outcomes. 'Endogeneity' makes it impossible to compare 'treated' and 'non-treated' individuals: no causal interpretation could be given to such a comparison, because the two groups are different irrespective of their treatment status.

A growing strand of applied economic literature has tried to identify causal effects of interventions from observational (i.e. non-experimental) studies using the conceptual framework of randomized experiments, and the so-called potential outcomes approach that allows causal questions to be translated into a statistical model.[1] While it is possible to find some identification strategies for causal effects even in non-experimental settings, data alone do not suffice to identify treatment effects. Suitable assumptions, possibly based on prior information available to the researchers, are always needed.

Guarcello, Mealli, and Rosati (2003), on which we draw in Chapter 6, uses the potential outcomes approach to causal inference, based on the statistical work on randomized experiments by Fisher and Neyman, and extended by Rubin (see Holland 1986). In recent years, many economists have accepted and adopted this framework[2] because of the clarity it brings to questions of causality. This approach defines a causal effect as the comparison of the

---

[1] See, for example, Angrist and Krueger (1999) and Heckman, Lalonde, and Smith (1999) for state-of-the-art papers.

[2] See, for example, Bjorklund and Moffit (1987), Pratt and Schlaifer (1988), Heckman (1989), Manski (1990), Manski et al. (1992), Angrist and Imbens (1995), Angrist and Krueger (1999).

potential outcomes on the same unit measured at the same time: $Y(0) =$ the value of the outcome variable Y if the unit is exposed to treatment $T = 0$, and $Y(1) =$ the value of Y if exposed to treatment $T = 1$. Only one of these two potential outcomes can be observed, yet causal effects are defined by their comparison, e.g. $Y(1) - Y(0)$. Thus, causal inference requires developing inferences able to handle missing data. The focus of the analysis is usually that of estimating the average treatment effect $\text{ATT} = E(Y(1) - Y(0))$, or the average treatment effect for subpopulations of individuals defined by the value of some variable, most notably the subpopulation of the treated individuals $\text{ATT} = E(Y(1) - Y(0)|T = 1)$.

The assignment mechanism is a stochastic rule for assigning treatments to units and thereby for revealing $Y(0)$ or $Y(1)$ for each unit. This assignment mechanism can depend on other measurements, i.e. $P(T = 1|Y(0), Y(1), X)$. If these other measurements are observed values, then the assignment mechanism is ignorable; if given observed values involve missing values, possibly even missing Ys, then it is non-ignorable. Unconfoundedness is a special case of ignorable missing mechanisms and holds when $P(T = 1|Y(0), Y(1), X) = P(T = 1|X)$ and X is fully observed.

Unconfoundedness is similar to the so-called 'selection on observables' assumption (also exogeneity of treatment assignment), which states that the value of the regressor of interest is independent of potential outcomes after accounting for a set of observable characteristics X. This approach is equivalent to assuming that exposure to treatment is random within the cells defined by the variables X. Although very strong, the plausibility of these assumptions relies heavily on the amount and on the quality of the information on the individuals contained in X.

Under unconfoundedness one can identify the average treatment effect within subpopulations defined by the values of X:

$$E(Y(1) - Y(0)|X = x) = E(Y(1)|X = x) - E(Y(0)|X = x)$$
$$= E(Y(1)|T = 1, X = x) - E(Y(0)|T = 0, X = x)$$

and also the overall ATT as:

$$E(Y(1) - Y(0)) = E(E(Y(1) - Y(0)|X = x))$$

where the outer expectation is over the distribution of X in the population. If we could simply divide the sample into sub-samples, dependent on the exact value of the covariates X, we could then take the average of the within-sub-sample estimates of the average treatment effects. Often the covariates are more or less continuous, so some smoothing techniques are in order: under unconfoundedness several estimation strategies can serve this purpose.

One such strategy is regression modelling. One usually starts by assuming a functional form for $E(Y(t)|X = x)$, for example a linear one, in a vector of functions of the covariates $E(Y(t)|X = x) = g(x)'\beta_t$. The estimates of the parameters' vectors $\beta_t (t = 0, 1)$ are usually obtained by least squares or maximum likelihood methods. Unless some restrictions are imposed on the β_t,[3] causal effects are rarely estimated from the value of the parameters (especially if the model is non-linear).

Using regression models to 'adjust' or 'control for' pre-intervention covariates, while being in principle a good strategy, has its pitfalls. For example, if there are many covariates, it can be difficult to find an appropriate specification. In addition, regression modelling obscures information on the distribution of covariates in the two treatment groups. In principle, one would like to compare individuals that have the same values for all the covariates: unless there is a substantial overlap of the covariates' distributions in the two groups, with a regression model one relies heavily on model specification (i.e. on extrapolation) for the estimation of treatment effects. Therefore, it is crucial to check the extent of the overlapping between the two distributions, and the 'region of common support' of these distributions. When the number of covariates is large, this task is not an easy one. An approach that can be followed is to reduce the problem to one dimension by using the propensity score, that is to say, the individual probability of receiving the treatment given the observed covariates $p(X) = P(T = 1|X)$. Under unconfoundedness the following results in fact hold (Rosenbaum and Rubin 1983a):

(i) T is independent of X given the propensity score $p(X)$,
(ii) $Y(0)$ and $Y(1)$ are independent of T given the propensity score.

From (i) we can see that the propensity score has the so-called balancing property, i.e. observations with the same value of the propensity score have the same distribution of observable (and possibly unobservable) characteristics independently of the treatment status. From (ii), we can see that exposure to treatment and control is random for a given value of the propensity score. These two properties allow us (a) to use the propensity score as a univariate summary of all the X, to check the overlap of the distributions of X, because it is enough to check the distribution of the propensity score in the two groups, and (b) to use the propensity score in the ATE (or ATT) estimation procedure as the single covariate that needs to be adjusted for, as adjusting for the propensity score automatically controls for all observed covariates (at least in large samples). In this paper we will use the estimated propensity score to serve purpose (a) to validate the regression results, and purpose (b) by estimating the ATT with a propensity score based matching algorithm.

The analysis of the propensity score alone can be very informative because it reveals the extent of the overlap in the treatment and comparisons groups in terms of pre-intervention variables. The conclusion of this initial phase may

---

[3] For example imposing that the treatment effect is constant (i.e. excluding the interaction terms of the treatment with the other covariates).

be that treatment and control groups are too far apart to produce reliable estimates without heroic modelling assumptions. The propensity score itself must be estimated: if the treatment is binary, any model for binary dependent variables can be used, although the balancing property should be used to choose the appropriate specification of the model, i.e. how the observed covariates enter the model. Some specification strategies are described in Becker and Ichino (2001) and Rubin (2002). Propensity score methods can be extended to include multiple treatments (Imbems 2000, Lechner 2001).

The assumption that the treatment assignment is ignorable, or even unconfounded, underlies much of the recent economic policy intervention evaluation strategies (Jalan and Ravallion 2003), so that one might have the impression that researchers no longer pay much attention to unobservables. The problem of the analyses involving adjustments for unobserved covariates, such as the Heckman's type corrections (Heckman and Hotz 1989), is that they tend to be quite subjective and very sensitive to distributional and functional specification. This has been shown in a series of theoretical and applied papers (Lalonde 1986, Dehejia and Wahba 1999, Copas and Li 1997). The adjustment for unobserved variables, however, strongly relies on the existence of valid instruments, i.e. on variables that are correlated with T but are otherwise independent of the potential outcomes. If such variables exist, they can then be used as a source of exogenous variation to identify causal effects (Angrist and Imbens 1995, Angrist and Rubin 1996).

The validity of a variable as an instrument, i.e. the validity of the exclusion restrictions, cannot be directly tested. In observational studies such variables are usually very hard to find, although there are some exceptions (see Angrist and Krueger 1999 for some examples). Thus, despite the strength of the unconfoundedness assumption, and the fact that it cannot be tested, it is very hard not to use this assumption in observational studies. It is then crucial to adjust the 'best' possible way for all observed covariates. Propensity score methods can help achieve this. The issue of unobserved covariates should then be addressed using models for sensitivity analysis (e.g. Rosenbaum and Rubin 1983b) or using non-parametric bounds for treatment effects (Manski 1990, Manski et al. 1992).

A.2 SENSITIVITY ANALYSIS

Many observational studies assume, implicitly or explicitly, that unobservables do not impinge on the effect of the exogenous variable of interest. This assumption ('unconfoundedness') lends itself to the criticism that it effectively rules out any role of the unobservable variables. Chapter 8 of this book reported the estimates in Guarcello, Mealli, and Rosati (2003) of the effects of uninsured shocks, and credit rationing, on education and child labour. In order to check whether the results are robust, that paper applies the sensitivity analysis method proposed by Rosenbaum and Rubin (1983a), extended here to a multinomial outcome. That method allows the researcher to assess the sensitivity of the causal effects to assumptions about an unobserved binary covariate associated with both the treatments and the response.

The unobservables are assumed to be summarized by a binary variable in order to simplify the analysis, although similar techniques could be used assuming other distributions for the unobservables. Note however that a Bernoulli distribution can be thought of as a discrete approximation to any distribution, and thus we believe that our distributional assumption will not severely restrict the generality of the results.

Suppose that the treatment assignment is not unconfounded given a set of observable variables X, i.e.

$$P(T = 1|Y(0), Y(1), X) \text{ is not equal to } P(T = 1|X),$$

but unconfoundedness holds given X and an unobserved binary covariate U, that is

$$P(T = 1|Y(0), Y(1), X, U) \text{ is equal to } P(T = 1|X, U).$$

We can then judge the sensitivity of the conclusions to certain plausible variations in assumptions about the association of U with T, $Y(0)$, $Y(1)$, and X. If such conclusions are relatively insensitive over a range of plausible assumptions about U, a causal inference is then more defensible.

Since $Y(0)$, $Y(1)$, and T are conditionally independent given X and U, the joint distribution of $(Y(t), T, X, U)$ for $t = 0, 1$ can be written as

$$\Pr(Y(t), T, X, U) = \Pr(Y(t)|X, U)\Pr(T|X, U)\Pr(U|X)\Pr(X),$$

where, for present purposes,

$$\Pr(U = 0|X) = \Pr(U = 0) = \pi,$$

$$\Pr(T = 0|X, U) = (1 + \exp(\gamma'X + \alpha U))^{-1}$$

and

$$\Pr(Y(t) = j|X, U) = \exp(\beta_j'X + \tau_j T + \delta_{tj}U)\left(1 + \sum_i \exp(\beta_i'X + \tau_i T + \delta_{ti}U)\right)^{-1}$$

j = (Working only: W, Studying only: S, Working and Studying: WS, Idle Children: I).

In these expressions, π represents the proportion of individuals with $U = 0$ in the population, and the distribution of U is assumed to be independent of X. This should render the sensitivity analysis more stringent, since, if U were associated with X, controlling for X should capture at least some of the effects of the unobservables. The sensitivity parameter α captures the effect of U on treatment receipt (e.g. credit rationing), while the δ_{ti}'s are the effects of U on the outcome.

Given plausible but arbitrary values to the parameters π, α, and δ_{ti}, the paper estimates the parameters γ and β_j by maximum likelihood, and derives estimates of the ATT as follows:

$$A\hat{T}T = \frac{1}{N^T} \sum_{i \in T} [\hat{Y}_i^1 - \hat{Y}_i^0]$$

where

$$\hat{Y}_i^t = \hat{\text{Pr}}(Y(t) = j|X) = \pi \hat{\text{Pr}}(Y(t) = j|X, U = 0) + (1 - \pi) \hat{\text{Pr}}(Y(t) = j|X, U = 1)$$

These estimates of the ATT are comparable with those obtained by the propensity score approach on the basis of a matching procedure, and very similar to the marginal effects obtained by that route.

By comparing the results obtained for different values of the sensitivity parameters with those obtained from the reference estimate, it is possible to assess the sensitivity of the conclusions reached with respect to the presence of unobservables. This was done in Chapters 6 and 8. The results of the sensitivity analysis carried out on the estimates presented in those chapters show that allowing for the presence of unobservables would not influence the results substantially.

References

Andersen, E. (1970), 'Asymptotic Properties of Conditional Maximum Likelihood Estimators', *Journal of the Royal Statistical Society*, 32: 238–301.

Angrist, J. D. (2001), 'Estimation of Limited-Dependent Variable Models with Dummy Endogenous Regressors: Simple Strategies for Empirical Practice', *Journal of Business and Economic Statistics*, 19: 2–16.

—— and Evans, W. N. (1998), 'Children and their Parents' Labor Supply: Evidence from Exogenous Variation in Family Size', *American Economic Review*, 88/3: 450–77.

—— and Imbens, G. W. (1995), 'Two-Stage Least Squares Estimation of Average Causal Effects in Models with Variable Treatment Intensity', *Journal of the American Statistical Association*, 90: 431–42.

—— and Rubin, D. B. (1996), 'Identification of Causal Effects Using Instrumental Variables', *Journal of the American Statistical Association*, 91: 444–72.

—— and Krueger, A. B. (1999), 'Empirical Strategies in Labor Economics', in O. Ashenfelter and D. Card (eds.), (1998) *Handbook of Labor Economics*, iii, Handbooks in Economics series, ed. K. J. Arrow and M. D. Intriligator, Amsterdam: North-Holland.

Ashagrie, K. (1998), *Statistics on Child Labor and Hazardous Child Labor in Brief*, Geneva: ILO.

Ashenfelter, O., and Krueger, A. (1994), 'Estimates of the Return to Schooling from a New Sample of Twins', *American Economic Review*, 84: 1157–73.

Atella, V., and Rosati, F. C., (2000), 'Uncertainty about Children's Survival and Fertility: A Test Using Indian Data', *Journal of Population Economics*, 13: 263–78.

Baland, J. M., and Robinson, A. (2000), 'Is Child Labor Inefficient?', *Journal of Political Economy*, 108: 663–79.

—— —— (2002), 'Rotten Parents', *Journal of Public Economics*, 84: 341–56.

Bales, K. (1999), *Disposable People: New Slavery in the Global Economy*, Berkeley and Los Angeles: University of California Press.

Bardhan, P. K. (1983), 'Labor Tying in a Poor Agrarian Economy: A Theoretical and Empirical Analysis', *Quarterly Journal of Economics*, 98: 501–14.

Barro, R. J. (1974), 'Are Government Bonds Net Wealth?', *Journal of Political Economy*, 82: 1095–118.

Basu, A. M. (1993), 'Family Size and Child Welfare in an Urban Slum', in C. B. Lloyd (ed.), *Fertility, Family Size and Structure*, New York: Population Council.

Basu, K. (1999), 'Child Labor: Cause, Consequence and Cure, with Remarks on International Labor Standards', *Journal of Economic Literature*, 37: 1083–119.

—— and Van, P. H. (1998), 'The Economics of Child Labor', *American Economic Review*, 88: 412–27.

Becker, G. S. (1960), 'An Economic Analysis of Fertility', in A. J. Coale (ed.), *Demographic and Economic Change in Developing Countries*, Princeton: Princeton University Press.

—— (1981), *A Treatise on the Family*, Cambridge, Mass: Harvard University Press.

—— and Barro, R. J. (1988), 'A Reformulation of the Economic Theory of Fertility', *Quarterly Journal of Economics*, 103: 1–25.

—— and Tomes, N. (1976), 'Child Endowment and the Quantity and Quality of Children', *Journal of Political Economy*, 87: 1153 –89.

Becker, S. O., and Ichino, A. (2001), 'Estimation of Average Treatment Effects Based on Propensity Score, *Stata Journal*, 2: 358–77.

Behrman, J. R., and Wolfe, B. L. (1989), 'Does More Schooling Make Women Better Nourished and Healthier?, *Journal of Human Resources*, 24: 644–63.

——, Foster, A. D., Rosenzweig, M. R., and Vashishtha, P. (1999), 'Women's Schooling, Home Teaching, and Economic Growth', *Journal of Political Economy*, 107: 682–714.

Bequele, A., and Myers, W. E. (1995), *First Things First in Child Labour: Eliminating Work Detrimental to Children*, Geneva: ILO.

Bergstrom, T. C. (1996), 'Economics in a Family Way', *Journal of Economic Literature*, 24: 1903–34.

Bernheim, B. D., and Ray, D. (1989), 'Collective Dynamic Consistency in Repeated Games', *Games and Economic Behaviour*, 1: 295–326.

Bhalotra, S. (2003), 'Is Child Warm Necessary?', *Department of Economics DP 03654*, University of Bristol.

—— and Heady, C. (2003), 'Child Farm Labour: The Wealth Paradox', *World Bank Economic Review*, 17/2.

Bhat, C. R. (2001), 'Quasi-Random Maximum Simulated Likelihood Estimation of the Mixed Multinomial Logit Model', *Transportation Research*, B35: 677–93.

Biggeri, M., Guarcello, L., Lyon, S., and Rosati, F. C. (2003), 'The Puzzle of "Idle" Children: Neither in School nor Performing Economic Activity: Evidence from Six Countries', UCW Working Paper, www.ucw-project.org.

Bingley, P., and Walker, I. (2001), 'Household Unemployment and the Labour Supply of Married Women', *Economica*, 68/270: 157–85.

Biswanger, H. P., Deininger, K., and Feder, G. (1995), 'Power, Distortions, Revolt and Reform in Agricultural and Land Relations', in J. Behrman and T. N. Srinavasan (eds.), *Handbook of Development Economics*, Amsterdam: North–Holland.

Bjorklund, A., and Moffit, R. (1987), 'Estimation of Wage Gains and Welfare Gains in Self-Selection Models', *Review of Economics and Statistics*, 69: 42–9.

Blundell, R., and Smith, R. J. (1994), 'Coherency and Estimation in Simultaneous Models with Censored or Qualitative Dependent Variables', *Journal of Econometrics*, 64: 355–73.

Bommier, A., and Dubois, P. (2005), 'Rotten Parents and Child Labor', *Journal of Political Economy*, 112: 240–8.

Bound, J., Jaeger, J. A., and Baker, R. (1995), 'Problems with Instrumental Variables when the Correlation between the Instruments and the Endogenous Explanatory Variables is Weak', *Journal of American Statistical Association*, 90: 443–50.

Brownstone, D., and Train, K. (1999), 'Forecasting New Product Penetration with Flexible Substitution Patterns', *Journal of Econometrics*, 89: 109–29.

Buchanan, J. (1987), 'Constitutional Economics', in *The New Palgrave: A Dictionary of Economics*, London: Macmillan.

Bureau of Labor Statistics (2000) Report on the Labour Force, Washington DC, United States Department of Labor.

Carrasco, R. (2001), 'Binary Choice with Binary Endogenous Regressors in Panel Data: Estimating the Effect of Fertility on Female Labor Participation', *Journal of Business and Economic Statistics*, 19: 385–94.

Chamberlain, G. (1980), 'Analysis of Covariance with Qualitative Data', *Review of Economic Studies*, 47: 225–38.

Cigno, A. (1991), *Economics of the Family*, Oxford: Clarendon Press.

—— (1993), 'Intergenerational Transfers without Altruism: Family, Market and State', *European Journal of Political Economy*, 7: 505–18.

—— (1998), 'Fertility Decisions when Infant Survival is Endogenous', *Journal of Population Economics*, 11: 21–8.

—— (2005), 'The Political Economy of Intergenerational Cooperation', in S. C. Kolm and J. Mercier Ythier (eds.), *The Handbook of Giving, Reciprocity and Altruism*, Handbooks in Economics series, ed. K. J. Arrow and M. D. Intriligator, Amsterdam: North-Holland.

—— (2006) 'A Constitutional Theory of the Family', *Journal of Population Economics*, 19 (forthcoming).

——, Casolaro, L., and Rosati, F. C. (2003), 'The Impact of Social Security on Saving and Fertility in Germany', *FinanzArchiv*, 59: 189–211.

—— and Pinal, C. (2004), 'Endogenous Child Mortality, the Price of Child-Specific Goods and Fertility Decisions: Evidence from Argentina', in E. Bour, D. Heymann, and F. Navajas (eds.), *Latin American Economic Crises: Trade and Labour*, Houndmills: Palgrave Macmillan.

—— and Rosati, F. C. (1992), 'The Effects of Financial Markets and Social Security on Saving and Fertility Behaviour in Italy', *Journal of Population Economics*, 5: 319–41.

—— —— (1996), 'Jointly Determined Saving and Fertility Behaviour: Theory, and Estimates for Germany, Italy, UK, and USA', *European Economic Review*, 40: 1561–89.

—— —— (1997), 'Rise and Fall of the Japanese Saving Rate: The Role of Social Security and Intra-Family Transfers', *Japan and the World Economy*, 9: 81–92.

Cigno, A., and Rosati, F. C. (2000), 'Mutual Interest, Self-Enforcing Constitutions and Apparent Generosity', in L. A. Gérard-Varet, S. C. Kolm, and J. Mercier Ythier (eds.), *The Economics of Reciprocity. Giving and Altruism*, London: MacMillan and St Martin's Press.

—— —— (2002), 'Child Labor, Education and Nutrition in Rural India', *Pacific Economic Review*, 7: 1–19.

—— —— and Guarcello, L. (2002), 'Does Globalization Increase Child Labor?', *World Development*, 30: 1579–89.

——, Giannelli, G. C., Rosati, F. C., and Vuri, D. (2004), 'Is There Such a Thing as a Family Constitution? A Test Based on Credit Rationing', IZA DP No. 1116.

Coale, A. J. (1991), 'Excess Female Mortality and the Balance of the Sexes: An Estimate of the Number of Missing Females', *Population and Development Review*, 17: 517–23.

Copas, J. B., and Li, H. G. (1997), 'Inference for Non-Random Samples, with Discussion', *Journal of the Royal Statistical Society*, B 59: 55–96.

Dasgupta, P. (1993), *An Enquiry into Well-Being and Destitution*, Oxford: Clarendon Press.

—— (1997), 'Nutritional Status, the Capacity for Work, and Poverty Traps', *Journal of Econometrics*, 77: 5–37.

Deb, P., and Rosati, F. C. (2002), 'Determinants of Child Labour and School Attendance: The Role of Household Unobservables', UCW working papers.

—— —— (2004), 'Estimating the Effect of Fertility Decisions on Child Labour and Schooling', UCW Working Paper, www.ucw-project.org.

Deheja, R. H., and Gatti, R. (2002), 'Child Labor: The Role of Income Variability and Access to Credit across Countries', NBER Working Paper 9018.

—— and Wahba, S. (1999), 'Causal Effects in Non Experimental Studies: Reevaluation of the Evaluation of Training Programs', *Journal of the American Statistical Association*, 94: 1053–62.

de Onis, M., and Habicht, J. P. (1996), 'Anthropometric Reference Data for International Use: Recommendations from a World Health Organization Expert Committee', *American Journal of Clinical Nutrition*, 64: 650–8.

Dessy, S. E. (2000), 'A Defense of Compulsive Measures against Child Labor', *Journal of Development Economics*, 62: 261–75.

Duranton, G. (1998), 'Globalisation, Productive Systems and Inequalities', LSE Centre for Economic Performance, Discussion Paper 401.

Edmonds, E. (2002), 'Will Child Labor Decline with Improvements in Living Standards?, mimeo, Dartmouth College.

—— (2005), 'Does Child Labor Decline with Improving Economic Status?', *Journal of Human Resources*, 40: 77–99.

—— and Pavcnik, N. (2001), 'Does Globalisation Increase Child Labor? Evidence from Vietnam', NBER Working Paper 8760.

—— —— (2005), 'The Effect of Trade Liberalization on Child Labor', *Journal of International Economics*, 65: 401–19.

Edmonds, E., and Sharma, S. (2004), 'Is Investment in Human Capital Influenced by Property Rights? Evidence from Families Vulnerable to Bondage', Dartmouth College, *mimeo*.

Edmonds, and Turk, C. (2004), 'Child Labor in Transition in Vietnam', in P. Glewwe, N. Agrawal, and D. Dollar (eds.), *Economic Growth, Poverty and Household Welfare in Vietnam*, Washington: World Bank, 505–50.

Ehrlich, I., and Zhong, J. H. (1998), 'Social Security and the Real Economy: An Inquiry into Some Neglected Issues', *American Economic Review*, 88: 151–7.

Entwisle, B., and Winegarden, C. (1984), 'Fertility and Pension Programs in LDCs: A Model of Mutual Reinforcement', *Economic Development and Cultural Change*, 32: 331–54.

Eswaran, M. (2002), 'The Empowerment of Women, Fertility, and Child Mortality', *Journal of Population Economics*, 15: 433–54.

——, Facchini, L. A., Dall'Agnol, M. M., and Christiani, D. C. (2000), 'Child Labor and Health: Problems and Perspectives', *International Journal of Occupational and Environmental Health*, 6/1: 55–62.

Fentiman, A., Hall, A., and Bundy, D. (2001), 'Health and Cultural Factors Associated with Enrolment in Basic Education: A Study in Rural Ghana', *Social Science and Medicine*, 52: 429–39.

Fogel, R. W. (1993), 'New Sources and New Techniques for the Study of Secular Trends in Nutritional Status, Health, Mortality, and the Process of Aging', *Historical Methods*, 26: 5–43.

Forastieri, V. (1997). *Children at Work: Health and Safety Risks*, Geneva: ILO.

Foster, A. D., and Rosenzweig, M. R. (2000), 'Financial Intermediation, Transfers, and Commitment: Do Banks Crowd out Private Insurance Arrangements in Low-Income Rural Areas?', in A. Mason and G. Tapinos (eds.), *Sharing the Wealth: Demographic Change and Economic Transfers between Generations*, New York: Oxford University Press.

Francesconi, M. (2002), 'A Joint Dynamic Model of Fertility and Work of Married Women', *Journal of Labor Economics*, 20: 336–80.

Genicot, G. (2002), 'Bonded Labor and Serfdom: A Paradox of Voluntary Choice', *Journal of Development Economics*, 67: 101–27.

Giuffrida, A., Iunes, R. F., and Savedo, W. D. (2001), 'Health and Poverty in Brazil: Estimation by Structural Equation Model with Latent Variables', *mimeo*.

Glewwe, P., Kock, S., and Linh Nguyen, B. (2002), 'Child Nutrition, Economic Growth and the Provision of Health Services in Vietnam in the 1990's, *Poverty Research Working Paper 2776*, Washington: World Bank.

—— and Nguyen, P. (2002), 'Economic mobility in Vietnam in the 1990s', *Poverty Research Working Paper 2838*, Washington: World Bank.

Gong, X., and van Soest, A. (2002), 'Family Structure and Female Labor Supply in Mexico City', *Journal of Human Resources*, 37: 163–91.

Gouriéroux, C., and Monfort, A. (1996), *Simulation Based Econometrics Methods*, New York: Oxford University Press.

Grootaert, C., and Patrinos, H. (1999), *The Policy Analysis of Child Labor: A Comparative Study*, New York: St Martin's Press.

—— and Kanbur, R. (1995), 'Child Labor: An Economic Perspective', *International Labor Review*, 134: 187–203.

Guarcello, L., Lyon, S., and Rosati, F. C. (2003), 'Child Labor and Access to Basic Services: Evidence from Five Countries', UCW Working Paper, www.ucw-project.org.

—— Mealli, F., and Rosati, F. C. (2003), 'Household Vulnerability and Child Labor: The Effects of Shocks, Credit Rationing and Insurance', World Bank Social Protection Discussion Paper 322.

Haddad, L., and Hoddinott, J. (1994), 'Women's Income and Boy–Girl Anthropometric Status in Côte d'Ivoire', *World Development*, 22: 543–53.

Hausman J. (1978), 'Specification Tests in Econometrics', *Econometrica*, 46 1251–71.

Heckman, J. (1989), 'Causal Inference and Nonrandom Samples', *Journal of Educational Statistics*, 14: 159–68.

—— and Hotz, V. J. (1989), 'Choosing among Alternative Nonexperimental Methods for Estimating the Impact of Social Programs: The Case of Manpower Training', *Journal of the American Statistical Association*, 84: 862–80.

——, Lalonde, R., and Smith, J. (1999), 'The Economics and Econometrics of Active Labor Market Programs', in O. Ashenfelter and D. Card (eds.), *Handbook of Labor Economics*, iii(a), Handbooks in Economics series, ed. K. J. Arrow and M. D. Intriligator, Amsterdam: North–Holland.

Hoddinott, J., and Haddad, L. (1995), 'Does Female Income Share Influence Household Expenditures? Evidence from Côte d'Ivoire', *Oxford Bulletin of Economics and Statistics*, 57: 77–96.

Hoff, K., and Lyon, A. (1995), 'Non-Leaky Buckets: Optimal Redistributive Taxation and Agency Costs', *Journal of Public Economics*, 58: 365–90.

Hohm, C. H. (1975), 'Social Security and Fertility: An International Perspective', *Demography*, 12: 629–44.

Holland, P. W. (1986), 'Statistics and Causal Inference', *Journal of the American Statistical Association*, 81: 945–60.

Holzmann, R., and Jorgensen, S. (2002), *Social Risk Management: A New Conceptual Framework for Social Protection and Beyond*, Washington, DC: World Bank.

Hotz, V. J., and Miller, R. A. (1988), 'An Empirical Analysis of Life Cycle Fertility and Female Labor Supply', *Econometrica*, 56: 91–118.

Idler, E. L., and Benyamini, Y. (1997), 'Self-Rated Health and Mortality: A Review of Twenty-Seven Community Studies', *Journal of Health and Social Behaviour*, 38/1: 21–37.

Imbens, G. W. (2000), 'The Role of Propensity Score in Estimating Dose-Response Functions', *Biometrika*, 87: 706–10.

—— and Angrist, J. (1994), 'Estimation and Identification of Local Average Treatment Effects', *Econometrica*, 62: 467–75.

Immink, M. D. C., and Payongayong, E. (1999), 'Risk Analysis of Poor Health and Growth Failure of Children in the Central Highlands of Guatemala', *Social Science and Medicine*, 48: 997–1009.

International Labour Office (2002), *Every Child Counts: New Global Estimates on Child Labour*, Geneva: ILO.

—— (2004), *Investing in Every Child: An Economic Study on the Costs and Benefits of Eliminating Child Labour*, Geneva: ILO.

International Labour Organization (1998), *Conference Report VI (I) Child Labor: Targeting the Intolerable*, Geneva: ILO.

—— (2002), *Every Child Counts: New Global Estimates of Child Labour*, Geneva: ILO.

International Programme for the Elimination of Child Labour (IPEC) (1997), *Defining Hazardous Undertakings for Young Workers below 18 Years of Age: A Country Report*, Manila: ILO.

Jacoby, H. G., and Skoufias, E. (1997), 'Risk, Financial Markets, and Human Capital in a Developing Country', *Review of Economic Studies*, 64: 311–35.

Jalan, J., and Ravallion, M. (2003), 'Estimating the Benefit Incidence of an Antipoverty Program by Propensity Score Matching', *Journal of Business and Economic Statistics*, 21(1): 19–30.

Jensen, P., and Nielsen, H. S. (1997), 'Child Labour or School Attendance? Evidence from Zambia', *Journal of Population Economics*, 10: 407–24.

Kaplan, G., and Camacho, T. (1983), 'Perceived Health and Mortality: A Nine Year Follow-up of the Human Population Laboratory Cohort', *American Journal of Epidemiology*, 117: 292–8.

Kassouf, A. L., McKee, M., and Mossialos, E. (2001), 'Early Entrance to the Job Market and its Effects on Adult Health: Evidence from Brazil', *Health Policy and Planning*, 16: 21–8.

Klasen, S. (1996), 'Nutrition, Health and Mortality in Sub-Saharan Africa: Is There a Gender Bias', *Journal of Development Studies*, 32: 913–32.

Kooiker, S. E. (1995), 'Exploring the Iceberg of Morbidity: A Comparison of Different Survey Methods for Assessing the Occurrence of Everyday Illness', *Social Science and Medicine*, 41: 317–32.

Krugman, P. (1995), 'Growing World Trade: Causes and Consequences', *Brookings Papers on Economic Activity*, 1: 327–77.

—— and Venables, A. (1995), 'Globalisation and the Inequality of Nations', *Quarterly Journal of Economics*, 110: 857–80.

Lalonde, R. J. (1986), 'Evaluating the Econometric Evaluations of Training Programs, Using Experimental Data', *American Economic Review*, 76: 602–20.

Lechner, M. (2001), 'Identification and Estimation of Causal Effects of Multiple Treatments under the Conditional Independence Assumption', in M. Lechner and F. Pfeiffer (eds.), *Econometric Evaluation of Labor Market Policies*, Heidelberg: Physica/Springer.

Leibenstein, H. (1957), *Economic Backwardness and Economic Growth*, New York: Wiley.

Lundberg, S., and Pollak, R. A. (1996), 'Bargaining and Distribution in Marriage', *Journal of Economic Perspectives*, 10: 139–58.

—— and Rose, E. (2002), 'The Effects of Sons and Daughters on Men's Labor Supply and Wages', *Review of Economics and Statistics*, 84: 251–68.

McElroy, M. B., and Horney, M. J. (1981), 'Nash-Bargained Household Decisions', *International Economic Review*, 22: 333–49.

McFadden, D., and Train, K. (1997) 'Mixed MNL Models for Discrete Response', Department of Economics, Working Paper, University of California, Berkeley.

Maddala, G. S. (1986), *Limited-Dependent and Qualitative Variables in Econometrics*, Cambridge: Econometric Society Monographs.

Maitra, P., and Ray, R. (2002), 'The Joint Estimation of Child Participation in Schooling and Employment: Comparative Evidence from Three Continents', *Oxford Development Studies*, 30: 41–62.

Manser, M., and Brown, M. (1980), 'Marriage and Household Decision Making: A Bargaining Analysis', *International Economic Review*, 21: 31–44.

Manski, C. F. (1990), 'Nonparametric Bounds on Treatment Effects', *American Economic Review Papers and Proceedings*, 80: 319–23.

——, Sandefur, G. D., McLanahan, S., and Powers, D. (1992), 'Alternative Estimates of the Effects of Family Structure during Adolescence on High School Graduation', *Journal of the American Statistical Association*, 87: 417, 25–37.

Martorell, R., and Ho, T. J. (1984). 'Malnutrition, Morbidity and Mortality', in W. H. Mosley and L. C. Chen (eds.), *Child Survival: Strategies for Research*, Cambridge: Cambridge University Press.

Maskin, E., and Farrell, J. (1989), 'Renegotiation in Repeated Games', *Games and Economic Behavior*, 1: 327–60.

Matz, P. (2004), 'Costs and Benefits of Education to Replace Child Labour', ILO Working Paper.

Mealli, F., and Rubin, D. B. (2003), 'Commentary: Assumptions Allowing the Estimation of Direct Causal Effects', *Journal of Econometrics*, 112: 79–87.

Moffitt, R. (1984), 'Profiles of Fertility, Labour Supply and Wages of Married Women: A Complete Life-Cycle Model', *Review of Economic Studies*, 51: 263–78.

Neher, P. (1971), 'Peasants, Procreation and Pensions', *American Economic Review*, 61: 380–9.

Neyman, J., and Scott, E. (1948), 'Consistent Estimates Based on Partially Consistent Observations', *Econometrica*, 16: 1–32.

O'Donnell, O., Rosati, F. C., and van Doorslaer, E. (2002), 'Child Labour and Health: Evidence and Research Issues', UCW Discussion Paper.

Patrinos, H. A., and Psacharopoulos, G. (1997), 'Family Size, Schooling and Child Labor in Peru', *Journal of Population Economics*, 10: 387–405.

Pitt, M. M., Rosenzweig, M. R., and Nazmul Hassan, M. D. (1990), 'Productivity, Health and the Intrahousehold Distribution of Food in the Low-Income Countries', *American Economic Review*, 80: 1139–56.

Pratt, J. W., and Schlaifer, R. (1988), 'On the Interpretation and Observation of Laws', *Journal of Econometrics*, 39: 23–52.

Psacharopoulos, G. (1997), 'Child Labor versus Educational Attainment: Some Evidence from Latin America', *Journal of Population Economics*, 10/4: 377–86.

Ralston, H. (1997), 'Health as an Input to Labour: Intrahousehold Food Distribution in Rural Indonesia', *Journal of Policy Modelling*, 19/5: 567–86.

Ravallion, M., and Wodon, Q. (2000), 'Does Child Labor Displace Schooling: Evidence from Behavioral Responses to an Enrolment Subsidy', *Economic Journal*, 110: 158–76.

Ray, R. (2000), 'Analysis of Child Labour in Peru and Pakistan: A Comparative Study', *Journal of Population Economics*, 13: 3–20.

Rivers, D., and Vuong, O.H. (1988), 'Limited Information Estimators and Exogeneity Tests for Simultaneous Probit Models', *Journal of Econometrics*, 39: 347–66.

Rodriguez, F., and Rodrik, D. (2000), 'Trade Policy and Economic Growth: A Skeptic's Guide to the Cross-National Evidence', www.ksghome.harvard.edu.

Rosati, F. C. (1996), 'Social Security in a Non-Altruistic Model with Uncertainty and Endogenous Fertility', *Journal of Public Economics*, 60: 283–94.

Rose, Andrew, K. (2002), 'Do we Really Know that the WTO Increases Trade', *NBER Working Papers*, 9273 (National Bureau of Economic Research, Inc.).

Rosenbaum, P., and Rubin, D. B. (1983*a*), 'The Central Role of the Propensity Score in Observational Studies for Causal Effects', *Biometrika*, 70: 41–55.

—— (1983*b*), 'Assessing Sensitivity to an Unobserved Binary Covariate in an Observational Study with Binary Outcome', *Journal of the Royal Statistical Society*, B 45: 212–18.

Rosenzweig, M. R., and Everson, R. (1977), 'Fertility, Schooling, and the Economic Contribution of Children in Rural India: An Econometric Analysis', *Econometrica*, 45: 1065–79.

—— and Schultz, T. P. (1982), 'Market Opportunities, Genetic Endowments, and Intra-family Resource Distribution: Child Survival in Rural India', *American Economic Review*, 72: 803–15.

—— and Wolpin, K. J. (1982), 'Governmental Interventions and Household Behavior in a Developing Country', *Journal of Development Economics*, 10: 209–25.

Rubin, D. B. (2002), 'Using Propensity Scores to Help Design Observational Studies: Application to the Tobacco Litigation', *Health Services Outcome Research Methodology*.

Sachs, J. D., and Warner, A. (1995), 'Economic Reform and the Process of Global Integration', *Brooking Papers on Economic Activity*, 1: 1–118.

Sadana, R., Mathers, C. D., Lopez, A. D., Murray, C. J. L., and Iburg, K. (2000), 'Comparative Analysis of more than 50 Household Surveys on Health Status, *GPE Discussion Paper No 15*, EIP/GPE/EBD., Geneva: WHO.

Satyanarayana, K., Krishna, T. P., and Rao, B. S. (1986). The Effect of Early Childhood Undernutrition and Child Labour on the Growth and Adult Nutritional Status of Rural Indian Boys around Hyderabad,' *Human Nutrition and Clinical Nutrition*, 40C: 131–9.

Shelbourne, R. (2001), 'An Explanation of the International Variation in the Prevalence of Child Labor', *World Economy*, 24: 359–78.

Smith, J. (1999), 'Healthy Bodies and Thick Wallets: the dual relation between health and economic status'. *Journal of Economic Respectives*, 13(2): 145–166.

Staiger, D., and Stock, J. (1997), 'Instrumental Variable Regressions with Weak Instruments', *Econometrica*, 65: 557–86.

Stark, O. (1993), 'Non-Market Transfers and Altruism', *European Economic Review*, 37: 1413–24.

Steckel, R. (1995), 'Stature and the Standard of Living,' *Journal of Economic Literature*, 33: 1903–40.

Stiglitz, J., and Weiss, A. (1981), 'Credit Rationing in Markets with Incomplete Information', *American Economic Review*, 71: 393–410.

Strauss, J., and Thomas, D. (1998), Health, Nutrition and Economic Development', *Journal of Economic Literature*, 36: 766–817.

Strulik, H. (2003), 'Mortality, the Trade-Off between Child Quality and Quantity, and Demo-Economic Development', *Metroeconomica*, 54: 499–520.

—— (2004), 'Child Mortality, Child Labour and Economic Development', *Economic Journal*, 114: 547–68.

Tesliue, E. D., and Lindert, K. (2002), 'Vulnerability: A Qualitative and Quantitative Assessment', World Bank, *mimeo*.

Train, K. (2003), *Discrete Choice Methods with Simulation*, New York: Cambridge University Press.

United Nations Organization (1998), *Debt Bondage*, Geneva: UN Economic and Social Council, Working Group on Contemporary Forms of Slavery.

Waaler, H. Th. (1984), 'Height, Weight and Mortality: The Norwegian Experience', *Acta Medica Scandinavica*, Supplement 67.

Wagstaff, A. and Van Doorslaer, E. (2003), 'Catastrophe and Impoverishment in Paying for Health Care: with Applications to Vietnam 1993–98', *Health Economics*, 12/11: 921–33.

Waldman, A. (2003), 'India's Poor Bet Precious Sums on Private Schools', *New York Times*, 15 Nov.

Waterlow, J. C. et al. (1977), 'The Presentation and Use of Height and Weight Data for Comparing the Nutritional Status of Groups of Children under the Age of 10 Yrs', *Bulletin of the World Health Organisation*, 55.

Wood, A. (1994), *North–South Trade, Employment and Inequality*, Oxford: Clarendon Press.

—— (1998), 'Globalisation and the Rise in Labour Market Inequalities', *Economic Journal*, 108: 1463–82.

—— and Ridao-Cano, C. (1999), 'Skill, Trade, and International Inequality', *Oxford Economic Papers*, 51: 89–119.

Wooldridge, J. M. (2002), *Econometric Analysis of Cross Section and Panel Data*, Cambridge, Mass.: MIT Press.

World Bank (2001), *Social Protection Sector Strategy: From Safety Nets to Springboard*, Washington DC: World Bank.

World Health Organization, (1995), 'Physical Status: Use and Interpretation of Anthropometry', Report of a WHO Expert Committee, *WHO Technical Report* 854, Geneva: WHO.

Zhang, J., and Zhang, J. (2004), 'How Does Social Security Affect Economic Growth? Evidence from Cross-Country Data', *Journal of Population Economics*, 17: 473–500.

Index